AF559871

ACADEMIC ACCREDITATION IN LIBRARIES

By
Deepak Kumar
BLISc, MLISc
Librarian
Sardar Patel Subharti Institute of Law
&
Subharti Institute of
Fine Art & Fashion Design
Subharti University, Meerut (U.P.)
(India)

DISCOVERY PUBLISHING HOUSE PVT. LTD.
NEW DELHI-110 002

Published by:
Tilak Wasan
DISCOVERY PUBLISHING HOUSE PVT. LTD.
4383/4B, Ansari Road, Darya Ganj
New Delhi-110 002 (India)
Phone : +91-11-23279245, 43596064-65
Fax : +91-11-23253475
E-mail : discoverypublishinghouse@gmail.com
sales@discoverypublishinggroup.com
parul.wasan@gmail.com
web : www.discoverypublishinggroup.com

Reprinted: 2019

First Edition: **2014**

ISBN: 978-93-5056-392-2

Academic Accreditation in Libraries

© 2014, Author

All rights reserved. No part of this publication should be reproduced, stored in a retrieval system, or transmitted in any form or by any means: electronic, mechanical, photocopying, recording or otherwise, without the prior written permission of the author and the publisher.

This book has been published in good faith that the material provided by authors is original. Every effort is made to ensure accuracy of material, but the publisher and printer will not be held responsible for any inadvertent error(s). In case of any dispute, all legal matters are to be settled under Delhi jurisdiction only.

Printed at:
Dynamic Printers
Delhi

Preface

Accreditation is a process developed specially to assemble the needs of colleges and universities. It is a system of quality declaration, based on the basis that the varied organizations of higher education can best be appraised through a procedure combining self-evaluation and examine assessment. Accreditation utilizes a two-step procedure of assessment, combining institutional self-study based on published values or criteria and visit from a team of experts. In this book, the essential ideas of accreditation and associated basic topics are competently involved. Extremely rich information restricted in topics like: A general introduction accreditation, the power of accreditation views of academics, principles and philosophy of accreditation, academic library environment, developing an accreditation system for LIS, etc., will hugely benefit the students, teachers and library professionals.

—*Author*

Contents

1

Accreditation

INTRODUCTION

Accreditation is a process in which certification of competency, authority, or credibility is presented. Organisations that issue credentials or certify third parties against official standards are themselves formally accredited by accreditation bodies; hence, they are sometimes known as 'accredited certification bodies'.

The accreditation process ensures that their certification practices are acceptable, typically meaning that they are competent to test and certify third parties, behave ethically and employ suitable quality assurance. One example of accreditation is the accreditation of testing laboratories and certification specialists that are permitted to issue official certificates of compliance with established technical standards, such as physical, chemical, forensic, quality, and security standards. Accreditation bodies in these fields usually operate according to ISO/IEC 17011.

Accredited entities in specific sectors must provide evidence to the accreditation body that they conform to other standards in the same series:

- *BS EN ISO/IEC 17020*: 'General criteria for the operation of various types of bodies performing inspection'.
- *BS EN ISO/IEC 17021*: "Conformity assessment. Requirements for bodies providing audit and certification of management systems".
- *BS EN ISO/IEC 17024*: "Conformity Assessment. General requirements for bodies operating certification of persons".

- *BS EN ISO/IEC 17025*: 'General requirements for the competence of testing and calibration laboratories'.

INSTITUTIONAL COMMITMENT AND RESPONSIBILITIES IN THE ACCREDITATION PROCESS

The effectiveness of self-regulatory accreditation depends upon an institution's acceptance of certain responsibilities, including involvement in and commitment to the accreditation process. An institution is expected to conduct an analytical self-study at the interval specified by the Commission and, at the conclusion of the self-study, accept peer assessment of institutional strengths and weaknesses with regard to the Commission's accreditation criteria.

The self-study is to assess every aspect of the institution; involve personnel from all segments of the institution, including faculty, staff, students, administration, and the governing board; and, provide a comprehensive analysis of the institution, identifying strengths and weaknesses. An institution must participate in the activities and decisions of the Commission. This commitment includes a willingness to participate in the decision-making processes of the Commission and to adhere to all policies and procedures, including those for reporting changes within the institution. Only if institutions accept seriously the responsibilities of membership will the validity and vitality of the accreditation process be ensured.

An institution of higher education is committed to the search for and dissemination of knowledge. Integrity in the pursuit of knowledge is expected, therefore, to govern the total environment of an institution. Each member institution is responsible for ensuring integrity in all operations dealing with its constituencies, in its relationships with other institutions, and in its accreditation activities with the Commission.

Each institution is expected to provide the Commission with access to all aspects of its operation. It should also provide accurate information about the institution's affairs, including reports of other accrediting, licensing, and auditing agencies. In the spirit of collegiality, institutions are expected to cooperate fully during all aspects of the process of evaluation: the preliminary visit in preparation for an evaluation visit, the evaluation itself, and any follow-up to the evaluation visit.

Institutions are also expected to provide the Commission, or its representatives, with information requested during evaluations, enabling evaluators to perform their duties with efficiency and effectiveness.

Each participating institution is to be in compliance with its programme responsibilities under Title IV of the *Higher Education Act of 1965*, as amended. Failure to comply with Title IV responsibilities will be considered when an institution is reviewed for initial accreditation or continued accreditation. In reviewing an institution's compliance with these programme responsibilities, the Commission will rely on documentation forwarded to it by the Secretary of the United States Department of Education.

INSTITUTIONAL COMPLIANCE WITH THE HIGHER EDUCATION ACT

The Commission expects candidate and member institutions to comply with the Title IV requirements of the *Higher Education Act of 1965*, as amended. Therefore, institutions will provide to evaluation committees for review and consideration the most recent default rates and any other documents concerning the institution's programme responsibilities under Title IV of the *Act*, including any results of financial or compliance audits and programme reviews.

Evaluation Committees evaluate the information and its relationship to the *Eligibility Requirements* and the *Standards* and *Policies* for Candidacy and Accreditation. The Commission reserves the right to review an institution's accreditation status when U.S.,. Department of Education findings demonstrate significant non-compliance with the *Higher Education Act of 1965*, as amended.

EVALUATION PROCESS

The evaluation process, which is periodically and jointly conducted by the institution and the Commission, may take a number of forms.

Regardless of the particular form employed, it includes the following steps:

- A representative of the Commission conducts a preliminary visit on campus 18 to 24 months before an evaluation committee visit.
- The institution analyses itself through a self-study. Approximately four to six weeks prior to the evaluation visit, the print and electronic copies of the self-study report are mailed to the evaluation committee and to the Commission office.
- Professional colleagues from other member institutions and appropriate agencies study the institutional self-study report, visit the campus as an evaluation committee, and prepare a written report of its findings.
- A draft report of the evaluation committee's report and findings is prepared and sent to the institution's chief executive officer who is given an opportunity to correct errors of fact before the final report is prepared.
- The committee's final report is submitted to the Commission Office. The Commission Office provides the institution's chief executive officer with a copy of the final version of the evaluation report.
- If it so chooses, the institution may provide the Commission with a written response to the evaluation committee report.
- The Commission reviews the institutional self-study report, the evaluation committee's written report, the institution's written response to the evaluation committee report, verbal statements of the evaluation committee chair and the institution's chief executive officer, and the evaluation committee's confidential recommendation in taking action on the accreditation status of the institution.
- The institution continues to consider and act on the results of its own self-study and the advice received.

The institutional self-study process is a major enterprise. It is an educational endeavor which requires time to reflect and engage in critical thinking. A full academic year is the minimum working time needed to complete the self-study. A two-year timeframe provides a better opportunity for organisation, staff involvement, and appraisal. If done well, self-study is abundantly rewarding. If rushed, the results are likely to be of limited value and not worth the effort expended by the institution.

INSTITUTIONAL SELF-STUDY

GENERAL DISCUSSION

Institutional self-study is the most significant part of the accreditation process. The benefits to the institution will be proportional to the incisiveness of the enquiry. The aim of self-study is to understand, evaluate, and improve—not merely to defend what already exists. A well-conducted self-study should result in a renewed common effort within the institution to improve the whole enterprise and document its achievements.

Self-study should be viewed as an ongoing process to:

- Analyse the resources and effectiveness of the institution in fulfilling its mission.
- Demonstrate that student achievement is commensurate with the certificates, diplomas, degrees, or other recognition awarded.
- Appraise the relationship of all the institution's activities to its purposes.
- Provide a sound basis for institutional planning and improvement.

It is important that the institutional self-study assess educational outcomes or results as well as structure and process. The institutional self-study should assess student achievement with respect to programmes and services offered to accomplish educational purposes. Prime consideration is to be placed on performance in achieving institutional mission and goals.

NATURE AND ORGANISATION

The concept of self-study as a continuing process does not mean that an institution is to be continuously involved in intensive, comprehensive self-analysis. The intensity of ongoing self-study may vary greatly from one institution to another, but the self-study presented to the Commission in preparation for an evaluation committee visit must be comprehensive, must evaluate the entire institution, and must address the Commission's accreditation criteria.

The objectives of the self-study effort should be clearly and specifically stated, the methodology worked out in advance, and a time schedule set. It is imperative that those involved in the effort have ready access to all relevant data and materials.

There must be frequent and widely disseminated reports of progress during the course of the ongoing self-study if a high level of interest is to be maintained. Once the methodologies to be employed in the self-study have been established, a survey should be undertaken to discover relevant data which may be available. Care should be taken to avoid gathering data that are not put to a constructive use.

The Commission, while requiring the submission of an analytical self-study report in connection with an evaluation for Candidacy or Accreditation, recognises that the self-study process is more beneficial to the institution when it is undertaken in response to significant needs identified by the institution itself.

A variety of approaches to self-study is acceptable. An institution is permitted to propose some variation in the design of the self-study which it considers to be of intrinsic value as long as the overarching purposes of a comprehensive self-study are met and all Commission accreditation criteria are addressed. Representatives of the institution and the Commission should come to a clear agreement well ahead of the initiation of the self-study process, concerning any particular institutional needs which the institution hopes to have the self-study address.

These understandings should be confirmed, in writing, by the President of the Commission. The question of cost of continuing self-study is frequently raised. Even though educational institutions are faced with many demands and limited resources, their quest for excellence mandates that they support a mechanism for ongoing self-analysis. This does not mean that small institutions must maintain a staff exclusively assigned to this function. Many significant data are, or easily could be, assembled by any institution in the course of its daily work. An overall design for continuing self-analysis, once it has been set up, provides a framework for data-gathering and analysis. This need not be costly.

Large complex institutions may find it feasible and desirable to maintain an office of institutional research for this particular purpose. The nature of the organisation of the self-study will, however, vary according to the characteristics of the institution and scope, nature, and emphasis of the self-study.

SELF-STUDY STEERING COMMITTEE

Selection of the right individuals to serve on the self-study steering committee is very important. Institutional groups characterised by lack of bias, by objectivity, and by the ability to work cooperatively to forge compromises can be organised to mount a self-study. Strong, skillful, and committed leadership is essential and the selection of the coordinator of the study is therefore of paramount importance.

It is important to have a steering committee broadly representative of the institution in order that objectivity may be promoted. Also, those whose interests might be affected by the results of the study should in some way be involved. How the leadership and the participating personnel are selected, whether by election, appointment, or some combination of both, must be resolved in accordance with the tradition and climate of the institution. Whatever the method of selection, it is imperative that sufficient time for effective participation be cleared and that adequate staff support be provided. Most institutions have multiple constituencies who have somewhat differing interests and values.

The faculty, staff, administrators, and students may group themselves around such issues as the relative importance of general, as contrasted with specialised, education or the broader outcomes of a general education as contrasted with skill acquisition. The relative importance of research productivity on the one hand, and teaching effectiveness on the other, is a commonly encountered basis for alignment, especially in large, complex institutions. Another common division groups those who would expand the institution's range of activities and broaden its constituency in contrast to those who would advocate a more limited role.

An institution organising for self-study should have these groupings in mind as it makes its plans and staffs its committees. The role of the governing board in the self-study process should be carefully considered. The institution should keep board members informed of policy matters addressed in the self-study. It is true that a self-study can founder on issues involving basic disagreement among stakeholder groups. Alternatively, self-study could be used to bring issues into sharper focus and provide a basis for their resolution. Indeed, a well-designed self-study might be a catalyst for such resolution.

DEVELOPMENT OF THE REPORT

Each committee or sub-group responsible for the various aspects of the study shall prepare a report setting forth the issue or issues addressed, the questions to which it sought answers, the data gathered and the means by which it gathered them, the techniques employed in analysing the data and a statement indicating how the results have been used to enhance institutional effectiveness.

The separate reports shall be brought together by the steering committee, which has the responsibility for preparing a single, unified institutional report. The final editing should usually be done by one person. The *Standards and Guide for Self-Study* provides a suggested framework of essential considerations for the self-study and for the evaluation committee. An institution is encouraged to design an analytic report best suited to its mission and supported by the necessary data presented in a concise and readable form.

A summary chapter of findings with institutional commendations and recommendations resulting from the self-study process should be prepared. Finally, though the experience of carrying on a self-study is, in itself, usually found to be salutary, a self-study which does not result in action is of limited benefit.

PROCESS SUMMARY

Recommendations for organising and conducting a comprehensive self-study:

- Highlight the role of the chief executive officer, which is to sustain maximum emphasis on the project, to stimulate without dominating, and to see that the results are translated into immediate action and/or long-range plans.
- Appoint a steering committee of a size appropriate to the complexity of the institution, with an active and interested coordinator to plan the work, hold it in balance, suggest new approaches, and monitor the editing of the final report. The task of the coordinator is a major assignment. Institutions are strongly encouraged to send representatives to the self-study workshop sponsored annually by the Commission.
- Provide members of the steering committee and key officials with copies of the *Accreditation Handbook*, or pertinent sections thereof.
- Set up whatever task forces and committees the steering committee decides are needed. Their first assignment is to become thoroughly familiar with the *Accreditation Handbook* and related documents.
- Determine how the institution will evaluate its effectiveness in fulfilling its mission, what evidence is needed to support institutional judgements, and what data need to be collected.
- Emphasise relationships among, as well as performance within, institutional units; encourage healthy cross-pollination of ideas. The study needs to present the entire institution.
- Avoid the temptation of asking outside consultants to provide answers to the institution's concerns. If consultants are used, draw upon their experience for suggestions to the institution as to ways in which it might address its concerns.

- Adopt a definite timetable; make it realistic and insist on maintaining it. Set a publication date to ensure the self-study report is available at least eight weeks before the evaluation committee is due to arrive so that it can be sent to the Commission office and to the evaluators four to six weeks prior the visit. Having determined the finish date, allow at least one month for final editing and duplicating. Then work back towards the beginning, allowing the necessary intervals for each stage. Set realistic timelines. Remember that self-study is a major undertaking involving many people. It must deal with the separate phases of the institution's life, but it must go beyond them in its concern with their relationships, with the focusing or directing of the institution's total effort, with its overall educational impact, as well as with the efficiency of each of its units.
- Implement the results of the study through to action. New thinking, new patterns, new proposals, and very likely new unity behind them will emerge during the process. The institution should see that each proposal is channeled in the proper direction and that follow-up is consistent. Perhaps the steering committee can remain helpful in the post-evaluation stage, too, but clearly the chief executive officer, the deans, and the faculty standing committees have continuing responsibili...

EVALUATION COMMITTEE

FUNCTION

Members of an evaluation committee function as colleagues as well as constructive critics. The purpose is to produce a committee report which will be useful to the institution and to the Commission which must make a decision on the institution's accreditation status.

COMMITTEE MAKE-UP

The number of reviewers that comprise an evaluation committee depends upon the characteristics of the institution and the scope of its programmes and services. Every principal area of the institution must be examined. Evaluators are assigned from peer, out-of-state member institutions. In some cases, evaluators represent appropriate agencies and peer institutions from other accrediting regions.

All evaluators will have completed evaluator training by the Commission and the committee chair will be an experienced evaluator. In selecting evaluators, care is taken to avoid a real or perceived conflict of interest. The evaluation committee roster is sent to the institution six to eight weeks in advance of the visit, and the chief executive officer is requested to notify the Commission office of any concern about the composition of the committee.

DATES

The dates for the committee evaluation are determined by the Commission office in consultation with the institution's chief executive officer. This is normally completed two years in advance of the visit. A concerted effort is made to arrange dates most suitable to the institution; however, compromises are sometimes necessary. Dates are selected to allow sufficient time for the committee report to be prepared for the summer or winter Commission meeting.

Evaluations in spring will be considered at the Commission's summer meeting and evaluation visits in fall will be considered at the Commission's winter meeting. The Commission's action will be reported in writing to the institution within one month following the Commission meeting at which the action was taken.

EVALUATION COMMITTEE REPORT

At the conclusion of the on-campus evaluation visit, each evaluator provides the committee chair with a report for the evaluator's area of responsibility. The committee chair, on behalf of the committee, is responsible for preparing a draft of the evaluation report. The draft evaluation report is sent to the institution's chief executive officer for review and correction of errors of fact. The committee chair then finalises the evaluation committee report and submits it to the Commission office. Prior to the summer or winter meetings the final version of the evaluation committee report is duplicated and sent to the institution's chief executive officer and to members of the Commission.

The evaluation committee's confidential recommendation on the institution's accreditation is not included in the evaluation committee report, but is communicated privately to the Commission. The committee's evaluation report is considered confidential. Unless authorisation is granted by the institution, the Commission does not distribute the evaluation committee report to other individuals or organisations. The institution's chief executive officer is given an opportunity to provide a written response to the evaluation committee report for consideration by the Commission.

The institution is also invited to send representatives to appear before the Commission when the institution's accreditation is being considered. Although there may be some disagreement with aspects of the report, it should be used to improve the institution. In order to achieve this goal, the trustees, administrators, and faculty members are expected to give serious consideration to the report and the findings of the committee. The Commission expects the institution to use the report objectively. In preparing public announcements, the institution should avoid quoting the report out of context or reporting only the favourable or unfavourable passages.

NEWLY ACCREDITED INSTITUTIONS

Institutions granted Initial Accreditation are not accredited for a specific number of years. They are expected to submit a progress report in the third year following the year of initial accreditation and to conduct a comprehensive self-study and host an evaluation committee in the fifth year following the year of initial accreditation. If, in the Commission's judgement, an institution is not ready for membership, it may defer a decision pending further reports on specific matters and/or a visit by a small committee, or it might deny initial accreditation. When Accreditation is initially granted by the Northwest Commission on Colleges and Universities, the effective date of accreditation is September 1 of the academic year in which the Commission took action. For example, if the Commission granted Initial Accreditation in summer of 2004, the effective date of Accreditation is September 1, 2003.

REAFFIRMATION OF ACCREDITATION

Continuing members are not accredited permanently or for a definite number of years. Accreditation must be reaffirmed periodically. Every institution is to conduct a self-study and be visited by an evaluation committee at least every ten years. In addition, each institution is to prepare an interim report and be visited by one or more representatives of the Commission at five year intervals between decennial visits.

At the time of reaffirmation, the Commission may request an institution to submit additional reports at specified times or to submit additional reports and receive a visit by a small evaluation committee. The Commission may also request that an institution conduct a complete self-study and be visited by a comprehensive evaluation committee.

COMMISSION DECISIONS ON INSTITUTIONS

Once the Commission has made a decision regarding candidacy or accreditation of an institution, it will provide written notification of the action to the institution within one month of the date the action was taken.

Commission action with regard to institutions include:

- Grant Candidacy or Initial Accreditation.
- Continue Candidacy or Reaffirm Accreditation.
- Request a Progress Report and/or a Focused Interim Report and Visit.
- Defer action on Candidacy or Accreditation.
- Issue or Continue *Warning*.
- Impose or Continue *Probation*.
- Issue or Continue a *Show-Cause* order with Candidacy or Accreditation to terminate unless the institution has

demonstrated, to the satisfaction of the Commission that it has satisfied the Commission's concerns or responded to its directives prior to a specified date.

- Deny Candidacy or Accreditation.
- Terminate Candidacy or Accreditation.

All of the Commission actions except number 5, are posted to the Commission's web site, published in the *Directory of Accredited and Preaccredited Institutions,* and in the minutes of the Commission meeting at which the action took place. In addition, the Commission may impose conditions on continued accreditation or candidacy status or request additional reporting or site visits.

REAPPLICATION FOR ACCREDITATION

An institution not granted Candidacy or Initial Accreditation may resubmit an Application for Consideration no fewer than two years following the date of the Commission's action to deny Candidacy or Initial Accreditation. An institution whose Candidacy or Accreditation has been terminated may resubmit an Application for Consideration no fewer than two years following the date of the Commission's action to terminate Candidacy or Accreditation.

COMMISSION RESPONSIBILITIES IN THE ACCREDITATION PROCESS

NATIONAL RECOGNITION OF ACCREDITING AGENCIES AND ASSOCIATIONS

For purposes of determining eligibility for United States government assistance under certain legislation, the Secretary of the U.S. Department of Education is required to publish a list of nationally recognised accrediting agencies and associations that he/she determines to be reliable authorities as to the quality of education offered by educational institutions and programmes. Most institutions thus attain eligibility for Federal funds by holding accredited or candidate status with one of the accrediting bodies recognised by the Secretary in addition to fulfilling other eligibility requirements.

The commissions of the regional associations and the national accrediting agencies recognised by the Secretary have no legal control over educational institutions or programmes. They promulgate standards of quality and admit to membership those institutions that meet the standards.

RELATIONSHIP WITH THE U.S. DEPARTMENT OF EDUCATION

The Northwest Commission on Colleges and Universities has been listed since, 1952 by the Secretary of the U.S. Department of Education as a nationally recognised accrediting agency for institutions offering programmes of at least one academic year in length at the post-secondary level. Recognition was most recently reaffirmed in December 2002 for a five-year period. The Commission notifies the Department of any changes in the scope of its activities.

Within thirty working days, the Commission files notification with the U.S. Department of Education the actions it has taken on institutions. However, it immediately files copies of institutional action letters that involve adverse action, *Probation*, or *Show-Cause*.

The Commission maintains communication with the Department of Education and other federal agencies. It responds to DOE enquiries regarding institutional eligibility for participation in the Higher Education Act programmes, including Title IV; on receipt, it forwards to the institution for comment claims of Title IV fraud and abuse; and it shares with the Department of Education clear evidence of possible Title IV fraud and abuse. The Commission notifies an institution whenever the Department provides such information.

ACTIONS OF STATE AGENCIES AND OTHER ACCREDITING BODIES

In considering whether to grant Candidacy or Initial Accreditation status to an institution, the Commission requires an institution to report to it actions taken by other recognised accrediting bodies which have:

- Denied such status to the institution.
- Placed the institution on public probation.

- Revoked the accreditation or preaccreditation status of the institution.

An institution accredited by or having Candidate for Accreditation status with the Commission is expected to remain in good standing with other recognised accrediting bodies or specialised accrediting bodies which accredit the principal programme of the institution with which it has accreditation or pre-accreditation status.

If another recognised accrediting body or governmental agency:

- Places an institution or a principal programme offered by the institution on public probationary status.
- Revokes such status, the institution shall report that action to the Northwest Commission on Colleges and Universities, which will promptly review the accreditation or candidacy status it has previously granted to the institution to determine if there is cause to alter that status.

In accordance with 34 CFR 602.28, the Commission will not reaffirm the candidacy or accreditation of an institution during a period in which the institution has:

- A pending or final action brought by a State agency to suspend, revoke, withdraw, or terminate the institution's legal authority to provide post-secondary education in the State.
- A decision by a recognised agency to deny accreditation or preaccreditation.
- A pending or final action brought by a recognised accrediting agency to suspend, revoke, withdraw, or terminate the institution's accreditation or preaccreditation.
- Probation or an equivalent status imposed by a recognised agency.

In adhering to these principles and, in cooperation with other appropriate recognised accrediting bodies and governmental agencies, the Commission will routinely share with other such bodies the accreditation or candidacy status of all of its Accredited and Candidate institutions.

RETENTION OF RECORDS

Through its records retention programme, the Commission maintains the official records of Commission actions on institutions. It also retains copies of institutional reports and materials, and copies of evaluation reports which formed the basis for those actions. These materials include applications for candidacy, comprehensive self-study reports and evaluation committee reports, progress reports, focused interim reports and evaluation reports, and regular fifth-year interim reports and evaluation reports. These documents are maintained through two complete evaluation cycles.

STANDARDS AND GUIDE FOR SELF-STUDY

STANDARDS AND THEIR USE IN SELF-STUDY

Structure of the Standards

Each of the nine Standards is identified by number and name. The scope of each Standard is provided in lettered Standard Elements. Each Standard Element is accompanied by a statement that represents the general intent of the Standard Element. Further definition of Standard Elements is provided in the form of numbered Standard Indicators. Related accreditation Policies follow several of the Standards.

These Policies are considered part of the Standard and are intended to further define the Standard. Following each Standard and the Related Policies is a section which identifies supporting documentation for the standard. The purpose of the supporting documentation is to provide evidence of the manner in which each standard and its elements are met. The evidence is to provide greater meaning to the narrative and analysis of the self-study.

The Commission has identified three kinds of documentation:

- Required Documentation: Documents or information embedded in the body of the self-study report, provided in the appendices, or included with the self-study materials sent to the Commission office.

- *Required Exhibits*: Documents or information to be summarised in the self-study, provided in the appendices, included with the self-study materials sent to the Commission office, or made available in the room on campus provided for the evaluation committee.
- *Suggested Materials*: Documents or information recommended to the institution for consideration in documenting the self-study report. They should be made available in the room on campus provided for the evaluation committee.

SELF-STUDY, SUPPORTING DOCUMENTATION, AND ACCREDITATION POLICIES

In preparing the self-study report and visit, the institution is expected to demonstrate that it meets each standard, each element of the Commission's *Eligibility Requirements* and accreditation Standards and Related Policies, and all other applicable policies. The self-study document should be succinct, thoughtful, and analytical including an appraisal of the institution's strengths, weaknesses, and achievements relative to each standard.

STANDARD ONE—INSTITUTIONAL MISSION AND GOALS, PLANNING AND EFFECTIVENESS

MISSION AND GOALS

The institution's mission and goals define the institution, including its educational activities, its student body, and its role within the higher education community. The evaluation proceeds from the institution's own definition of its mission and goals.

Such evaluation is to determine the extent to which the mission and goals are achieved and are consistent with the Commission's Eligibility Requirements and standards for accreditation.

- The institution's mission and goals derive from, or are widely understood by, the campus community, are adopted by the governing board, and are periodically re-examined.
- The mission, as adopted by the governing board, appears in appropriate institutional publications, including the catalogue.

- Progress in accomplishing the institution's mission and goals is documented and made public.
- Goals are determined consistent with the institution's mission and its resources-human, physical, and financial.
- The institution's mission and goals give direction to all its educational activities, to its admission policies, selection of faculty, allocation of resources, and to planning.
- Public service is consistent with the educational mission and goals of the institution.
- The institution reviews with the Commission, contemplated changes that would alter its mission, autonomy, ownership or locus of control, or its intention to offer a degree at a higher level than is included in its present accreditation, or other changes in accordance with Policy A-2 *Substantive Change.*

PLANNING AND EFFECTIVENESS

The institution engages in ongoing planning to achieve its mission and goals. It also evaluates how well, and in what ways, it is accomplishing its mission and goals and uses the results for broad-based, continuous planning and evaluation.

Through its planning process, the institution asks questions, seeks answers, analyses itself, and revises its goals, policies, procedures, and resource allocation.

- The institution clearly defines its evaluation and planning processes. It develops and implements procedures to evaluate the extent to which it achieves institutional goals.
- The institution engages in systematic planning for, and evaluation of, its activities, including teaching, research, and public service consistent with institutional mission and goals.
- The planning process is participatory involving constituencies appropriate to the institution such as board members, administrators, faculty, staff, students, and other interested parties.

- The institution uses the results of its systematic evaluation activities and ongoing planning processes to influence resource allocation and to improve its instructional programmes, institutional services, and activities.
- The institution integrates its evaluation and planning processes to identify institutional priorities for improvement.
- The institution provides the necessary resources for effective evaluation and planning processes.
- The institution's research is integrated with and supportive of institutional evaluation and planning.
- The institution systematically reviews its institutional research efforts, its evaluation processes, and its planning activities to document their effectiveness.
- The institution uses information from its planning and evaluation processes to communicate evidence of institutional effectiveness to its public.

SUPPORTING DOCUMENTATION FOR STANDARD ONE

Required Documentation:

- Official statement of the institutional mission: Indicate how and when it was developed, approved, and communicated to the institution's constituencies.
- Evidence that demonstrates the analysis and appraisal of institutional outcomes. Examples may include:
  - Annual goals and assessment of success in their accomplishments;
  - Studies of alumni and former students;
  - Studies regarding effectiveness of programmes and their graduates;
  - Studies that indicate degree of success in placing graduates;
  - Pre-and post-test comparisons of student knowledge, skills, and abilities;
  - Surveys of satisfaction-students, alumni, and employees.
- *Required Exhibits*: Institutional short term, strategic, or long term plans, including system master plans.

- *Suggested Materials*: Planning studies, enrollments for the past five years, enrollment projections, programme and personnel needs analyses, fund development plans, and other institutional research results.

STANDARD TWO—EDUCATIONAL PROGRAMME AND ITS EFFECTIVENESS

GENERAL REQUIREMENTS

The institution offers collegiate level programmes that culminate in identified student competencies and lead to degrees or certificates in recognised fields of study. The achievement and maintenance of high quality programmes is the primary responsibility of an accredited institution; hence, the evaluation of educational programmes and their continuous improvement is an ongoing responsibility.

As conditions and needs change, the institution continually redefines for itself the elements that result in educational programmes of high quality.

- The institution demonstrates its commitment to high standards of teaching and learning by providing sufficient human, physical, and financial resources to support its educational programmes and to facilitate student achievement of programme objectives whenever and however they are offered.
- The goals of the institution's educational programmes, whenever and however offered, including instructional policies, methods, and delivery systems, are compatible with the institution's mission. They are developed, approved, and periodically evaluated under established institutional policies and procedures through a clearly defined process.
- Degree and certificate programmes demonstrate a coherent design; are characterised by appropriate breadth, depth, sequencing of courses, synthesis of learning, and the assessment of learning outcomes; and require the use of library and other information sources.

- The institution uses degree designators consistent with programme content. In each field of study or technical programme, degree objectives are clearly defined: the content to be covered, the intellectual skills, the creative capabilities, and the methods of enquiry to be acquired; and, if applicable, the specific career-preparation competencies to be mastered.
- The institution provides evidence that students enrolled in programmes offered in concentrated or abbreviated timeframes demonstrate mastery of programme goals and course objectives.
- The institution is able to equate its learning experiences with semester or quarter credit hours using practices common to institutions of higher education, to justify the lengths of its programmes in comparison to similar programmes found in regionally accredited institutions of higher education, and to justify any programme-specific tuition in terms of programme costs, programme length, and programme objectives.
- Responsibility for design, approval, and implementation of the curriculum is vested in designated institutional bodies with clearly established channels of communication and control. The faculty has a major role and responsibility in the design, integrity, and implementation of the curriculum.
- Faculty, in partnership with library and information resources personnel, ensure that the use of library and information resources is integrated into the learning process.
- The institution's curriculum is planned both for optimal learning and accessible scheduling.
- Credit for prior experiential learning is awarded only in accordance with Policy 2.3 *Credit for Prior Experiential Learning*.
- Policies, regulations, and procedures for additions and deletions of courses or programmes are systematically and periodically reviewed.

- In the event of programme elimination or significant change in requirements, institutional policy requires appropriate arrangements to be made for enrolled students to complete their programme in a timely manner and with a minimum of disruption.

EDUCATIONAL PROGRAMME PLANNING AND ASSESSMENT

Educational programme planning is based on regular and continuous assessment of programmes in light of the needs of the disciplines, the fields or occupations for which programmes prepare students, and other constituencies of the institution.

- The institution's processes for assessing its educational programmes are clearly defined, encompass all of its offerings, are conducted on a regular basis, and are integrated into the overall planning and evaluation plan. These processes are consistent with the institution's assessment plan as required by Policy 2.2 *Educational Assessment*. While key constituents are involved in the process, the faculty have a central role in planning and evaluating the educational programmes.
- The institution identifies and publishes the expected learning outcomes for each of its degree and certificate programmes. Through regular and systematic assessment, it demonstrates that students who complete their programmes, no matter where or how they are offered, have achieved these outcomes.
- The institution provides evidence that its assessment activities lead to the improvement of teaching and learning.

UNDERGRADUATE PROGRAMME

The undergraduate programme is designed to provide students with a substantial, coherent, and articulated exposure to the broad domains of knowledge.

The Commission encourages a tripartite structure for baccalaureate and academic or transfer associate degree programmes:

- General education requires students to master competencies for independent learning and to develop an awareness of the fundamental areas of knowledge;
- The major requires students to achieve a knowledge base in a specific area of concentration; and
- Electives provide the opportunity for students to pursue other intellectual interests.

The instructional programme, as a whole, is based on a clear rationale with the component parts designed to reflect that rationale. Degree and certificate programmes are characterised by clarity and order which are discernible in model curricula shown in official publications and are recorded in official student records of actual programmes pursued.

Baccalaureate and academic or transfer associate degree programmes include a substantial core of general education instruction with identifiable outcomes and require competence in:

- Written and oral communication;
- Quantitative reasoning;
- Critical analysis and logical thinking; and
- litreacy in the discourse or technology appropriate to the programme of study.

Associate degree programmes are designed to prepare students for careers in vocational and technical fields, and for transfer to a senior institution. The educational requirements for these degrees must be carefully determined in order to fulfill their respective purposes.

Programmes of study for which applied or specialised associate degrees are granted, or programmes of an academic year or more in length for which certificates are granted, contain a recognisable body of instruction in three programme-related areas:

- Communication;
- Computation; and
- Human relations described in *General Education/*

Related Instruction Requirements.

- The institution requires of all its degree and pre-baccalaureate programmes a component of general education and/or related instruction that is published in its general catalogue in clear and complete terms.
- The general education component of the institution's degree programmes is based on a rationale that is clearly articulated and is published in clear and complete terms in the catalogue. It provides the criteria by which the relevance of each course to the general education component is evaluated.
- The general education programme offerings include the humanities and fine arts, the natural sciences, mathematics, and the social sciences. The programme may also include courses that focus on the interrelationships between these major fields of study.
- The institution's policies for the transfer and acceptance of credit are clearly articulated. In accepting transfer credits to fulfill degree requirements, the institution ensures that the credits accepted are comparable to its own courses. Where patterns of transfer from other institutions are established, efforts to formulate articulation agreements are demonstrated.
- The institution designs and maintains effective academic advising programmes to meet student needs for information and advice, and adequately informs and prepares faculty and other personnel responsible for the advising function.
- Whenever developmental or remedial work is required for admission to the institution or any of its programmes, clear policies govern the procedures that are followed, including such matters as ability to benefit, permissible student load, and granting of credit. When such courses are granted credit, students are informed of the

institution's policy of whether or not the credits apply towards a degree.

- The institution's faculty is adequate for the educational levels offered, including full-time faculty representing each field in which it offers major work.
- In an effort to further establish an institution's success with respect to student achievement, the Northwest Commission on Colleges and Universities shall require those institutions that offer pre-baccalaureate vocational programmes to track State licensing examination pass rates, as applicable, and job placement rates.

GRADUATE PROGRAMME

A graduate programme is a set of advanced academic experiences beyond the baccalaureate level which must be satisfactorily completed to warrant the award of a graduate degree such as a master's or doctorate. Graduate degree programmes may generally be classified into two categories: those that prepare students mainly as scholars and researchers and those that prepare students for a profession. The objective of a research-oriented graduate degree programme is to develop scholars—that is, students with skills necessary to discover or acquire, organise, and disseminate new knowledge.

The objective of the professional graduate degree is to develop in students their competence in interpreting, organising, and communicating knowledge and to develop the analytical and performance skills needed for the conduct and advancement of professional practice.

- The level and nature of graduate-degree programmes are consistent with the mission and goals of the institution.
- Programmes of study at the graduate level are guided by well-defined and appropriate educational objectives and differ from undergraduate programmes in requiring greater depth of study and increased demands on student intellectual or creative capacities.

- When offering the doctoral degree, the institution ensures that the level of expectations, curricula, and resources made available are significantly greater than those provided for master's and baccalaureate level programmes.

GRADUATE FACULTY AND RELATED RESOURCES

Essential to graduate education are the recruitment and retention of a faculty that excels in scholarship, teaching, and research. To provide an acceptable level of instruction for the graduate student, faculty whose responsibilities include a major commitment to graduate education are involved in keeping pace with, and advancing the frontiers of, knowledge.

Successful graduate programmes demand a substantial institutional commitment of resources for faculty, space, equipment, laboratories, library and information resources.

- The institution provides evidence that it makes available for graduate programmes the required resources for faculty, facilities, equipment, laboratories, library and information resources wherever the graduate programmes are offered and however delivered.
- The institution demonstrates a continuing commitment of resources to initiate graduate programmes and to ensure that the graduate programmes maintain pace with the expansion of knowledge and technology.
- Institutions offering graduate degrees have appropriate full-time faculty in areas appropriate to the degree offered and whose main activity lies with the institution. Such faculty are related by training and research to the disciplines in which they teach and supervise research.
- Faculty are adequate in number and sufficiently diversified within disciplines so as to provide effective teaching, advising, scholarly and/or creative activity, as well as to participate appropriately in curriculum development, policy development, evaluation, institutional planning, and development.

Small graduate programmes ordinarily require the participation of several full-time faculty whose responsibilities include a major commitment to graduate education.

- In the delivery of off-campus programmes, full-time faculty whose responsibilities include a major commitment to graduate education provide physical presence and participation in the planning, delivery, and assessment of the programmes.
- The institution that offers the doctoral degree has a core of full-time faculty active in graduate education at its main campus and at each off-campus location where doctoral programmes are offered.

GRADUATE RECORDS AND ACADEMIC CREDIT

Graduate admission and retention policies ensure that student qualifications and expectations are compatible with institutional mission and goals.

Graduate programme faculty are involved in specifying admission criteria, transfer of graduate credit, and graduation requirements.

- Graduate programme admission policies and regulations are consistent with and supportive of the character of the graduate programmes offered by the institution. These policies and regulations are published and made available to prospective and enrolled students.
- Admission to all graduate programmes is based on information submitted with the formal application such as undergraduate and graduate transcripts, official reports on nationally recognised tests, and evaluations by professionals in the field or other faculty-controlled evaluation procedures.
- Faculty teaching in graduate programmes are involved in establishing both general admission criteria for graduate study as well as admission criteria to specific graduate programmes.
- Graduation requirements for advanced degrees

offered by the institution are determined by the faculty teaching in the applicable graduate programmes. At minimum, the policies governing these graduation requirements include:

- — The specified time period in which the degree must be completed.
- — The number of credit hours that must be completed at the degree-granting institution, normally at least two-thirds of those required for the degree.
- — The minimum number of graduate-level credits, normally at least 50 per cent of those required for the degree.
- — For the master's degree, a minimum of one academic year of full-time study or its equivalent, with a minimum of 24 semester or 36 quarter hours.
- — The number of graded credit hours that must be earned for the degree.
- — The minimum standard of performance or acceptable grade point average, normally a B or its equivalent.
- — The types of qualifying and exit examinations which the candidate must pass.
- — The proficiency requirements the candidate must satisfy.
- — The thesis, dissertation, writing, or research requirement which the candidate must satisfy.

- Transfer of graduate credit is evaluated by faculty based on policies established by faculty whose responsibilities include a major commitment to graduate education, or by a representative body of such faculty who are responsible for the degree programme at the receiving institution. The amount of transfer credit granted may be limited by the age of the credit, the institution from which the transfer is made, and the appropriateness of the credit earned to the degree being sought.
- Graduate credit may be granted for internships, field

experiences, and clinical practices that are an integral part of the graduate degree programme. Consistent with Policy 2.3 *Credit for Prior Experiential Learning,* credit may not be granted for experiential learning which occurred prior to the student's matriculation into the graduate degree programme. Unless the graduate student's faculty advisor structures the current learning experience and monitors and assesses the learning and its outcomes, no graduate credit is granted for current learning experiences external to the student's formal graduate programme.

CONTINUING EDUCATION AND SPECIAL LEARNING ACTIVITIES

The changing nature of the demands placed upon individuals in today's society requires many of them to engage in life-long education. Many higher education institutions have incorporated into their missions an extension and public service component to provide for life-long learning opportunities.

These opportunities are referred to as continuing education, professional development, extension education, outreach, special programmes, public and community service programmes.

Such programmes may be for either undergraduate or graduate credit, or non-credit, may be offered on and off campus, and may be offered through a variety of instructional formats.

The provisions of this standard apply to:

- Off-campus programmes and courses for credit, including those at branch campuses, extension centers or satellite sites, external degree programmes, and military base programmes.
- Degree-completion programmes.
- Distance learning courses and courses taught exclusively on or off campus by special delivery systems, such as computer-based instruction, correspondence, television, video or audio cassette, or through other electronically-accessed means.

- Practices providing credit for prior experiential learning.
- Travel/study and study abroad programmes.
- Courses certified by the institution offered in secondary schools for college or university academic credit.
- Non-credit community service programmes and courses, including those that offer *Continuing Education Units* (CEU).
- Relicensure courses, in-service, and credential programmes.
- Testing, evaluation, and examination procedures for granting degree credit.
- Workshops, seminars, short courses, conferences, institutes, special evening and summer programmes.

Off-Campus and Other Special Programmes Providing Academic Credit

Continuing education and special learning activities, programmes, and courses offered for credit are consistent with the educational mission and goals of the institution. Such activities are integral parts of the institution and maintain the same academic standards as regularly offered programmes and courses. The institution maintains direct and sole responsibility for the academic quality of all aspects of all programmes and courses through the management and supervision by faculty and institutional administrators.

Adequate resources to maintain high quality programmes are ensured.

- The institution provides evidence that all off-campus, continuing education, and other special programmes are compatible with the institution's mission and goals, and are designed, approved, administered, and periodically evaluated under established institutional procedures.
- The institution is solely responsible for the academic and fiscal elements of all instructional programmes it offers. The institution conforms to Policy A-6 *Contractual Relationships with Organisations Not Regionally Accredited.*

- Full-time faculty representing the appropriate disciplines and fields of work are involved in the planning and evaluation of the institution's continuing education and special learning activities.
- The responsibility for the administration of continuing education and special learning activities is clearly defined and an integral organisational component of the institution's organisation.
- Programmes and courses offered through electronically-mediated or other distance delivery systems provide ready access to appropriate learning resources and provide sufficient time and opportunities for students to interact with faculty.
- There is an equitable fee structure and refund policy.
- The granting of credit for continuing education courses and special learning activities is based upon institutional policy, consistent throughout the institution, and applied wherever located and however delivered. The standard of one quarter hour of credit for 30 hours or one semester hour of credit for 45 hours of student involvement is maintained for instructional programmes and courses.
- Continuing education and/or special learning activities, programmes, or courses offered for academic credit are approved in advance by the appropriate institutional body and monitored through established procedures.
- Credit for prior experiential learning is offered only at the undergraduate level and in accordance with Policy 2.3 *Credit for Prior Experiential Learning*.
- An institution offering an external degree, degree-completion programme, or special degree has clearly articulated policies and procedures concerning admission to the programme, transfer of prior-earned credit, credit by examination, credit for prior experiential learning, credit by evaluation, and residency requirements.
- When credit is measured by outcomes alone or other

non-traditional means, student learning and achievement are demonstrated to be at least comparable in breadth, depth, and quality to the results of traditional instructional practices.

- Travel/study courses meet the same academic standards, award similar credit, and are subject to the same institutional control as other courses and programmes offered by the sponsoring or participating institution. Credit is not awarded for travel alone. The operation of these programmes is consistent with Policy 2.4 *Study Abroad Programmes,* and Policy A-6 *Contractual Relationships with Organisations Not Regionally Accredited.*

NON-CREDIT PROGRAMMES AND COURSES

Non-credit programmes and courses, including those that award *Continuing Education Units* (CEU), are consistent with the mission and goals of the institution.

These offerings are characterised by high quality instruction with qualified instructors.

- Non-credit programmes and courses are administered under appropriate institutional policies, regulations, and procedures. Faculty are involved, as appropriate, in planning and evaluating non-credit programmes.
- The institution maintains records for audit purposes which describe the nature, level, and quantity of service provided through non-credit instruction.
- When offering courses that award *Continuing Education Units* (CEU), the institution follows national guidelines for awarding and recording such units which call for one CEU being equivalent to 10 hours of instruction and appropriate to the objectives of the course.

GENERAL EDUCATION/RELATED INSTRUCTION REQUIREMENTS

The Commission endorses the concept of general education and requires of all undergraduate programmes a substantial and coherent programme of general education or a programme of related instruction. By design, the policy is intended to be qualitative rather than quantitative in nature. No formula for specific application or particular pattern of general education is endorsed. However, every institution is expected to publish in its general catalogue a clear and complete statement of its requirements for general education and/or related instruction, as appropriate.

A substantial core of general education instruction is regarded as an essential component of all baccalaureate degree programmes and of all academic or transfer associate degree programmes. Similarly, a core of related instruction is regarded as a necessary integral part of all applied or specialised associate degree programmes and of all certificate programmes of an academic year or more in length. General education in degree programmes shall be of collegiate level.

The contents of general education, and of related instruction in applied or specialised degree and certificate programmes, should be comparable, though not necessarily identical, to traditional academic offerings and should be taught by faculty who are clearly appropriately qualified. In some cases, institutions may provide for general education through admission or graduation requirements. Institutions are encouraged to include broad general education instruction as part of non-degree specialised programmes in addition to directly utilitarian-related instruction.

GENERAL EDUCATION

General education introduces students to the content and methodology of the major areas of knowledge—the humanities and fine arts, the natural sciences, mathematics, and the social sciences and helps them develop the mental skills that will make them more effective learners. General education may, of course, be taught in different ways, and an institution must judge whether its students are better served by curricula or requirements that approach the disciplines through content and methodology, or that approach the disciplines by concentrating on outcomes.

The rationale and plan for the general education requirements should be cooperatively developed by the faculty, administrative staff, and trustees, and the expected outcomes should be stated in relation to the institution's mission and goals.

RELATED INSTRUCTION

Programmes of study for which applied or specialised associate degrees are granted, or programmes of an academic year or more in length for which certificates are granted, must contain a recognisable body of instruction in programme-related areas of.

- Communication;
- Computation;
- Human relations.

Additional topics which should be covered as appropriate include safety, industrial safety, and environmental awareness.

Instruction in the related instructional areas may be either embedded within the programme curriculum or taught in blocks of specialised instruction. Each approach, however, must have clearly identified content that is pertinent to the general programme of study.

EDUCATIONAL ASSESSMENT

The Northwest Commission on Colleges and Universities expects each institution and programme to adopt an assessment plan responsive to its mission and its needs. In so doing, the Commission urges the necessity of a continuing process of academic planning, the carrying out of those plans, the assessment of the outcomes, and the influencing of the planning process by the assessment activities. As noted in Standard Two, implicit in the mission statement of every institution of higher education is the education of students. Consequently, each institution has an obligation to plan carefully its courses of instruction to respond to student needs, to evaluate the effectiveness of that educational programme in terms of the change it brings about in students, and to make improvements in the programme dictated by the evaluative process.

Assessment of educational quality has always been at the heart of the accreditation process. In earlier times, this assessment tended to focus more upon process measures and structural features; hence, there was considerable emphasis placed upon resources available to enhance students' educational experiences such as the range and variety of graduate degrees held by members of the faculty, the number of books in the library, the quality of specialised laboratory equipment, and the like.

More recently, while still stressing the need to assess the quantity and quality of the whole educational experience, the communities of interest served by the accreditation enterprise have come to appreciate the validity and usefulness of using output evaluations and assessment as well as input measures. Nearly every institution accredited by the Northwest Commission on Colleges and Universities engages in some type of outcomes assessment. Some are more formalised than others; some more quantified; some less so; some well- developed and long-utilised, and some of more recent origin and implementation.

The intent of Commission policy is to stress outcomes assessment as an essential part of the ongoing institutional self-study and accreditation processes, to underline the necessity for each institution to formulate a plan which provides for a series of outcomes measures that are internally consistent and in accord with its mission and structure, and, finally, to provide some examples of a variety of successful plans for assessing educational outcomes.

Central to the outcomes analyses or assessments are judgements about the effects of the educational programme upon students. These judgements can be made in a variety of ways and can be based upon a variety of data sources. The more data sources that contribute to the overall judgement, the more reliable that judgement would seem to be. There follows a list of several outcomes measures which, when used in appropriate combinations and informed by the institutional mission, could yield an efficacious programme of outcomes assessment.

This list is intended to be illustrative and exemplary as opposed to prescriptive and exhaustive.

- *Student Information*: From what sources does the institution acquire its students? What percentage directly from high school? Community college transfers? Transfers from other institutions? What blend of gender, age group, and ethnicity has the institution attracted over time? Retained over time? Graduated over time? What is the mean measured aptitude, over time, of entering students? What are the local grade distribution trends? What changes have appeared over time?

- *Mid-Programme Assessments*: If the institution has some kind of required writing course or an emphasis on writing across the curriculum, what evidence is there that students are better writers after having been exposed to the course or curriculum? How are these judgements rendered? If student writing improves, do students appear to retain this newly acquired proficiency? If so, why, and if not, why not? What changes are planned as a result of the assessment exercise? A required course, programme, or sequence in mathematics can be assessed in a similar fashion. What evidence is there that the skills improved or declined as a result of the programme? How are these judgements rendered? Does the improvement appear permanent or transitory? How has the programme been changed as a result of the assessment programme? A required course, programme, or sequence in any subject matter can be addressed in a similar fashion, as can nearly any part of the programme in general education or the programme as a whole.
- *End of Programme Assessment*: What percentage of those students who enter an institution graduate? Is the percentage increasing or decreasing? Why? What is the mean number of years in which students graduate? Is that mean increasing or decreasing? Why? What are the criteria for these judgements? What is the severalyear retention pattern from one class to the next, such as freshman to sophomore? If patterns reflect significant losses between one level

and another, what are the reasons? Similar questions may be asked by gender and/or ethnic background. If the institution or programme requires a capstone experience at the end of the curriculum, are present students performing better or worse than their predecessors? What are the reasons? What are the bases for the judgements?

- *Programme Review and Specialised Accreditation*: Some institutions require periodic programme review of each academic programme, either through an institutionally approved internal process and/or through seeking and achieving specialised accreditation, or by utilising external experts. Either or both of these activities can provide a wealth of outcomes assessment data, particularly if the methodology remains somewhat standardised over time.
- *Alumni Satisfaction and Loyalty*: A number of institutions engage in a variety of alumni surveys which elicit, over time, the judgements of alumni of the efficacy of their educational experience in a programme or at an institution. Use of such a mechanism can assist an institution in understanding whether alumni satisfaction with various aspects of the educational programme, particularly those facets which the institution stresses, appears to be growing or diminishing over time. If satisfaction is increasing, why? If decreasing, why? What are the bases for the judgements? What curricular implications do these findings have?
- *Dropouts/Non-completers*: What methods has the institution utilised to determine the reasons why students drop out or otherwise do not complete a programme once they have enrolled in it? What is the attrition rate over the past five years? Is it increasing or decreasing? What are the reasons? What programmes or efforts does the institution engage to enhance student retention? Which tactics have proved to be effective?

- *Employment and/or Employer Satisfaction Measures*: One relatively straightforward outcomes measure used by some institutions concerns that number and/or percentage of former students who have sought and found employment. Are they happy with what they have found? Do they think the programme prepared them well for their chosen occupations? If trained in a particular area, teacher education, for example, have they found a teaching position?

CREDIT FOR PRIOR EXPERIENTIAL LEARNING

The Northwest Commission on Colleges and Universities recognises the validity of granting credit for prior experiential learning, provided the practice is carefully monitored and documented. Credit for prior experiential learning may be offered under the conditions enumerated. This policy is not designed to apply to such practices as CLEP, Advanced Placement, or ACE-evaluated military credit.

Credit for courses taken from non-accredited institutions must be addressed pursuant to Policy 2.5 Transfer and Award of Academic Credit.

- Policies and procedures for awarding experiential learning credit must be adopted, described in appropriate institutional publications, and reviewed at regular intervals.
- Credit for prior experiential learning may be granted only at the undergraduate level.
- Credit may be granted only upon the recommendation of teaching faculty who are appropriately qualified and who are on a regular appointment with the college on a continuing basis.
- Credit may be granted only for documented learning which ties the prior experience to the theories and data of the relevant academic fields.
- Credit may be granted only for documented learning which falls within the regular curricular offerings of the institution.
- An institution that uses documentation and interviews in lieu of examinations must demonstrate in its self-

study that the documentation provides the academic assurances of equivalence to credit earned by traditional means.

- Credit for prior experiential learning should not constitute more than 25 per cent of the credits needed for a degree or certificate.
- No assurances are made as to the number of credits to be awarded prior to the completion of the institution's review process.
- Credit may be granted only to enrolled students and is to be identified on the student's transcript as credit for prior experiential learning.
- Policies and procedures must ensure that credit for prior experiential learning does not duplicate other credit awarded.
- Adequate precautions must be provided to ensure that payment of fees does not influence the award of credit.

STUDY ABROAD PROGRAMMES

Study abroad can be an important phase of undergraduate and graduate programmes in American colleges and universities. Carefully planned and administered, foreign study may add significant dimensions to a student's educational experience.

As guidelines for institutions which conduct programmes of foreign study or whose students participate in such programmes, the Northwest Commission on Colleges and Universities urges that a study abroad programme should:

- Be clearly related to the mission and goals of the sponsoring or participating institution.
- Have a well-defined rationale stating the specific nature and purposes of the programme, and be accurately represented in the institution's catalogue and all promotional litreature.
- Provide educational experiences related to the institution's curriculum.
- Be available to students carefully selected according to ability and interest.

- Have a carefully articulated policy regarding the availability of financial assistance to students for programmes required by the institution.
- Have clearly specified language proficiency requirements when appropriate to the programme and place of study, and clearly defined methods of testing proficiency prior to acceptance into the programme.
- Provide extensive information to intended participants, honestly and specifically describing the program's opportunities and limitations, indicating how and where instruction will be given and the relationship to the foreign institution, describing grading practices, identifying especially significant differences between a home campus experience and what can be expected abroad, including information about local living conditions and the extent of responsibility assumed by the programme for housing participants.
- Provide extensive orientation for participants prior to departure for, and on arrival in, the foreign country with respect to the matters in item, augmented with more detailed information and instruction related to the specific programme.
- Have a resident director carefully selected on the basis of professional competence and interest, appointed for a minimum of two years with provision for overlapping replacement appointments to allow for transition, and assured of the same professional rights, privileges, and consideration as colleagues on the home campus, with due respect for the responsibilities of the overseas assignment.
- Provide counseling and supervisory services at the foreign center, with special attention to problems peculiar to the location and nature of the programme.
- Guarantee adequate basic reference materials to offset any limitations of local libraries or inaccessibility to them.
- Include clearly defined criteria and policies for judging performance and assigning credit in accordance with

prevailing standards and practices at the home institution; where several institutions are involved with a single overseas institution or in a consortium, a common basis for determining grade equivalents is essential.

- Stipulate that students will ordinarily not receive credit for foreign study undertaken without prior planning or approval on the students' home campuses;
- Include provisions for regular follow-up studies on the individual and institutional benefits derived from such programmes.
- Ensure fair reimbursement to participants if the programme is not delivered as promised for reasons within the sponsor's control.

Cooperative arrangements are urged among American institutions seeking to provide foreign study opportunities for their students. In many cases, resident directors, faculty, and facilities could be shared, resulting in significant improvement in the efficiency and economy of the operation. One basic reference collection, for example, supported and used by students from several programmes is likely to be more satisfactory than several separate ones. Travel programmes *per se* or commercially sponsored 'study-travel programmes' should be thoroughly investigated by an institution before granting degree credit for these activities. The regional accrediting commissions do not evaluate these activities as foreign study programmes of member institutions, nor will they evaluate independent foreign study programmes which are not related to the curricula of specific colleges or universities in the United States.

2

Academic Fraud Accreditation and Quality Assurance

INTRODUCTION

Three major trends affect the demand for higher education today: the global growth of student enrolment figures, the redistribution of student enrolment among regions and the increased traffic of students from country to country. These trends arguably pose major challenges for transparency and accountability in higher education management.

THE MASSIFICATION OF EDUCATION

In 1970, the number of students in higher education was 28.2 million. By 1990, it had grown to 70.8 million and by 2004 to 132 million. These are minimum figures, as they only account for countries with available data.

The many reasons for this expansion in higher education include: the increasing complexity of the demand of modern societies and economies for more highly trained personnel; the fact that, in many fields, training that would have once been provided 'on the job' has become formalised in institutions of higher education, including corporate universities; the emergence of new fields that rely on universities as key sources of training, such as biology and computer science; the restructuring of higher education systems in Central and Eastern Europe and Central Asia after the fall of communism, which has led to the emergence of new public and private institutions and an increased number of students being admitted to higher education institutions. These trends, in generating further competition among students—not only to be admitted to universities, but also to enter the best institutions and get the most highly valued degrees or diplomas—have paradoxically encouraged a rat race in higher education.

THE CHANGING GEOPOLITICAL ENVIRONMENT

The demand for higher education has evolved greatly in recent years. The following are the dominant countries in terms of size and growth of enrolment figures: China, which had 19.4 million students in 2004; the United States, which had about 17 million students in 2004; India, which had 11.3 million students in 2004; Russia, which had 8.6 million students in 2004; Brazil, Indonesia, Japan, which had between 3 and 4 million students each in 2004; and, finally, Argentina, Egypt, France, Italy, South Korea, Mexico, the Philippines, Poland, Thailand, Turkey, the United Kingdom and Ukraine, which had between 2 and 3 million students each in 2004.

With the collapse of the Soviet Union and the regional unification of Europe, new models are gaining popular support, such as combining courses at different universities and campuses in different countries, which at times blurs the overall picture. Finally, while nations control what happens within their borders via various regulations and requirements, the vast enrolment figures for transnational education, which had about 2.5 million students in 2004, has naturally led to an increasing demand for quality assurance, mutual accreditation of institutions and awards, and mutual recognition of qualifications.

THE CROSS-BORDER PHENOMENON OF OVERSEAS STUDENTS AND COURSES

Economic globalisation has contributed to the international mobility of labour and students. This has generated a huge market in the international trade in higher education, which now moves billions of dollars and is a major source of income for a few provider countries. However, the cross-border phenomenon is also characterised by the development of overseas courses with at times extremely complex and even opaque administration.

Pebble Hills University offers a striking example of this: not only does it claim to offer degrees in a variety of fields, it also claims to be incorporated in Hutt River Province Principality in Western Australia and to have a licence to grant degrees from the Principality of Seborga in Italy. Moreover, the degrees offered are taught in learning centres in what are referred to as *knowledge villages* in Dubai, Hong Kong, Singapore, Taiwan, Lebanon and Nigeria.

The explosion of new information and communication technologies has rendered the current situation even more complex, with the multiplication of both virtual institutions and distance education programmes. The financing and quality assurance mechanisms of these educational providers are rather different from those of conventional higher education establishments. These major trends are certainly promising, as they reveal that more students have access to universities, new regions are emerging and new opportunities for studying abroad are rapidly developing.

At the same time, they contribute to increasing competition among students and institutions, to changes in roles and functions of universities, to the emergence of new providers, and so on. All of these factors could generate new incentives for academic fraud and corrupt behaviour.

The Increased Competition Among Students and Institutions

The increased competition among students and between institutions is today a worldwide phenomenon. Unless well regulated and controlled, this pressure increases the risk of academic fraud and cheating by students and by higher education institutions. In Georgia, for example, some private tutors take bribes to help guarantee that students are admitted to the department of their choice. These private tutors are generally on examination committees and therefore have connections within universities, are familiar with the content of exam papers, and can manipulate admission procedures to improve the chances of an applicant gaining entry to a particular university. Competition in the area of research is also having detrimental effects. For example, higher education institutions, as producers of research, are now even more susceptible to plagiarism. As they are also consumers of research, they are also more vulnerable to the manipulation of research results.

The More Dominant Gate-keeping Function of Universities

A university degree is gradually becoming a prerequisite for an increasing number of occupations. Certification is now indispensable for most positions of power, authority and prestige in modern societies. This puts immense responsibility in the hands of higher education institutions and, at the same time, opens enormous opportunities for corrupt practices. Testing for admission to higher education has become a key role of higher education institutions, which they share with the ministry of education in some cases.

Tests are the main tools used in the admissions process and are the major determinants of future success in education, employment, income and social status. Because of competition between institutions and for access to specific professions, the pressure of the demand for access to the 'right institution' and the 'right courses' generates and sustains corrupt behaviours. Furthermore, universities are playing a greater role as examining bodies.

This is due to various reasons, in particular the expansion in education and the consequent need to provide ever more competitive sorting mechanisms to control access to high-prestige occupations. Universities are seen *de facto* as meritocratic institutions that can be trusted to provide fair and impartial testing. However, when their testing mechanisms break down (for example in China) or are subject to corrupt practices (for example in India), their image is significantly weakened.

The Emergence of New Higher Education Providers

The emergence of new providers of higher education has contributed to the diversification of the higher education market, with the creation of technical institutes, community colleges, liberal arts colleges, mega-universities, on and off campuses, and so on. Many countries have therefore experienced a boost in private secondary education initiatives; an exodus of students abroad; a diversification of production and delivery technologies; and the development of a significant market for the providers of e-training and other distance and open institutions (as early as the Open University in the United Kingdom had more than 120,000 students).

For the higher education market to operate effectively and fairly within this context, there is a strong need for certified information about what is being offered by each institution and the actual value in terms of learning achievements, skill development and qualification. However, there is a two-fold obstacle to achieving this: not all stakeholders agree to respect the need for accreditation, and even accredited entities and programmes do not always provide services of similar quality.

The Diversification of Higher Education Markets

Advances in information and communication technologies have assisted in the development of new ways of delivering higher education and demonstrated the possibility of enhancing the quality and quantity of learning. For well-established and large-scale distance teaching universities, the shift to using new technologies necessitates a major overhaul of activities and huge investments in entirely new infrastructure for the development and delivery of new courses.

The major decisions required to initiate these changes cannot be taken easily or quickly. However, it is evident that if distance education universities do not positively face the challenges of merging and continuously evolving technologies, they may lose students and government support. International joint ventures, financed by global networks, could help speed up the adoption of new e-learning technologies on an even wider scale. The question, however, is: in this scenario, who will be regarded as accountable, to whom and how? Due to the mushrooming of new degree programmes and private institutions, sometimes with a high likelihood of the delivery of fake services and certification, there is also a growing need for the recognition of certificates, diplomas, courses, training programmes and institutions. This need is being translated into more demand for quality assurance and accreditation from institutions and delivery mechanisms.

The Demand for Professional Governance of Higher Education

Despite imponderables, it is likely that demand for access to education by an ever-widening segment of the population will continue overall. However, limited funds and the desire for efficient allocation of resources will come into direct conflict with demands for access, which will put greater pressure on higher education. As institutions become larger and more complex, there will also be increasing pressure for a greater level of professional administration.

At the same time, traditional forms of governance will come under increasing pressure to reform, as they will become inefficient in institutions that are growing larger and more bureaucratic. Moreover, the overall administration of higher education will be professionalised. The demands for accountability will also increase, causing institutions considerable difficulty. And as academic budgets increase, there will be an inevitable demand to monitor and control expenditures and a call for more transparency and accountability in resource management.

ACADEMIC FRAUD AND QUALITY ASSURANCE—KEY ISSUES

Corruption occurs at all levels in universities. The Georgian case study exemplifies this. There, widespread misconduct affects university examinations, the conferring of academic credentials, the procurement of goods and services, and the licensing and accreditation of institutions. It is also now accepted that academic fraud and corrupt practices involve a variety of stakeholders, including examination candidates, teachers, faculty members, supervisors, officials and employees of examination authorities, in addition to managers of courses, programmes, institutions, universities, and so on. Entities in charge of quality assurance and accreditation are also susceptible to corrupt practices, which is even more worrisome. Within this context, and given the complexity and diversity of the trends, it is extremely difficult to produce a comprehensive list of all opportunities for academic fraud.

This would be a useful exercise, however, as it would help to analyse the causes of corruption in higher education and to design strategies to address it. This chapter thus focuses on a broad cluster of opportunities for corrupt practice. In doing so, it maintains a distinction between the existing forms of higher education and the new forms emerging both within and outside of traditional public and private higher education sectors, despite there being blurred boundaries between the two.

ACADEMIC FRAUD AND CORRUPTION IN TRADITIONAL FORMS OF HIGHER EDUCATION

Academic fraud and corruption in traditional forms of higher education take various forms, namely agreements between students and faculty members or administrators, such as students paying professors for good grades or administrators charging students' families for admission to their university. However, examinations are the key area for a variety of malpractices. These can take place before, during or after exams. Some examples of these malpractices follow.

Before the Examination

- University professors offering university applicants expensive tutorial sessions that serve as a condition for entry or success.
- Officials, paper-setters, moderators or school administrators leaking the content of exam papers prior to the exam because of nepotism, favouritism or bribery.

- Preparing the actual topics of an examination beforehand (for example in Pakistan, some paper-setters were found to be operating their own tuition centres for exam candidates, who, upon payment of substantial fees, were granted access to at least part of their exam papers).

During the Examination

- Impersonation (that is, unregistered candidates taking the examinations of registered candidates, sometimes with the full knowledge of the supervisor).
- Candidates smuggling in cheating material (for example written notes or textbooks hidden in garments).
- External assistance (from helpers, for example, with the use of cell phones).
- Plagiarism in answering examination questions or in writing term papers.
- Copying and collusion among candidates.
- Irregularities during the examination process (for example the amount of time allotted to a candidate being altered for no justifiable reason).
- Intimidation of supervisory staff (for example by candidates, external helpers, parents, politicians, and so on).
- Improper assignment of candidates by officials to targeted centres.
- The use of *ghost centres* (that is, fictitious exam centres established by corrupt examination officials, where candidates can complete exams with the support of helpers and/or without supervision).
- The purchase of finished term papers, particularly on the Internet (for example via so-called 'paper mills').
- Substitution of scripts (that is, scripts written during an examination being replaced with scripts written either before or after the examination).

After the Examination (Admission to Universities)

- Grading malpractices (that is, collusion between the candidate and the grader, intimidation of graders by parents, or intimidation of parents by graders seeking rewards from candidates' parents).

- Bribery of the academic authorities responsible for admissions and/or for officially awarding scholarships to candidates on the basis of academic qualifications or exam results.
- Falsification of data files and result sheets, often by corrupt officials (for example admission test scores or the ranking of students in the admission list being illegally changed).
- Illegally changing fee-paying and non-fee-paying quotas.
- Sale of seats to students whose test scores do not qualify them for a position (at times through a bidding process, if the number of seats is limited).
- Issuing fake credentials and diplomas (for example via diploma mills).
- Manipulation of curricula vitae in order to obtain a job or pay increase (for example using fake diplomas, non-existent publications, and so on).
- Selling academic posts (for gifts, bribes, free work or other emoluments) or granting them based on ethnic or religious backgrounds.

Many malpractices are also found in the area of research, academic journals and publications, such as plagiarism, fabrication or falsification of data, distortions or manipulations of research results, manipulation of statistics, biases and conflicts of interest among reviewers, and so on. Some university lecturers and researchers, for example, give consultations to private firms without any form of control by their university hierarchy. At times, this practice has a strong impact on the rate of attendance, influences teaching content and introduces bias in research conclusions.

CORRUPTION IN NEW FORMS OF HIGHER EDUCATION

In recent years, extensive developments in ICTs have immensely widened the scope for fraud in academia and, at the same time, introduced innovative new methods of malpractice. The Internet (and all forms of e-learning) is now arguably the leading vehicle for fraudulent practices. Among other things, it has facilitated the practices of selling essays and term papers (rendering plagiarism a major problem), as well as fake degrees, at times even from reputable colleges and institutions such as Harvard and Yale or others in London and Paris. The Swedish National Agency for Higher Education, Sweden is now affected by academic fraud to a greater extent than ever before.

The country's problems include: bogus PhDs supposedly from Swedish higher education institutions, students applying for courses based on fake qualifications and individuals applying for posts using fake degrees. In addition, there are many fake universities, some of which advertise in the international press, circulate information by sending spam and rank high on the hit lists of search engines.

These universities also sell qualifications from Swedish higher education institutions, claiming that they are members of the institutions. Indeed, web sites specialising in fraudulent services are numerous today.

The transnational education boom has also contributed to the emergence of new opportunities for fraud. The following are some illustrations of this involving the management of overseas students and the franchising of overseas courses.

Management of Overseas Students

- Overseas students being offered financial incentives to enrol.
- Applicants being given false hope or promised admission on the spot.
- Applicants not eligible for admissions unduly charged a variety of fees.
- Applicants using fake credentials to gain admission.
- Applicants being charged by education agents for the falsification of documents that will qualify them for university entry.

- Indiscriminate recruitment of foreign students as a means of chasing money (that is, the acceptance of fake diplomas, lack of language skills, and so on).
- Bogus institutions that do not deliver the services they advertise. These are often unsustainable institutions that close down after the receipt of money.
- Bogus institutions promising visas to overseas students who enrol in their courses.
- Institutions and courses without proper accreditation being included on the official lists prepared for international students.
- Lowering of academic standards for overseas students (that is, with regard to admission, performance, graduation, and so on).
- Overseas students being allowed to repeat courses several times, even when they have no prospect of passing.

Franchising of Overseas Courses

- Corrupt officers making money by issuing licences and franchise rights and collecting fees/bribes from those wanting franchises.
- Students enrolling at franchised institutions assuming that since, they are paying fees they will automatically qualify.
- Reducing the number of failing students by inflating the grades of those at risk of failing and turning a blind eye to plagiarism.
- Students, parents, the franchisee or the franchising institution pressuring faculty members to adjust grading standards so that everyone passes examinations and assessments (for example, in institutions in China, Malaysia and Vietnam).

CORRUPTION IN QUALITY ASSURANCE AND ACCREDITATION MECHANISMS

Accreditation and certification processes worldwide are increasingly being undermined by fraud.

According to Bear and Bear:

- There are more than 300 unaccredited universities

now operating. While a few are genuine start-ups or online ventures, the great majority range from simply being of dreadful quality to being outright diploma mills, which are fake institutions that sell degrees for between US$3,000 and US$5,000. It is not uncommon for a large bogus school to 'award' as many as 500 PhD's each year and, as a consequence, earn an aggregate income easily in excess of US$200 million. Data shows that a single phony school can earn between US$10 million and US$20 million annually.

More specific forms of malpractice in quality assurance and accreditation include:

- Payment of bribes to obtain successful certification or accreditation.
- Distortion in the application of accreditation criteria, for example admitting below-standard candidates to meet enrolment criteria (*ex ante*) or over-grading students to meet achievement criteria (*ex post*).
- Accreditation processes based on non-transparent criteria (because rectors have an interest in preventing competition).
- Higher education providers circumventing accreditation procedures through franchising schemes or introducing courses in segments of the education system where accreditation is not compulsory.
- Establishing schools for the sole purpose of making a profit by lying about their accreditation status, thus preventing their students from taking national licensing exams.
- Non-accredited institutions falsely issuing accredited degrees.
- Creation of fraudulent or bogus accreditation agencies (accreditation mills, which are at times established by higher education institutions themselves).

DIFFERENCES BASED ON CONTEXT

Because opportunities for corruption may depend on the model in place, certain distinctions may arise based on the context. Indeed, a brief glance at higher education throughout the world reveals a continuum of academic systems: from highly centralised models (for example France and China) to almost completely decentralised ones (for example Australia, Canada and India); from federal systems (for example Germany and the United States) to systems where the private sector is in competition with the public sector (for example Latin America and Japan); from systems which, until quite recently, were fragmented, with numerous and over-specialised establishments (as in the former communist European countries), to systems that are virtually carbon copies of others (as in some countries in Africa and the Arab region). Similarly, systems of quality assurance and accreditation vary from country to country.

A distinction should therefore be made between the following two models: quality assurance and accreditation regulated and controlled by central public bodies (for example ministries of education, University Grants Commissions, and so on) and quality assurance and accreditation regulated and controlled by non-governmental bodies (for example independent commissions, private entities, professional associations, and so on).

Quality Assurance and Accreditation Regulated and Controlled by Central Public Bodies

This is the prevailing model in many societies, typically those with a strong tradition of centralised education administration, as in France and some former Soviet countries. In this case, quality assurance mechanisms are often confined to the educational activities of institutions within national boundaries and are not always consistent nationwide.

Moreover, the monopoly power exerted by public bodies and the regular occurrence of collusion of interests open doors for a variety of corrupt practices, such as the payment of bribes for university admission or to successfully obtain accreditation, accreditation processes based on non-transparent criteria, distortion in the application of accreditation criteria, and so on.

A study undertaken in Ukraine, where there are some 175 accredited private higher education institutions, shows that the main areas of corruption in the education sector include large state universities that control licensing and accreditation.

Interviews conducted with 43 rectors, vice rectors and administrators from five private universities revealed that successful licensing or accreditation applications, with few exceptions, required some form of bribery; that licensing, mandatory only for private institutions, may require a bribe of US$200 (about two months' salary for a typical academic); and that accreditation might call for a 'gratuity' of 10 or 20 times that amount.

Quality Assurance and Accreditation Regulated and Controlled by Non-governmental Bodies

With the higher education market now becoming liberalised, this is the model currently in vogue. In principle, this model offers low risks of collusion and conflict of interest between the bodies in charge of accreditation and the beneficiaries of its service.

But de-linking the bodies in charge of quality assurance and accreditation from higher education institutions does not address the other manifold causes of corruption and academic fraud, such as: illegitimate regulatory bodies; the partial or inconsistent scope of quality assurance and accreditation, leaving room for managers to misuse procedures; non-compliance of higher education institutions with quality assurance procedures, and so on.

Experience shows that this regulation model can also be distorted. For example, higher education providers can circumvent accreditation procedures through franchising schemes, schools can lie about their accreditation status, bogus accredited agencies can be created (particularly via the web), and so on.

ACADEMIC FRAUD AND QUALITY ASSURANCE—GUIDING PRINCIPLES

Given the enormous complexity of the problems, the variety of opportunities for academic fraud, and the importance of contextual and societal factors, universally applicable solutions cannot be provided to address these challenges. Each country, and institution, must be properly diagnosed and the appropriate strategies to meet the challenges must be identified. However, from the experience gained worldwide in this area, three guiding principles could be proposed for designing strategies.

PRINCIPLE 1
QUALITY ASSURANCE POLICIES SHOULD CONTRIBUTE TO A VIRTUOUS CYCLE (AND NOT A VICIOUS ONE)

In most cases, quality assurance supports accreditation and accredited institutions are fraud-free. By addressing the issues based on the type of provider, what needs to be provided, the mode, media and location of the delivery system, and the curricula and teaching content, internal and external quality assurance arrangements provide the key elements for accreditation and reduce or eliminate opportunities for academic fraud. Put differently, accredited institutions assume that quality assurance is addressed and contribute to combating academic fraud.

This is the *virtuous cycle*. Under this circumstance, quality assurance and accreditation are central approaches for combating fraud for both new and existing forms of higher education. When in some societies, for political reasons or because of lack of resources, it is impossible to adopt quality assurance and impose accreditation procedures on institutions, there are still some pragmatic means of addressing corruption, addressing the challenges.

However, a *vicious cycle* can occur when the challenges of quality assurance are not properly addressed and the quality assurance process offers opportunities for corruption. This is the case when the accountability of the accrediting institution or mechanism is not well established; when the accrediting institution or mechanism is not free of collusion of interests or when it is a tool of social, political or financial pressure on the delivery system requesting accreditation. Worst of all, this occurs when the team in charge of quality assurance manipulates data and the accrediting mechanism is based on dishonest grounds.

An unaccredited institution, however, is not necessarily a diploma mill. Some truck-driving schools, massage therapy colleges and even computer schools, for example, choose not to be accredited and yet still hold classes, teach students and hold them accountable for learning.

PRINCIPLE 2
SOUND POLICIES SHOULD CONSIDER THE WIDE DISSEMINATION OF THE SOCIAL, FINANCIAL AND ETHICAL COSTS OF FRAUD

The costs of fraud are generally either ignored or overlooked by higher education stakeholders. However, in order to mobilise authorities and the public at large against fraud, there is a need to raise their awareness about the enormous social, financial and ethical implications it can have. Consequences of fraud include greater inequity and unfairness in selection procedures, scepticism about the performance of higher educational systems, costs involved in introducing reliable security measures, and so on.

The different categories of stakeholders affected by different types of fraud include the following:

- The honest *clients* who are the victims of fraud. They are charged fees and other costs and receive in exchange fake services and certificates or the person they think is a trained teacher, business consultant, or engineer may not have the degree or even the knowledge required.
- The *employers* who are victims of unqualified employees using fake credentials, which causes them financial liability and may also cause injury to people or property. In a recent survey of human resource managers in 1,500 major UK companies, over half said that lying on CVs was a serious problem for their organisation and over 70 per cent said that they had encountered cases of serious lying on CVs from prospective job applicants.

- The *citisens* who as taxpayers subsidise higher education, and therefore may gradually question the *raison d'être* of the tax system and the legitimacy of financing higher education. Fake institutions can indeed take millions from good institutions and foul the waters of non-traditional higher education.

Within this context, the ethical cost of fraud should be taken very seriously, as its consequences are potentially devastating. Two illustrations of this are: a prominent paediatrician was discovered to have forged his medical degree from the University of California; and for more than 20 years an expert witness provided scientific testimony in more than 300 cases before the California Superior Court without having the adequate credentials.

PRINCIPLE 3

POLICIES SHOULD BE COMPREHENSIVE AND TARGET NOT ONLY ACADEMIC FRAUD BUT ALSO OTHER CORRUPT PRACTICES

Higher education, like any other sector, is subject to corrupt practices, as it involves the management of different kinds of resources. Corrupt practices are known to affect all kinds of expenditures, including construction, purchase of equipment and materials, payment of salaries, and so on. It can take the form of misuse of physical and human resources and accompany the outsourcing of activities (for example support services to students and academics). Like at other levels of education, corrupt practices can develop when financing mechanisms (that is, per capita grants) offer opportunities for misbehaviour.

A recent illustration of the possible manipulation of statistics is offered by El Alto, the public university of Bolivia, which failed to certify its enrolment figures. As a consequence, it could not receive its financial allocation from the Bolivian gas royalty until quite recently.

Beyond these similarities, in order to assess the various costs of corruption in higher education, it is important to keep in mind that higher education is distinctive as a socioeconomic activity in the following two respects:

- First, it is *intensive* in 'specific capital investment, both human and physical', meaning that its capital must be designed and defined specifically for the construction of buildings, the installation of training equipment and the recruitment of staff and lecturers, and so on. Because physical and human capital is to a large extent different in each case, it is difficult to standardise and therefore benchmark investment costs. Unlike manufactured goods, for instance, the supplier has much more information about the true costs than the purchaser does (the 'information asymmetry'), which translates into greater opportunities for corruption, even when competitive bidding is in place and adhered to. This is all the more true with cross-border providers, when education is delivered via open or distance methods (especially in the case of e-teaching), and when a programme or course offered is a small or marginal part of the services offered by a mega-university or corporate institution that can easily transfer investment costs between various services.
- Second, higher education is a *network* activity. It is not fundamentally a heap of structures but rather a flow of services, that is, training, research, certification, support services to the community, contractual arrangements with industry and services, partnership and other linkages with sponsors, and so on. Being a network activity, higher education runs two major risks: one, the range of services offered often includes areas with monopoly power, which are in the hands of either the training institution or one of its counterparts; and two, the services are not always offered by a single stakeholder or controlled in a transparent way, thus offering easy opportunities for corrupt practices supported by potential collusion of interests (sponsors may interfere in the choice of a

service delivery method, a provider, equipment, and so on).

This is why government authorities usually regulate the operation of institutions of higher education and require that external audits be conducted on a regular basis.

At the same time, when regulators (accrediting bodies) include areas with monopoly power, and even more so, when collusion of interests occurs in regulating bodies and higher education institutions, corruption can become rampant or even pandemic. Regulators themselves may need to be regulated. On a different yet relevant note, in many countries, including the European region, access to jobs in higher education (particularly teaching positions) is not regulated by an entirely free and well-informed job market, which leads to opportunities for corrupt practices. All of these issues need to be properly taken into consideration when addressing corruption problems.

ADDRESSING THE CHALLENGES

SIX LINES OF ACTION

Six main lines of action are presented below to address the various challenges.

LINE 1
REGULATING THE MARKET WITH TRANSPARENT CRITERIA

Whether the system is centralised or decentralised, with predominant control by the state or non-governmental procedures, it is necessary to regulate the operating conditions of the higher education market so as to combat fraud. This means that clear admission criteria and procedures must be set.

This concern has led certain former Soviet countries to establish reliable, transparent mechanisms for administering exams for graduation from higher education. Ukraine, for instance, has created standardised national exams and Kyrgyzstan has set up a unified testing system. It also means that clear assessment guidelines and transparent standards and processes for quality assurance and accrediting bodies must be developed. UNESCO and OECD have paved the way by formulating guidelines for quality in crossborder higher education. Of course, the issue is not only setting up transparent criteria and procedures, but also ensuring that they have been actually enforced.

There have been many successful systems for checking qualifications and credentials. All of these systems are gradually turning to e-mechanisms, either independently at the national level (for example in South Africa, China and the United States) or by soliciting the help of specialised organisations such as QualSearch in Australia or Experian in the United Kingdom. China also claims to have developed a central verification system through which the legitimacy of qualifications can be verified, but there is no evidence that it is fully operational.

LINE 2
REDUCING THE RISK OF CONFLICTS OF INTEREST

An efficient means of reducing the risk of conflicts of interest among agents in charge of certification and accreditation is to establish autonomous professional bodies with fair representation of stakeholders (public and private). Apromising development in this regard is the outsourcing and subcontracting of exam management in order to limit interferences and thus lower the probability of academic fraud. Another is the establishment of independent organisations, such as the Australian Universities Quality Agency. Private consulting firms that offer their services online to provide judgements on accredited and non-accredited institutions can also be very useful.

Such institutions must comply with codes of conduct that protect against distorted behaviour such as conflicts of interest. Another important approach is to de-link bodies in charge of certification and accreditation. For example, in the medical field, Heyneman suggests that the process by which individuals apply to practise or become certified in their professions should be separate from the realm of higher education institutions: 'No matter how excellent, no university should provide a license to practice medicine. This licence should be awarded by a board of medical examiners that also manages a system of testing that all medical students must pass. Similar systems must be established for law, accounting and others. The key to this new system is to allow many higher education institutions to compete with one another.' However, in some societies, institutional control tends to take the form of political repression. As a result, universities in these countries put up enormous resistance to quality assurance and accreditation by outside bodies.

The real dilemma is that countries with a lack of social control may fuel corruption by demanding accreditation and pressing for more accountability and that countries with more established democratic traditions may limit the autonomy and thus distort the behaviour of academic institutions so as to serve the public opinion agenda.

To be effective, an accountability system should:

- Clearly state the rules and procedures associated with managing the education system;
- Provide a mechanism for monitoring compliance;
- Specify the consequences of non-compliance; and
- Be consistently enforced.

LINE 3
DEVELOPING STANDARDS AND CODES OF PRACTICE OF ACADEMIC INTEGRITY

Another important component of a strategy to fight academic fraud is the design and adoption of professional, ethical and honour codes of conduct for both students and teachers. A number of countries such as Canada, Hong Kong, India and the United States have had particularly relevant experiences in this regard.

Comparative studies carried out by the International Institute for Educational Planning (IIEP) in this area conclude that a number of conditions are required for such codes to be effective and complied with, namely: participatory procedures for their design and maintenance; a proper information system on their content and the 'rules of the game', including the penalties for non-compliance; and the training of key stakeholders, including members of the education and administrative professions. The main concern is not to identify and prosecute individuals but to change the ethos and quality assurance culture by accrediting entities and academic institutions. In a context of internationalisation and even more so of the globalisation of higher education, special guidelines and codes of practice are required for the recruitment and support of overseas students.

LINE 4
USING MORE EFFECTIVE AND TRANSPARENT MANAGEMENT TOOLS

More effective and transparent management tools are needed for both traditional and new forms of higher education, and for the mechanisms and bodies in charge of quality assurance and accreditations.

The more systematic use of ICTs, for instance, offers the potential to detect fraud, check for plagiarism and increase the costs of corrupt practices in examination processes and in access to the labour market for higher education graduates.

There are many examples of this. In the Philippines, an electronic device is used to detect fraud in exams by identify statistically improbable results (for example when grades appear to have risen sharply, or when the statistical distribution of the scores is erratic or difficult to interpret). Other countries, particularly in Europe and North America, recommend using a web site to detect plagiarism. Others recommend adopting automated procedures to manage all stages of examination.

These procedures are based on the experience of Azerbaijan, where the higher education admissions process is run entirely by computer: designing tests, administering exams, grading tests, processing university admissions and informing candidates of the results. The University Grants Commission of India has decided to request that universities add computer microchips to the degrees they award to students in order to reduce the circulation of fake university degrees.

LINE 5
FACILITATING PUBLIC ACCESS TO INFORMATION

Reliable and user-friendly information systems are needed in higher education and accrediting institutions. In particular, many English-speaking countries have developed directories of courses or institutions accredited by their recognised institutions and approved accreditation agencies.

In the United States, the state of Oregon has an Office of Degree Authorisation and the state of Michigan has compiled a list of unapproved accreditation agencies. Furthermore, the International Association of University Presidents has created a register of reliable accreditation agencies. However, in the context of internationalisation and the globalisation of higher education, access to international reference databases on accredited higher education institutions and courses needs to be facilitated.

The Council for Higher Education Accreditation (CHEA), a coordinating body for higher education accreditation, has paved the way by creating a database with examples of US accreditation obtained by higher education institutions located in 31 different countries. In addition, information on reliability, quality and standards could be made available to applicants interested in overseas courses.

For example, for all cross-border higher education, there is a need to widely publicise (on web sites) recruitment fairs, course requirements and help lines, as well as rules, regulations, agreements, placement schemes for new students, and so on. One good example is South Africa, which seeks to maintain web sites listing accredited overseas universities. Finally, systems to penalise institutions that provide unreliable or false information could be established.

LINE 6
ESTABLISHING AND USING AWARENESS INDICATORS OR 'RED FLAGS'

These indicators could help various stakeholders with different levels of responsibility, including accrediting institutions, entities in charge of quality assurance, presidents and rectors of universities, department directors, academics, managers of e-training companies, funding and sponsoring agencies, students, and users of higher education graduates.

FUTURE TRENDS, LESSONS LEARNED AND CONCLUSION

The persistent growth in the demand for higher education services, coupled with the variety of agencies involved in the market, will sustain the pressure for more distorted practices. Fortunately, and as a direct consequence, a trend towards more transparency, accountability and ethics is simultaneously on the rise.

Table 2.1 Forecasts of Global Demand for International Higher Education for the top five Source Countries

Countries	2000	2005	2010	2020	2025	Growth (per cent)
China	218,437	437,109	760,103	1,937,129	2,973,287	11.0
South Korea	81,370	96,681	114,269	155,737	172,671	3.1
India	76,908	141,691	271,193	502,237	629,080	8.8
Japan	66,097	65,872	68,544	71,974	73,665	0.4
Greece	60,486	68,285	75,339	84,608	89,903	1.6

This trend demands more regulation, the design of codes of conduct, training to fight academic fraud, better access to reliable information, separating examinations from access to jobs, and so on. At the same time, recent trends show that the nature of certification and accreditation is changing. Greater emphasis is being placed on the results and skills obtained by students rather than on the processes or means involved. In this context, the notion of 'accountability' of accrediting institutions and quality assurance systems might change and there may be a significant movement towards more transparency.

Furthermore, complementary action trends are already addressing the challenge of adapting existing quality assurance and accreditation mechanisms to the development and diversification of demand. These trends include voluntary cooperation among partners within the higher education profession, the creation of international lists of quality-assured and accredited institutions and programmes, and the introduction of consultancy services for potential students and users.

The principle of subsidiarity, a cascade of mechanisms and entities sharing different degrees of responsibility for certification are thus expected to progressively develop at different levels, as follows:

- At the *institutional level,* internal evaluation and audit systems will develop to complement external audit mechanisms. This is the case in Slovakia, where the law has introduced internal university auditing as 'an objective activity focussed mainly on operative and independent assessment of the appropriateness and efficiency of the operation of the entity covered by the audit.
- At the *national level,* quality assurance arrangements will depend on historical factors: centralised *versus* decentralised higher education and the private sector share. U21 is a good example: quality assurance is not managed by prestigious universities but by an independent institution linked to a profit-making company called Thomson Learning.
- At the *sub-regional level,* independent regional, public or private accreditation agencies (for example the Central and Eastern European Network of Quality Assurance Agencies) will evaluate institutions and providers.
- At the *regional level,* regional mechanisms for monitoring and recognising national quality assurance and accreditation systems will be strengthened. The Bologna process in Europe, for instance, favours the creation of bodies such as the

European Consortium for Accreditation (ECA), which aim to make national quality assurance systems transparent – not to replace them.

- At the *international level,* international mechanisms for monitoring and recognising regional and national quality assurance and accreditation systems may improve and enjoy more support by stakeholders. UNESCO, the World Bank, OECD and other international institutions—public and private—will pursue initiatives in this regard. However, no excessive optimism is warranted here.

Observers say that a comprehensive international quality assurance system is unlikely to develop in the near future as a substitute for national policies and procedures because of inertia, national resistance and the practical difficulties of imposing coordination and rules of the game on an uneven galaxy of providers. Put differently, a comprehensive international higher education market is unlikely to be established soon. At the same time, some arguments suggest that, because of globalisation, it is likely that strong pressure will encourage the concentration of the market of higher education providers.

It may have some of the following features:

- Stable elite higher education sector (both public and private).
- Agrowing share of corporate institutions.
- The deterioration, if not closing down, of some traditional public higher education institutions.
- The disappearance of many private institutions.
- Great volatility and instability of small institutions. This may have important consequences for transparency and accountability issues. Indeed, depending on the segment of the higher education sector concerned (that is, small private higher education institutions, which are not regarded as part of the 'elite'), opportunities for corruption may remain high or grow in the future – and so will the need to address them.

3

The Power of Accreditation
Views of Academics

The paper draws on many years' experience of analysing external evaluations of quality and standards. It is important to note that quality and standards are not the same. The paper will draw on the views of those who have been involved in accreditation in Britain and in North America.

Both countries have had forms of accreditation for decades. These views will, at a surface level, help to identify the perceived benefits and problems of accreditation. However, those same views, when critically deconstructed, will also raise fundamental issues about accreditation. Overall, the view underpinning this paper is that Europe is rushing precipitously into accreditation and that the approach being taken is based on naïve views of what accreditation is and what it can achieve.

More fundamentally, there is an underlying but unspecified and unexamined set of taken-for-granteds that legitimate accreditation. Accreditation is neither neutral nor benign; it is not apolitical. Quite the contrary, the accreditation route is highly political and is fundamentally about a shift of power but a shift concealed behind a new public management ideology cloaked in consumerist demand and European conformity. The paper intends to demonstrate this. Also, accreditation is not a process somehow set aside from audit, assessment, or standards monitoring such as external examining. Accreditation uses methods and has purposes that overlap with audit, assessment and external examining.

ACCREDITATION

Before exploring these issues, some orientation on what accreditation is and how it relates to other external processes. Accreditation may be of programmes or institutions. Accreditation is the establishment or re-statement of the status, legitimacy or appropriateness of an institution, programme or module of study.

INSTITUTIONAL ACCREDITATION

Institutional accreditation effectively provides a licence to operate. It is usually based on an evaluation of whether the institution meets specified minimum standards such as staff qualifications, research activities, student intake and learning resources. It might also be based on an estimation of the potential for the institution to produce graduates that meet explicit or implicit academic standard or professional competence.

Institutional accreditation or re-accreditation, in Europe for example, is usually undertaken by national bodies either government departments or government-initiated agencies or quangos that make formal judgements on recognition. In some countries, with a total or preponderant public sector higher education system, there is little need for institutional accreditation, *per se,* but there is a growing need for a mechanism to validate 'upgrading' of non-university higher education institution to university status, as has happened, for example, in the UK and Sweden. The focus of US institutional accreditation has changed. Initially accreditation was a device 'used by a college or university to convince other institutions that its students and courses should be accepted by them, and *vice versa*'.

It evolved into a form of public accountability providing assurances 'to those outside the higher education community as well as those inside it that the institution had capacity to offer its programs'. Furthermore, despite the voluntary nature of the process, there has been a funding link through eligibility for federal aid. Increasingly, there has been a shift in accreditation to focus more on outputs, in particular, student learning outcomes. In Canada, the government of Ontario has established The Post-secondary Education Quality Assessment Board to examine applications to offer degrees from institutions other than the provinces' publicly-funded universities.

Institutional accreditation, especially initial recognition, tends to be more prominent in countries with a significant new private higher education provision, such as those in the Americas and Eastern Europe. For example, the Consejo Nacional de Univeridades in Venezuela evaluated and granted licences to new, experimental higher education institutions and continued to evaluate them until they attained full autonomy. Delegates at the international seminar *The End of Quality?* accepted that institutional accreditation was useful, in theory, to ensure the integrity of higher education—including international integrity.

However, the context and stage of development of higher education within any system is a key variable in determining the importance of accreditation. The more new development the more, it was thought, is the need for institutional accreditation. In the US, for example, institutional accreditation with established institutions is not providing much return on the monitoring process.

PROGRAMME ACCREDITATION

Programmes may be accredited for their academic standing or they may be accredited to produce graduates with professional competence to practice; usually referred to as professional accreditation. Accreditation of courses in North America tends to focus on professional areas. About 14 different non-governmental voluntary associations recognise provision in institutions that have been found to meet stated criteria of quality.

These accreditors judge whether the study programmes appropriately prepare graduates to enter a profession. This is very similar to the role played by the professional and regulatory bodies in the UK, who also control access to the profession by making accreditation of the programme a prerequisite for graduate entry.

Perhaps more draconian than their US counterparts, some bodies in the UK set and grade their own examinations and require a period of work experience before registering graduates as full professionals. The newer accreditation in Eastern European countries such as Hungary, the Czech Republic and Slovakia has, at least initially, opted for programme accreditation in all academic fields. This appears to be designed principally to provide academic rather than professional accreditation in the wake of the Soviet era.

The mushrooming of new programme accreditation proposals in some Western European countries, linked to bachelor-masters conversion, also predominantly appears to be academic accreditation. Instead of accrediting institutional processes for the creation of bachelor-masters courses based on existing provision, it seems some countries intend to accredit every new programme

LICENCE TO PRACTICE AND ACCREDITATION

There is a distinction between graduating from an accredited programme and having a licence to practice. In some cases, these are coincident, especially for graduates from some postgraduate programmes. Sometimes an undergraduate degree in a specified subject is a prerequisite for progression to a postgraduate course or diploma in that area.

In some cases *any* good undergraduate degree is a prerequisite for further professional training; for example, in law in the UK there is a one-year postgraduate conversion course that non-law graduates take before joining the law society postgraduate qualification programme. In many professional areas, graduation from an appropriately accredited academic programme is a preliminary step and full professional certification, and thus a licence to practice, follows only after some period of work experience. In some instances, such as teaching, a licence to practice may be virtually independent of studying on an accredited programme. In many US states, obtaining a teaching licence is *not* dependent on having an accredited teacher education degree.

VALIDATION AND ACCREDITATION

When examining subject or programme accreditation it is important also to distinguish between validation, revalidation, accreditation and re-accreditation. Validation refers to internal processes in institutions. So, a validation process would ensure that a new programme fulfilled internal institutional criteria. Validation is the internal acknowledgement of the establishment and legitimacy of a programme.

In some countries, such as the UK, the introduction of new programmes of study and new component modules in some areas, such as social science, is solely an internal process. In others, new programmes require external approval, from an agency or government department and if they are in 'professional' areas they may need additional accreditation. In other countries, there are limits on new developments, for example, in Norway, if a subject area is already well-established at an institution, new programmes up to 90 credits can be opened. Revalidation is the formal renewal of that acknowledgement.

Most institutions have processes for periodic review of existing programmes of study and of their constituent modules. This process may be linked to external accreditation but is often an internal process within permitted parameters and, usually, conforming to explicit guidelines. External re-accreditation may be 'delegated' to the internal revalidation procedure. Accreditation is the formal or official external recognition of a programme.

This may be for funding purposes or it may be registration of the programme as a provider of professional education. The external accreditation agency may be a national agency or a discipline-specific agency or a regulatory or professional body with delegated authority. Re-accreditation is, thus, the formal renewal of an accredited programme.

ACCREDITATION CRITERIA AND DECISIONS

Accreditation has been described as a public statement that a certain threshold of quality has been achieved or surpassed. However, one might argue that accreditation is more about minimum standards than about the quality of the process. None the less, accreditation decisions are, or at least should be, based on transparent agreed, pre-defined standards or criteria. Not all accreditation criteria are as transparent as they might be. Accreditation is a binary state, either a programme or an institution is accredited, or it is not. However, the absolute of this binary state is blurred or softened by a 'holding' decision that permits, in effect, progression to accreditation. This ranges from accreditation subject to further action, through probationary accreditation to permission to reapply for accreditation.

FOCUS OF ACCREDITATION

Accreditation may be focussed on inputs, process or outputs or any combination of these. Programme accreditation tends to focus on inputs such as staffing, programme resources, and curricula design and content.

Sometimes it addresses the teaching process and the level of student support. Occasionally programme accreditation explores outcomes such as the graduate abilities and employability. In some cases, the medium of delivery might be the key focus, especially when it differs from the norm. For example, the *Council for National Academic Awards* (CNAA) initial accreditation process that used to operate in the British polytechnic system, focussed on the inputs to a programme and the proposed syllabus, booklist and teaching method.

A programme could, thus, be accredited before any students were enrolled. The US, *Teacher Education Accreditation Council* (TEAC), for example, only gives new teacher training programmes pre-accreditation status. Full accreditation follows only when the academics make the case that the 'professional education programme has succeeded in preparing competent, caring, and qualified professional educators', that is once students have been through the programme. Here the focus for full accreditation is on the outputs of the programme. This is not untypical of professional programme accreditation undertaken in the UK or US. Institutional accreditation tends to focus on the overall infrastructure, especially the physical space, along with the IT and library resources and the staffing. It might address this from the point of view of the overall student learning experience. In addition, institutional accreditation might focus on financial arrangements and viability, governance and regulation and administrative support. Where an institution offers distance or on-line learning, the medium of delivery might be a focus of accreditation procedures.

Increasingly, the US regional institutional accreditation agencies are focusing on outcomes and effectiveness. For example, the Northwest Association of Schools, Colleges and Universities identifies the assessment of institutional effectiveness as an essential eligibility requirement for candidacy for accreditation. Similarly, a core requirement for college accreditation of the *Southern Association of Colleges and Schools* (SACS) is that 'the institution must engage in ongoing, integrated and institution-wide research-based planning and evaluation processes that incorporate a systematic review of programmes and services to demonstrate that the institution is effectively accomplishing its mission'.

In principal, though, rather than the input-process-output focus, accreditation might be based on recognition that the institution has in place appropriate control and monitoring processes to ensure satisfactory quality and standards. However, identifying appropriate mechanisms is normally viewed as an auditing function distinct from, but possibly contributing to, a formal process of accreditation of an institution. However, the term audit is not restricted to an exploration of organisational process.

For example, the TEAC accreditation process includes 'academic audit during which auditors visit a campus to verify the evidence that supports the claims made in the Enquiry Brief'.

RATIONALE

Rather more complex is the ostensive rationale for accreditation. Accreditation is primarily about control of the sector; this is much more explicit in accreditation than in other external quality processes such as audit, assessment or external examining. Although accreditation involves compliance and indirect accountability, its main function is to maintain control of the sector and the programmes offered.

Improvement is a spinoff from accreditation processes, which some agencies emphasise more than others. Institutional accreditation is designed to ensure that institutions of dubious merit do not become established as *bona fide* higher education institutions. Accreditation also monitors the sector to ensure that accredited institutions continue to fulfil the expectations of a university or college. A key concern is the need to control 'for-profit' organisations, whose motivation is different from the public sector. In many countries, with a predominant public sector higher education system, there is little or no institutional accreditation *per se*, but there has been a growing tendency, fuelled by new public management ideology, to require institutions to demonstrate accountability for public funds.

Although not the same as accreditation, in the extreme, failure to exhibit satisfactory accountability can result in the 'de-accreditation' in the form of closure or merger of unsatisfactory institutions, as has happened in the further education college sector in the UK. Accreditation at the programme level is also about control. In Eastern Europe, academic accreditation of programmes is about ensuring adequate standards, a function fulfilled, in effect, in the UK by the external examining system.

Although the latter is not accreditation *per se*, unsatisfactory examiners reports might lead to the closure or sanctioning of a programme either by the institution management or as a result of other forms of external monitoring such as external subject review or academic audit. Professional accreditation is even more about ostensive control.

It is about an external agency maintaining control of a subject area that links into professional employment, especially where to practice requires certification separate from academic qualification.

Although such bodies provide guidelines with which successful accreditees comply, these guidelines are manifestations of the organisation's control of the sector.

Sometimes this control is grounded in legislation, such as the British General Medical Council's regulatory function. Sometimes, despite having no regulatory power, the professional body is so well established in the profession that it is impossible to gain work in some areas without it, such as chartered engineering status to work for British local authorities.

ACCREDITATION METHODS AND MECHANISMS

Accreditation involves a set of procedures designed to gather evidence to enable a decision to be made about whether the institution or programme should be granted accredited status. The onus is on the applicants to 'prove' their suitability; that they fulfil minimum criteria. Methods by which this evidence is gathered overlap with methods used in audits, assessments and external examining.

The component methods include self-assessments, document analysis, scrutiny of performance indicators, peer visits, inspections, specially-constituted panels, delegated responsibility to internal panels often via proxy entrustment to external examiners or advisors; stakeholder surveys, such as student satisfaction surveys, alumni and employer surveys, direct intervention, such as direct observation of classroom teaching or grading of student work. In the UK for example, the evidence used by professional bodies is derived from one or more of the following: exchange of correspondence, scrutiny of documentation, special on-site visits or attendance at internal validation events. In Russia the emphasis is on statistical data. Following increased demand for higher education and widespread structural changes including the founding of non-state universities, accreditation in Russia is now based on comparative statistical assessment.

ACCREDITATION, AUDIT, ASSESSMENT AND EXTERNAL EXAMINING

Although accreditation is distinct from audit, assessment and external examining there is a degree of overlap between these different external processes. There is overlap in the object, focus, rationale and methods of the different forms of external monitoring and evaluation. For example, in the United States, accreditation processes are increasingly being called upon by higher education's internal and external constituencies to demonstrate accountability and improvement.

Furthermore, The National Council of Regional Accrediting Commissions reports that members' focus is shifted from inputs to student learning outcomes and the regional accreditors expect institutions to provide direct evidence of achievement of outcomes. One big difference, though, is that audit, assessment and external examining operate on the premise that the institution or programme is functioning appropriately and the external process has to demonstrate otherwise. For example, audits often involve a methodology designed to test the verisimilitude of institutional or programme claims.

Accreditation, though, shifts this round and institutions or programmes have to prove that they are worthy. For example, TEAC denies accreditation 'when the preponderance of evidence is insufficient and inconclusive'.

NUANCES

Accreditation thus has three nuances. *First,* accreditation as a process applied to applicant organisations. *Second,* accreditation is the label that institutions or programmes may acquire as a result of the accreditation procedures. *Third,* underpinning the first two, accreditation is an 'abstract notion of a formal authorising power', enacted via official decisions about recognition. It is this underpinning abstraction that gives accreditation its legitimacy.

Ironically, this abstraction, frequently taken-for-granted, is not a traditionally intrinsic aspect of accreditation. As Jones has pointed out, 'The original audience for accreditation was the academy itself. The process did not arise in response to concerns about quality expressed by external audiences....' This third nuance chimes with the issue, alluded to throughout the forgoing, of the underpinning ideology and politics of accreditation. It leads to an investigation of the power relationships embodied in the accreditation process. An examination of the perceptions of those who have engaged with accreditation of various types reveals surface views about the benefits and draw-backs.

A second-order examination of the comments will, though, also uncover the political and ideological dimensions. Professional and Regulatory Bodies (PRBs) play three roles. However, professional bodies also represent the interest of the professional practitioners and here they act as a professional association or trade union or as a learned society contributing to continuous professional development.

Third, the professional or regulatory body represents its own self-interest: the organisations act to maintain their own privileged and powerful position as a controlling body. This is where control, legitimated by public interest becomes confounded by control based on self-interest.

VIEWS OF PARTICIPANTS

The following views are derived from what little litreature there is on participants' views of accreditation and the responses of 53 academics and administrators who have been involved in accreditation processes.

This group, are mainly from the UK with some US, Canadian and Australian input. The qualitative perceptions were gathered on-line via e-mail correspondence. The majority of respondents comment on subject accreditation rather than institutional processes and their comments relate to 24 different discipline areas, as well as accreditation of learning and teaching practices *per se*. Quotes are included but for reasons of confidentiality the source is assigned a number, and the remainder of the reference relates to country and the subject area the respondent is talking about.

As far as possible, the quote is contextualised without making it too long and AT TIMES ostensibly deconstructed, using Barthesian semiological notions of denotation, connotation and 'myth', the latter informed by prevailing ideology. Programme accreditation in the UK is enormously varied and about 100 regulatory and professional bodies are involved in some form of accreditation of higher education programmes in British higher education institutions.

NECESSITY: EMPLOYMENT AND MARKETING

However, for most respondents this necessity was closely linked to a concern that the marketability of programmes in some areas is closely tied to accredited status and that failure to achieve accreditation would be problematic:

- Professional accreditation is liked by employers and students and courses with it recruit more students than those that do not have it. This may mean the difference between them running and not running.
- Overall, I feel that the process is a valuable one. However it also depends on what valuable means to the University. In our case it not only enable us to ensure that we will creating a programme that was up-to-date but also one that was marketable as professional recognition is an important decision to applicants.
- My impression from the central administration is that accreditation is highly valued: students are looking for an accredited programme, therefore the absence or loss of accreditation would cause great anxiety from the point of view of student recruitment.

The allusion to real-world relevance is also recognised by others:

- Our engagement with these emerging bodies has been helpful to us in shaping the playwork course, even where we have not agreed with policy directions of some of them. It certainly keeps us current in social policy and public opinion fashion.

However, comments about real-world relevance, suggests that the accreditors are in tune with the real world, which is a moot point.

One US respondent, though asked, 'were accreditation not tied to federal funding or professional licensure, would your institution or programme seek it anyway?' The assumption, here is that there is an objective external view that is the province of the external accrediting body. The 'objectivity', though, may be tempered by the controlling function of the organisation, itself possibly a function of its own self-interest.

UNIFORMITY

The presumption is that uniformity is important and desirable and thus that all courses should 'cover' the same content. This assumes that covering the same course content equates with uniformity of learning and understanding of the subject area.

The question remains, though whether the demand for uniformity is the professional body safeguarding the public, representing its members' interests or reinforcing its own status? The assumption is that there is an external guiding hand that knows what's best and that academia has to conform to it.

An alternative view is less benign:

- Sometimes it seems to be about how powerful the agencies are—the professional body or the institution and I've had experience of it going both ways.... In relation to psychology, it initially resulted in inflexibility in relation to residential schools—mandatory to get a named degree and this disadvantaged women with childcare needs. We then renegotiated after much feedback and because student voted with their feet and we then found money to provide an alternative, and an on-line experience was developed.

Do we read this as safeguarding of the public or is this inflexibility born of the society invoking its public security mission to reinforce its political power and omniscience? What would it matter if undergraduate psychology students on different degree courses took different syllabuses taught in different ways?

Tony Gale, ex- Honourary General Secretary of the *British Psychology Society* (BPS), argues that, given a first degree in psychology does not give you a licence to practice, the society accredits undergraduate courses for political reasons.

Which have little to do with public security or pedagogy.

- In 1967 rebellious heads of department met at Brown's Hotel in Mayfair, to protest against the

Society's move towards a national curriculum. The Society wanted to specify not only a curriculum but also the teaching time allocated to every element in it. The heads argued that university departments should maintain their autonomy and decide themselves what and how much they should teach. They believed the bureaucratic tail was seeking to wag the academic dog. But they lost the battle. For many years the Society has accredited the psychology degree and has awarded GBR to approved degrees.

ACADEMIC OR PRACTITIONER

This leads to the relative influence of academics and practitioners in each other's realms. 'There is often a clear tension between academic priorities and professional ones in say engineering or social work'.

I think they are valuable when:

- They focus on the professional rather than the academic side of the programme;
- They explicitly acknowledge that the students are being educated and not just trained for a profession;
- They are conducted by peers;
- They ask to see only strictly essential documentation;
- They are willing to respect and take on trust the expertise and judgements of, for example, external examiners.
- They can be harmful and irritating, though, when the opposite of any of the happens. I think it is a matter of particular concern when professional bodies try to overrule academic judgements on academic matters, for example, curriculum design and content and assessment of academic aspects of the course.

The principle concern here seems to be the perceived infringement of practitioners into the academic realm, notably requiring specific course content, making demands about teaching and learning approaches, as was noted with psychology, and even questioning assessment judgements.

- For example on your accounting degree, they require specific areas to be covered in, say, economics but the economist who teaches the subject may not think so and this at times causes a problem. However, if you take the professional requirements for recognition to be the minimum standards then it might be useful. However, quite often the professional standards are not and they focus on ensuring that students do not get through too easily rather than requiring them to have well-rounded development.

The tail wagging dog analogy recurs in comments of respondents:

- We have found the RICS accreditation an ongoing problematic saga with because of allegedly inadequate A-level points at entry. We have a large number of mature students for whom this is irrelevant and besides pride ourselves in how far we raise our students' capacity during the degree not how well qualified they are before they come here. RICS, like so many other institutions, seem to be allowing the bureaucratic tail to way the dog. The actual membership claim to be horrified at the bureaucratic requirements but seem powerless to their educational department
- We had a particular problem with one Engineering institution over regulations that allow Honours degrees to be awarded to students who have been reassessed. I think we got into a tail wagging dog situation and included a 'notwithstanding' clause in the regulations to appease the accrediting body.
- I am also aware, from my old NVQ days of training and development, that meeting awarding body requirements can galvanise centres into improving numerous aspects of their programmes, but can also end up with the tail wagging the dog.

It is curious that these respondents should all use exactly the same phrase about accreditation implying a clear perception in the sector about confusion of the locus of decision making. It is also interesting that the analogy is used rather than any direct statement made about where the power should lie. Indeed, only one respondent, an administrator, actually directly talked about accrediting bodies and academics struggling for power.

It is almost as though it is a taboo subject. Even the different political agendas embedded in the accreditation process rarely seem to get publicly aired. The tension occurs mainly in three areas; programme content, programme delivery and bureaucratic requirements. The issues around delivery are particularly about contested control and consequent inhibition of innovation. Bureaucracy is as much about synchronicity of processes as it is burdensome workloads and unnecessary requirements.

CONTENT

The issue over programme content is not so much the specification of what subjects should be taught but how restrictive that specification is perceived. Academics tend to think that externals/practitioners only need specify what is an essential core that would enable a student to become a practitioner and then leave it to the academy to develop a coherent educational programme delivered in a manner that they consider is pedagogically sound.

DELIVERY AND INNOVATION

Some respondents thought there was potential in accreditation to rethink and develop innovative ideas.

- We have been a leader in programme innovation ... We have found that our accreditation agencies have been quite supportive of these efforts and, in fact, have provided a wonderful forum for us to share its innovations with the broader academic community. With accreditation agencies allowing institutions to develop programmes consistent with their missions, we have found that early restrictions provided by accrediting bodies experienced have made way for support of meaningful programme innovation. In a sense, as programmes have developed to meet today's needs, so too have accreditation bodies changed to meet the issues of contemporary management education.

However, despite the potential there was no guarantee, for various reasons, that this would happen.

The structural constraints and the membership of visiting panels impacted on innovation.

- Overall it really depends on the accreditation body and level of the subject area. I found from my experience that it was restrictive in some ways but there were also opportunities to be innovative and cover the same areas in a different way.
- Professional body accreditation does stimulate programme teams to rethink what they are doing and encourage innovation but often within a predefined area. For example, CIPD requirements have stimulated higher education providers to build in competence outcomes to programmes which might otherwise be purely academic.
- Depends entirely on the organisation and indeed the panel who visits. My experience has been RIBA good and developmental, as are RTPI. The Institute of Environmental Health—a real pain—they are policing things not developing. The opportunity again depends—especially on the nature of the guidelines and degrees of discretion. Environmental Health is compliance; the others much more developmental
- How valuable it is must surely depend on how it is handled, but my fear is that it can deteriorate to ticking boxes and compliance. A notable exception is the accreditation of academics by ILTHE, which is based on the SEDA scheme. This is wholly qualitative. Hence, it most emphatically can and does lead to rethinking....The SEDA scheme has led to a substantial amount of innovation.

This perception of the positive, innovatory effects of the ILTHE process resonates with earlier views and is further endorsed by another respondent:

- All the team thought that the discussions were really useful and productive, and that the ILTHE processes were very worthwhile. I also think that the processes actually encourage innovation, while at the same time helping innovators to think hard enough about how their ideas are actually going to work in practice.

The key to the satisfaction with this process might be that it encourages self-reflection and drives innovative thinking, requiring academic legitimation rather than compliance. The control element, in effect, is minimised and the trust, innovative and reflective element is maximised.

One respondent, referring to engineering, noted:

- Constraints of accreditation seem to be on content rather than style of delivery, so doesn't necessarily restrict innovation in learning and teaching methods.

This sceptical response is consistent with a discussion below about the alliance some academics make with the professional bodies against their institutions. It was not just in engineering that respondents thought accreditation stifled innovation.

Respondents were particularly concerned about situations where accreditors went beyond content and made requirements about delivery:

- The Geological Society had just taken upon itself a new role as watchdog over professional qualifications for geologists, and was in the vanguard, applying for accreditation of its courses. Not all of the courses could actually be accredited because the Geological Society put some very stringent requirements on the fieldwork component of an accreditable course.... My perception is that we believed that we had to do it to retain credibility and that it was indeed just a hoop to jump through. We even see accreditation as a force for stasis, because it prevents us from accrediting innovative new courses that we might want to run

The terminology here is instructive: 'watchdog' and 'hoop to jump through' imply not only the compliance requirement of the latter but also that the organisation set itself up as a controller of the discipline, although no evident public interest is served by the requirements.

Other respondents also implied that the control function inhibits innovation:

- All your questions triggered immediate recognition. Particularly the danger of constraining new developments and fixing a national curriculum in concrete.
- At present any innovations I make, which I see as positive, I must always share but not in a constructive manner...more in an 'asking permission' type situation. I can see that this might restrict others who may see that they must continue to comply in a middle-of-the-road fashion.

In seeking permission the last respondent denotes a process of supplication. However, the second-order connotation is a lack of trust of the academic and the underlying Barthesian, third order, 'myth' is that there is a body that indeed has the knowledge and wisdom to grant permission.

An alternative take is to see professional bodies as disengaged from the reality of the higher education setting

- There is little understanding by the statutory bodies of the workload requirements for HEI staff. Time for lecturing, preparation, marking, etc., is in short supply. Add to that the requisite visits to the clinical areas, the need to carry out research, clinical caseloads, publish or present papers and to serve on boards, external examinations and so on and the professional bodies can quickly be seen as busybodies out of touch with daily academic life.

One respondent with an institutional overview of accreditation noted:

- On the point about encouraging or restricting changes -I have heard departments voice both views. For one particular PRB the view is that it is constraining the curriculum. However, we have said that the School needs to work with the PRB to effect change. Another down side is that a different PRB cannot make up its mind about what it wants and this is having a knock-on effect in delaying desired curriculum change.

Some respondents cited the variability of the visiting panel as a reason for inconsistency in effecting innovatory change:

- In answer to your question re innovation I think the extra burden of yet more self-justifying representatives on validation panels does nothing to encourage improvements in teaching and/or learning.
- The RIBA visit was always a clubby sort of thing and you were either in or out of the club. The panel coming to visit us next week is almost entirely made up of thrusting young professional climbers from the south east of England, who have the time to be on endless RIBA committees. They will have little idea of how we are working in the hothouse of education today and almost certainly will never have heard of the RAE! They will concentrate almost exclusively on 'Design' and ignore the rest of the course.

A holistic view was provided by a respondent who argued that the accreditation process was cyclical and this impacted on the innovative potential of accreditation.

- The bottom line is that there seems to be a cycle—first the educational process gets behind 'real life', if the Body is on the ball it writes a report, generates a new specification, etc. The profession's education process catches up, the Body can then stagnate for a bit, and so on. Depends on the Body and which bit of the cycle you are in. Until 1993, nothing much had changed in medical education for 100 years. A relatively radical document changed all that. Problem-based learning is alive and well and so are graduate entry courses. But much of that comes from government imperatives—new medical schools, workforce issues, etc.

Here, the external body is reduced to anything but knowledgeable and wise. Indeed it is seen as essentially pragmatic and propelled into action by historical necessity.

In the US, it seems that the real motive force for innovative change in learning and teaching is not the accreditation process per se but the potential of the consequent assessment of student learning outcomes, which research provides a basis for engaging with innovative pedagogy.

- Clearly institutional accreditation now focuses on student learning outcomes ... so it would be more feasible for institutions to use that information to initiate changes in teaching and learning.

BUREAUCRACY AND BURDEN

A recurrent theme was the amount of work involved in accreditation.

A problem accentuated by rigidity of requirements, perceived at best as heavy-handed bureaucracy and at worst as an unnecessary degree of control.

- Well, it is obviously a bit of a 'chore', especially when the PRB insists on receiving documentation in its own prescribed formats and won't accept 'substitute' documents, addressing the same issues or needs, that the university or programme already has for its own purposes. But we are working towards trying to come to some mutual understanding with PRBs on this, and trying to find ways of involving PRBs at relevant in-house 'quality' events such as validations, reviews, audits or whatever as an alternative to a separate formal visit, for example. This sometimes works.

When asked how might the bureaucracy be reduced, the respondent answered:

- In many ways. For example:
- By accepting information already existing in the department/school in the form already available. We spent days transferring information and recasting it in the format required, different from ours.
- By not insisting on producing the 'progression of students through the programme' charts - unless the universities have appropriate software to do it automatically.

- By accepting information in electronic format. For example our entire operation of the School is on intranet and everything the IEE wanted was there - but admittedly not in the format the IEE forms expected it, hence, a lot of our time was spent on pulling the bits of info out and plugging them into appropriate tables or boxes.
- I would go even further by suggesting that accreditation institutions should NOT insist on any particular format in which the information is submitted, but they of course should expect that information does exist and they should indeed be making judgements and assessments whether the way in which information is kept is appropriate or not. We feel, for example, that our way is better than what IEE wanted from us, so in that sense we were wasting time by reformatting the content. Currently there is far too much duplication of presentation of the same information in many different formats.

Others, noting the amount of work required, were less negative in the connotations of their remarks:

- *Yes Valuable*: Although one has to put up with the inevitable requirements for oodles of paperwork

The connotation of 'oodles' is benign; someone who has oodles of food has a joyous surfeit and this is re-presented in the parenthetical comment. The implication being that, if the process is worthwhile, the paperwork requirement is an appropriate price to pay.

Going further, one respondent talking of the process in biomedical sciences noted:

- I cannot think of any alternative procedure that could ever be as effective as a one-day intensive look at the syllabus, facilities and staffing. This is streamlined, mutually beneficial to all concerned, encourages innovation, and yet is acceptable to the IBMS and the Health Professions Council.

Despite the apparent compatibility in the biomedical sciences setting, an issue that annoyed many respondents was that of synchronisation between external agencies:

- My difficulties with the current system are the huge amount of paperwork which is spilling out and the lack of cohesion regarding validation-type visits. I often find the QAA, the NMC and NAO are visiting an institution at the same time but rarely share the same documents!
- Here I do have strong views. I think the accreditations institutions, RAE, QAA, and anyone else subjecting the universities to continuous assessment processes should agree once and for all in consultation with universities—the format in which information should be kept and presented for all purposes. Then it is just the question of pressing appropriate button to retrieve information for a particular exercise. We do have all necessary information all the time and yet every time an assessment takes place we spend weeks or months preparing the documentation.

The lack of synchronisation and incompatible documentation is indicative of the desire for different agencies to control their corner of the quality and standards monitoring process and, again, one might ask whether this is in the public interest or the monitoring organisations' self-interest? However, not all the extra burden was externally imposed.

Sometimes the burden is increased by the quality control processes within institutions.

- We also try to keep a much stricter audit and control of submission documents than in the past. A sub group of our Academic Quality Assurance Committee (AQAC) checks the submissions to ensure that they are of appropriate quality to go out as university documents. All this takes a lot of time and we are beholden to academic colleagues to read the documentation. I also read everything.

The argument might be that this is the inevitable self-preservation response of institutions subject to increasing accreditation demands. Certainly, the proposed new accreditation processes in some Western European countries are ludicrously bureaucratic and evidence of a lack of trust in academia.

ALLIANCE

Curiously, at first sight academics sometimes make use of the professional or regulatory body to support their own ends. Knowing the power of accreditation in the marketplace, they ally themselves with the professional body. Sometimes this alliance is used to conserve existing practices and sometimes to make demands on institutional resources.

Gale noted that:

- As the teaching of psychology spread from a handful of old universities to the whole higher education system, heads have found Society accreditation a useful political tool. They have used the threat of withdrawal of accreditation by the Society as a means of securing enhanced facilities for their undergraduate programmes.

Respondents on both sides of the Atlantic remarked on this:

- There are some disadvantages to accreditation. It is expensive and sometimes accrediting teams will make recommendations that cause money to be shifted from unaccredited programmes to accredited ones so that the accredited ones can retain their accreditation. This is an unfortunate consequence.
- Find professional body accreditation provides a 'bulwark' against senior management initiatives to reduce resources
- Accreditation is most valued by those who are closest to not having it and by those who know how to use it creatively to conduct innovative self-evaluations or to strong-arm funders with 'what the accreditors say we absolutely need to retain accreditation'

The apparent curious alliance is resolved relatively easily. Not only is this a manipulative ploy based on academic self-interest, using whatever support comes to hand, especially in resource-straightened times, but professional bodies are not mutually exclusive of academics.

Indeed, sometimes seem to be controlled by them:

- Some employers seemed to be critical of the actions of the Engineering professional bodies in raising the academic requirements for full chartered status, partly to enhance the status of their profession are dominated by academics reinforces this emphasis on educational needs rather than the needs of the industry.

SPECIALIST ACTIVITY

What emerges from all the responses is that accreditation is a game for specialists; it is not something that engages the majority of staff nor, to any significant extent, exercises the students. For the latter, accreditation means the kitemark rather than the process. It is about uniformity of curricula, as one medical student noted, 'we all need to be doing the same syllabus'. Part of the controlling element of accreditation is that it does not engage everyone and retains an element of mystification.

POWER

Accreditation is a struggle for power and it is not a benign process. Nor does it engage all those involved. It is also not a pure process of identifying those who have met minimum criteria to join the club. The evidence from the UK and North America shows clearly that accreditation is just one of a raft of ongoing processes that demand accountability and compliance as managerialism continues to bite into academic autonomy and undermine the skills and experience of educators. Accreditation is yet another layer alongside assessment, audit and other forms of standards and output monitoring.

THE ACCREDITATION—IMPROVEMENT PARADOX

The quality debate in higher education has, for a decade, attempted to engage with the apparent incompatibility, in practice, of accountability function of external quality monitoring and the hoped-for improvement function.

This is mirrored in the analyses of voluntary accreditation in the United States. Graham, Trow, and Lyman argued that the accreditation process is fundamentally flawed because the process of certification and assurance to the public of the soundness of the institution's practices is incompatible with the improvement of an institution's performance based on its continual assessment and evaluation of its strengths and weaknesses.

The certification function invariably overwhelms improvement because the process leads to the production of a public relations document that overstates the institution's strengths and conceals its weaknesses. This is precisely the opposite of what is needed if the improvement function is to be served by accreditation.

More to the point, as Murray notes, accreditation in the United States has not satisfactorily persuaded the public that the quality of the professions is safeguarded.

- We should also expect to find that the assurance of quality in the other learned professions is, like teaching, beyond the capacity of accreditation itself and that it inevitably entails the mechanisms of licensure, certification, peer review, employment, and so forth. The decisions made about the granting of employment, the professional license, certificate, merit award and honours, should be based more on solid evidence of accomplishment than on conformity to standards, largely unvalidated, and established by mere consensus of the members of the profession.

Although the surge towards accreditation in many parts of Europe is not being delegated to self-interest membership bodies in the main there remain issues of bureaucratic self interest. Self-perpetuation and a growing desire to control are characteristic of all types of quality monitoring agencies, especially those with control remits. Furthermore, as the American experience shows, accreditation is not distinct from quality issues and there is nothing to suggest that accreditation will not be wrapped round with audit, assessment and other forms of quality evaluation. As the edifice grows and becomes more specific and directive, so academic alienation increases, staff perceive a lack of trust and their own academic judgement being undermined. The resultant perception of deskilling and diminution of autonomy and freedom to make pedagogic decisions creates a context of compliance and, ultimately, as has been seen in other areas of quality control, game playing, manipulation and subversion of the process. Improvement is a long way down the agenda, if it is really on it at all. Most frustration is expressed at the loss of control of the pedagogic situation and the potential for improvement.

The positive view of the ILTHE process is precisely because it encourages innovation and reflection and delegates control to the academic. Although educators may not be aware of the specific concerns of a professional practice workplace, practitioners are equally unaware of the learning process. Teachers, if not 'up-to-date' understand the principles of the professional realm they teach about: it is far from evident that professionals representing accrediting agencies are so well versed in the principles of pedagogy.

CONCLUSION

However, the concern is not so much whether accreditation is a benign protector of the public interest or a process to sustain the self-interest of the accrediting agency. Nor, indeed, whether processes are bureaucratic or restrictive and inhibit innovation. Important as these are, they are indicative of a more deep-seated ideological presumption summed up in Jon Haakstad's third nuance of an 'abstract notion of a formal authorising power'. Repeatedly we saw references to jumping through hoops, tail wagging dogs, asking permission and the like.

Even one of the strongest supporters of accreditation, who noted that 'a one-day intensive look at the syllabus, facilities and staffing... is streamlined, mutually beneficial to all concerned and encourages innovation', made it clear that the process needed to be 'acceptable' to the professional and regulatory bodies. The underlying, third-level, 'myth' is that of the abstract authorising power, which legitimates the accreditation activity.

Yet, although taken for granted, this 'myth' of benign guidance is perpetuated by the powerful as a control on those who provide the education. Accreditation is fundamentally about a shift of power from educators to managers and bureaucrats. It accentuates the trends already evident in the UK towards 'delegated accountability' but reverses the delegation trend in most of the rest of the Europe. To understand staff perceptions of accreditation requires a holistic view that sets the control function of accreditation within the wider context of higher education as a public good.

It is necessary to dig beyond the surface legitimations of European unity and consumerist rhetoric to reveal the power processes and the ideology that legitimates the control function of accreditation. Only then can we approach accreditation openly and critically.

4

Principles and Philosophy of Accreditation

GENERAL OVERVIEW

The Commission on Colleges of the Southern Association of Colleges and Schools is the regional body for the accreditation of higher education institutions in the Southern states (Alabama, Florida, Georgia, Kentucky, Louisiana, Mississippi, North Carolina, South Carolina, Tennessee, Texas, and Virginia) and Latin America that award associate, baccalaureate, master's, or doctoral degrees. Accreditation by the Commission on Colleges signifies that an institution has a purpose appropriate to higher education and has resources, programmes, and services sufficient to accomplish and sustain that purpose.

Accreditation indicates that an institution maintains clearly specified educational objectives that are consistent with its mission and appropriate to the degrees it offers, and that it is successful in achieving its stated objectives. Self-regulation through accreditation embodies a traditional U.S.,. philosophy that a free people can and ought to govern themselves through a representative, flexible, and responsive system.

Accreditation is best accomplished through a voluntary association of educational institutions. Accreditation enhances educational quality throughout the region by improving the effectiveness of institutions and ensuring that institutions meet standards established by the higher education community, and serves as a common denominator of shared values and practices among the diverse institutions. Both a process and a product, accreditation relies on integrity, thoughtful and principled judgement, rigourous application of requirements, and a context of trust.

It provides an assessment of an institution's effectiveness in the fulfillment of its mission, its compliance with the requirements of its accrediting association, and its continuing efforts to enhance the quality of student learning and its programmes and services. Based upon reasoned judgement, the process stimulates evaluation and improvement, while providing a means of continuing accountability to constituents and the public.

The product of accreditation is a public statement of an institution's continuing capacity to provide effective programmes and services based on agreed-upon requirements. The statement of an institution's accreditation status with the Commission on Colleges is also an affirmation of that institution's continuing commitment to the Commission's principles and philosophy of accreditation.

The Commission on Colleges supports the right of an institution to pursue its established educational mission; the right of faculty members to teach, investigate, and publish freely; and the right of students to access opportunities for learning and for the open exchange of ideas. However, the exercise of these rights should not interfere with the overriding obligation of an institution to offer its students a sound education.

The Commission on Colleges adheres to the following fundamental characteristics of accreditation:

- Participation in the accreditation process is voluntary and is an earned and renewable status.
- Member institutions develop, amend, and approve accreditation requirements.
  Member institutions develop, amend, and approve accreditation requirements.
- The process of accreditation is representative, responsive, and appropriate to the types of institutions accredited.
- Accreditation is self-regulation.

- Accreditation requires institutional commitment and engagement.
- Accreditation is based upon a peer review process.
- Accreditation requires an institutional commitment to student learning and achievement.
- Accreditation acknowledges an institution's prerogative to articulate its mission within the recognised context of higher education and its responsibility to show that it is accomplishing its mission.
- Accreditation expects an institution to develop a balanced governing structure designed to promote institutional autonomy and flexibility of operation.
- Accreditation expects an institution to ensure that its programmes are complemented by support structures and resources that allow for the total growth and development of its students.

The first task of the Commission when considering accreditation status is to determine the institution's integrity and its commitment to quality enhancement. These two principles serve as the foundation of the relationship between the Commission and its member and candidate institutions.

INTEGRITY

Integrity, essential to the purpose of higher education, functions as the basic contract defining the relationship between the Commission and each of its member institutions. It is a relationship in which all parties agree to deal honestly and openly with their constituencies and with one another. Without this commitment, no relationship can exist or be sustained between the Commission and its member institutions.

The Commission's requirements, policies, processes, procedures, and decisions are predicated on integrity. The Commission on Colleges expects integrity to govern the operation of institutions. Therefore, evidence of intentionally withholding information, deliberately providing inaccurate information to the public, or failing to provide timely and accurate information to the Commission will be seen as the lack of a full commitment to integrity and may result in the loss of membership in the Commission on Colleges.

QUALITY ENHANCEMENT

The Commission on Colleges expects institutions to dedicate themselves to enhancing the quality of their programmes and services within the context of their missions, resources, and capacities, and to create an environment in which teaching, public service, research, and learning occur.

The concept of quality enhancement is at the heart of the Commission's philosophy of accreditation; this presumes each member institution to be engaged in an ongoing programme of improvement and able to demonstrate how well it fulfills its stated mission. Although evaluation of an institution's educational quality and its effectiveness in achieving its mission is a difficult task requiring careful analysis and professional judgement, an institution is expected to document quality and effectiveness in all its major aspects.

AN ORGANISATIONAL OVERVIEW

The Southern Association of Colleges and Schools is a private, non-profit, voluntary organisation founded in 1895 in Atlanta, Georgia. The Association comprises the Commission on Colleges, the Commission on Secondary and Middle Schools, and the Commission on Elementary and Middle Schools. The three Commissions carry out their missions with considerable autonomy: they develop their own standards and procedures, and govern themselves by a delegate assembly.

All three operate under the Association's Board of Trustees. The College Delegate Assembly includes one voting representative (the chief executive officer or the officer's designee) from each member institution. Its responsibilities include electing the seventy seven-member Commission on Colleges to guide the organisation's work; to approve all revisions of accrediting standards as recommended by the Commission; to approve the dues of candidate and member institutions as recommended by the Commission; and to elect an Appeals Committee to hear appeals of certain accreditation decisions.

The Commission on Colleges is responsible for preparing a statement on the standards for candidacy and membership; authorising special visits; taking final action on the accreditation status of institutions based only on its published standards, policies, and procedures; nominating to the College Delegate Assembly persons to succeed outgoing members of the Commission; electing an Executive Council of the Commission that will act for the Commission while it is not in session; appointing *ad hoc* study committees as needed; and approving the policies and procedures consistent with the Association's charter and bylaws.

The thirteen-member Executive Council is the executive arm of the Commission and functions on behalf of the Commission and the College Delegate Assembly between sessions. However, the actions of the Council are subject to the review and approval of the Commission.

The Council interprets Commission policies and procedures; develops procedures for and supervises the work of *ad hoc* and standing committees of the Commission; approves goals and objectives of the Commission; reviews and approves the Commission's budget; oversees and annually evaluates the work of its executive director; and initiates new programmes, projects, and policy proposals.

The Council receives and acts on reports from all *ad hoc* and standing committees and submits them to the Commission. In the case of institutions applying for candidacy, membership, or reaffirmation of accreditation, the Executive Council receives recommendations from the Committees on Compliance and Reports, the standing evaluation committees of the Commission, and in turn submits its recommendations on these institutions to the Commission for final action.

THE PROCESS OF ACCREDITATION

The process for initial and continued accreditation involves a collective analysis and judgement by an institution's internal constituencies, an informed review by peers external to the institution, and a reasoned decision by the elected members of the Commission on Colleges.

Accredited institutions periodically conduct internal reviews involving their administrative officers, staffs, faculties, students, trustees, and others appropriate to the process. The internal review allows an institution to consider its effectiveness in achieving its stated mission and its compliance with the accreditation requirements established by the member institutions.

Furthermore, it helps an institution evaluate its efforts in enhancing the quality of student learning and the quality of programmes and services offered to its constituencies as well as challenge itself to examine its successes in accomplishing its mission.

At the culmination of the internal review, peer evaluators representing the Commission apply their professional judgement through a preliminary assessment of the institution; elected Commissioners make the final determination of an institution's compliance with the accreditation requirements.

APPLICATION OF THE REQUIREMENTS

The Commission on Colleges accredits degree-granting higher education institutions and entities based on requirements in its *Principles of Accreditation: Foundations for Quality Enhancement*. The requirements apply to all institutional programmes and services, wherever located and however delivered.

The *Principles of Accreditation* is designed to guide institutions in all stages of membership, from application through initial accreditation and reaffirmation of accreditation. Compliance with the requirements is intended to help an institution achieve overall effectiveness. The Commission on Colleges applies the requirements of its *Principles* to all applicant, candidate, and member institutions, regardless of the type of institution; private for profit, private not-for-profit, or public.

The Commission evaluates an institution and makes accreditation decisions based on the following:

- Compliance with the *Principles of Accreditation*, defined as integrity and commitment to quality enhancement.

- Compliance with the Core Requirements.
- Compliance with the Comprehensive Standards
- Compliance with additional Federal Requirements

The Commission's philosophy of accreditation precludes denial of membership to a degree-granting institution of higher education on any ground other than an institution's failure to meet the requirements in the professional judgement of peer reviewers, or failure to comply with the policies and procedures of the Commission.

COMPLIANCE WITH THE CORE REQUIREMENTS

Compliance with the Core Requirements is essential for gaining and maintaining accreditation with the Commission on Colleges. The requirements establish a level of development required of an institution seeking initial or continued accreditation. Compliance with the Core Requirements is necessary but not sufficient to warrant accreditation or reaffirmation of accreditation.

To maintain accreditation, an institution must meet all Core Requirements, including Requirement 2.12. An institution responds to each Core Requirement by either confirming compliance or explaining those situations for which there is non-compliance. Core Requirement 2.12 requires an institution to develop an acceptable Quality Enhancement Plan (QEP) and show that the plan is part of an ongoing planning and evaluation process.

Engaging the wider academic community, the QEP is based upon a comprehensive and thorough analysis of the effectiveness of the learning environment for supporting student learning and accomplishing the mission of the institution. It is used to outline a course of action for institutional improvement by addressing one or more issues that contribute to institutional quality, with special attention to student learning.

An applicant institution seeking membership with the Commission on Colleges is required to document compliance with Core Requirements 2.1 - 2.11 in order to be awarded candidacy, candidacy renewal, or membership.

COMPLIANCE WITH THE COMPREHENSIVE STANDARDS

The Comprehensive Standards set forth requirements in the following three areas: institutional mission, governance, and effectiveness; programmes; and resources. The Comprehensive Standards represent good practices in higher education and establish a level of accomplishment expected of all member institutions.

Institutions respond to each Comprehensive Standard either by confirming compliance or by explaining those situations that constitute non-compliance. Guidelines for faculty credentials contained in Comprehensive Standard 3.7.1 reflect the commonly accepted standards of good practice within the larger community of the Commission's membership and describe one method for documenting faculty competence. Guidelines are not Comprehensive Standards.

COMPLIANCE WITH ADDITIONAL FEDERAL REQUIREMENTS

The U.S. Secretary of Education recognises accreditation by the Commission on Colleges in establishing the eligibility of higher education institutions to participate in programmes authorised under Title IV of the 1998 *Higher Education Amendments* and other federal programmes.

Through its compliance with these federal regulations, the Commission assures the public that it is a reliable authority on the quality of education provided by its member institutions.

The federal statute includes mandates that the Commission review an institution in accordance with criteria outlined in the regulations of the *Amendments* developed by the U.S. Department of Education.

As part of the review process, institutions are required to document compliance with those criteria and the Commission is obligated to consider such compliance when the institution is reviewed for initial membership or continued accreditation.

COMPONENTS OF THE PEER REVIEW PROCESS

REVIEW BY THE INSTITUTION

The institution will provide two separate documents as part of its reaffirmation review.

Compliance Certification

The Compliance Certification, submitted fifteen months in advance of an institution's scheduled reaffirmation, is a document completed by the institution that demonstrates its judgement of the extent of its compliance with each of the Core Requirements and Comprehensive Standards. Signatures by the institution's chief executive officer and accreditation liaison will be required to certify compliance. By signing the document, the individuals certify that the process of institutional self-assessment has been thorough, honest, and forthright, and that the information contained in the document is truthful, accurate, and complete.

Quality Enhancement Plan

The Quality Enhancement Plan (QEP), submitted six weeks in advance of the on-site review by the Commission, describes a carefully designed and focussed course of action that addresses a well-defined issue or issues directly related to improving student learning. The development of the QEP involves significant participation by the institution's academic community. The plan should be focussed and succinct (no more than seventy-five pages of narrative text and no more than twenty-five pages of support documentation or charts, graphs, and tables).

REVIEW BY THE COMMISSION

The Off-Site Peer Review

The Off-Site Review Committee, composed of a chair and normally eight evaluators, meets at an off-site location and reviews Compliance Certifications of a group of institutions to determine whether each institution is in compliance with all Core Requirements and Comprehensive Standards, and with federal regulations. The group of institutions, called a cluster, normally will consist of five institutions similar in governance and degrees offered.

At the conclusion of the review, the Off-Site Review Committee will prepare a separate report for each institution, recording and explaining its decisions regarding compliance. A report is forwarded to the respective institution's On- Site Review Committee which makes the final determination on compliance.

The On-Site Peer Review

Following review by the Off-Site Committee, an On-Site Review Committee of peers will conduct a focussed evaluation at the campus to finalise issues of compliance with the Core Requirements and Comprehensive Standards, evaluate the acceptability of the QEP, and provide consultation regarding the issues addressed in the QEP.

At the conclusion of its visit, the On-Site Review Committee will prepare a written report of its findings noting areas of non-compliance and will make a recommendation to the Commission on Colleges regarding the institution's accreditation status. The committee's report, along with the institution's response to areas of non-compliance, will be forwarded to the Commission for review and action.

INSTITUTIONAL RESPONSIBILITY FOR REPORTING SUBSTANTIVE CHANGE

The Commission on Colleges accredits the entire institution and its programmes and services, wherever they are located and however they are delivered. Accreditation, specific to an institution, is based on conditions existing at the time of the most recent evaluation and is not transferable. When an accredited institution significantly modifies or expands its scope, or changes the nature of its affiliation or its ownership, a substantive change review is required. The Commission is responsible for evaluating all substantive changes that occur between an institution's scheduled reviews (normally ten years) to determine whether the change has affected the quality of the total institution and to assure the public that the institution continues to meet defined standards.

A member institution is responsible for following the substantive change policy by informing the Commission of changes in accord with the Commission's procedures and, when required, seeking approval prior to the initiation of the change. If an institution fails to follow the procedures, its total accreditation may be placed in jeopardy. If an institution is unclear as to whether a change is substantive in nature, it should contact Commission staff for consultation. An applicant or candidate institution may not undergo substantive change prior to action on initial membership.

REPRESENTATION OF STATUS

An institution must be accurate in reporting to the public its status with the Commission.

In all official institutional publications, a member institution describes its status with the Commission only according with the following statement:

- (Name of institution) is accredited by the Commission on Colleges of the Southern Association of Colleges and Schools to award (name specific degree levels).

A candidate institution describes its status with the Commission only according to the following statement:

- (Name of institution) is a candidate for accreditation with the Commission on Colleges of the Southern Association of Colleges and Schools to award (name specific degree levels).

No statement may be made about the possible future accreditation status with the Commission on Colleges of the Southern Association of Colleges and Schools nor may an institution use the logo or seal of the Southern Association in any of its publications or documents.

CORE REQUIREMENTS

- The institution has degree-granting authority from the appropriate government agency or agencies. (Degree-granting Authority)

- The institution has a governing board of at least five members that is the legal body with specific authority over the institution. The board is an active policy-making body for the institution and is ultimately responsible for ensuring that the financial resources of the institution are adequate to provide a sound educational programme. The board is not controlled by a minority of board members or by organisations or interests separate from it. Neither the presiding officer of the board nor the majority of other voting members of the board have contractual, employment, or personal or familial financial interest in the institution. A military institution authorised and operated by the federal government to award degrees has a public board in which neither the presiding officer nor a majority of the other members are civilian employees of the military or active/retired military. The board has broad and significant influence upon the institution's programmes and operations, plays an active role in policy-making, and ensures that the financial resources of the institution are used to provide a sound educational programme. The board is not controlled by a minority of board members or by organisations or interests separate from the board except as specified by the authorising legislation. Neither the presiding officer of the board nor the majority of other voting board members have contractual, employment, or personal or familial financial interest in the institution. (Governing Board)
- The institution has a chief executive officer whose primary responsibility is to the institution and who is not the presiding officer of the board. (Chief Executive Officer)
- The institution has a clearly defined and published mission statement specific to the institution and appropriate to an institution of higher education, addressing teaching and learning and, where applicable, research and public service. (Institutional Mission)

- The institution engages in ongoing, integrated, and institution-wide research-based planning and evaluation processes that incorporate a systematic review of programmes and services that
  - Results in continuing improvement; and
  - Demonstrates that the institution is effectively accomplishing its mission. (Institutional Effectiveness)
- The institution is in operation and has students enrolled in degree programmes. (Continuous Operation)
- The institution:
  - Offers one or more degree programmes based on at least 60 semester credit hours or the equivalent at the associate level; at least 120 semester credit hours or the equivalent at the baccalaureate level; or at least 30 semester credit hours or the equivalent at the post-baccalaureate, graduate, or professional level. The institution provides a written justification and rationale for programme equivalency. (Programme Length)
  - Offers degree programmes that embody a coherent course of study that is compatible with its stated purpose and is based upon fields of study appropriate to higher education. (Programme Content)

    a. Requires in each undergraduate degree programme the successful completion of a general education component at the collegiate level that.

    b. Is a substantial component of each undergraduate degree.

    c. Ensures breadth of knowledg.

    d. Is based on a coherent rationale. For degree completion in associate programmes, the component constitutes a minimum of 15 semester hours or the equivalent; for baccalaureate programmes, a minimum of 30 semester hours or the equivalent. These credit hours are to be drawn from and include at least one course from each of the following areas: humanities/fine arts; social/behavioural sciences; and natural science/ mathematics. The courses do not narrowly focus on those skills, techniques, and procedures specific to a particular occupation or profession. The institution provides a written justification and rationale for course equivalency. (General Education)

— Provides instruction for all course work required for at least one degree programme at each level at which it awards degrees. If the institution makes arrangements for some instruction to be provided by other accredited institutions or entities through contracts or consortia, or uses some other alternative approach to meeting this requirement, the alternative approach must be approved by the Commission on Colleges. In all cases, the institution demonstrates that it controls all aspects of its educational programme. (Contractual Agreements for Instruction)

- The number of full-time faculty members is adequate to support the mission of the institution. The institution has adequate faculty resources to ensure the quality and integrity of its academic programmes. In addition, upon application for candidacy, an applicant institution demonstrates that it meets Comprehensive Standard 3.7.1 for faculty qualifications. (Faculty)
- The institution, through ownership or formal arrangements or agreements, provides and supports student and faculty access and user privileges to adequate library collections as well as to other learning/ information resources consistent with the degrees offered. These collections and resources are sufficient to support all its educational, research, and public service programmes. (Learning Resources and Services)
- The institution provides student support programmes, services, and activities consistent with its mission that

promote student learning and enhance the development of its students. (Student Support Services)

- The institution has a sound financial base, demonstrated financial stability, and adequate physical resources to support the mission of the institution and the scope of its programmes and services. The member institution provides the following financial statements:
  - an institutional audit (or Standard Review Report issued in accordance with Statements on Standards for Accounting and Review Services issued by the AICPA for those institutions audited as part of a systemwide or statewide audit) and written institutional management letter for the most recent fiscal year prepared by an independent certified public accountant and/or an appropriate governmental auditing agency employing the appropriate audit (or Standard Review Report) guide;
  - a statement of financial position of unrestricted net assets, exclusive of plant assets and plant-related debt, which represents the change in unrestricted net assets attributable to operations for the most recent year; and
  - an annual budget that is preceded by sound planning, is subject to sound fiscal procedures, and is approved by the governing board. Audit requirements for applicant institutions may be found in the Commission policy entitled 'Accreditation Procedures for Applicant Institutions.' (Resources)
- The institution has developed an acceptable Quality Enhancement Plan and demonstrates that the plan is part of an ongoing planning and evaluation process. (Quality Enhancement Plan)omprehensive Standards Institutional Mission: The institution has clear and comprehensive mission statement that

guides it; is approved by the governing board; is periodically reviewed by the board; and is communicated to the institution's constituencies.

- Governance and Administration:
  - The governing board of the institution is responsible for the selection and the evaluation of the chief executive officer.
  - The legal authority and operating control of the institution are clearly defined for the following areas within the institution's governance structure:
    a. Institution's mission;
    b. Fiscal stability of the institution;
    c. institutional policy, including policies concerning related and affiliated corporate entities and all auxiliary services; and
    d. Related foundations (athletic, research, etc.,) and other corporate entities whose primary purpose is to support the institution and/or its programmes.
  - The board has a policy addressing conflict of interest for its members.
  - The governing board is free from undue influence from political, religious, or other external bodies, and protects the institution from such influence.
  - Members of the governing board can be dismissed only for cause and by due process.
  - There is a clear and appropriate distinction, in writing and practice, between the policy-making functions of the governing board and the responsibility of the administration and faculty to administer and implement policy.
  - The institution has a clearly defined and published organisational structure that delineates responsibility for the administration of policies.
  - The institution has qualified administrative and academic officers with the experience, competence, and capacity to lead the institution.

- The institution defines and publishes policies regarding appointment and employment of faculty and staff.
- The institution evaluates the effectiveness of its administrators, including the chief executive officer, on a periodic basis.
- The institution's chief executive officer has ultimate responsibility for, and exercises appropriate administrative and fiscal control over, the institution's intercollegiate athletics programme.
- The institution's chief executive officer has ultimate control of the institution's fund-raising activities.
- Any institution-related foundation not controlled by the institution has a contractual or other formal agreement that
  a. Accurately describes the relationship between the institution and the foundation; and
  b. Describes any liability associated with that relationship. In all cases, the institution ensuresthat the relationship is consistent with its mission.
- The institution's policies are clear concerning ownership of materials, compensation, copyright issues, and the use of revenue derived from the creation and production of all intellectual property. This applies to students, faculty, and staff.

• Institutional Effectiveness:
- The institution identifies expected outcomes for its educational programmes and its administrative and educational support services; assesses whether it achieves these outcomes; and provides evidence of improvement based on analysis of those results.

PROGRAMMES

• *Educational Programmes*: All Educational Programmes (includes all on-campus, off-campus, and distance learning programmes and course work):

— The institution demonstrates that each. educational programme for which academic credit is awarded.

a. Is approved by the faculty and the administration, and

b. Establishes and evaluates programme and learning outcomes.

— The institution's continuing education, outreach, and service programmes are consistent with the institution's mission.

— The institution publishes admissions policies consistent with its mission.

— The institution has a defined and published policy for evaluating, awarding, and accepting credit for transfer, experiential learning, advanced placement, and professional certificates that is consistent with its mission and ensures that course work and learning outcomes are at the collegiate level and comparable to the institution's own degree programmes. The institution assumes responsibility for the academic quality of any course work or credit recorded on the institution's transcript.

— The institution publishes academic policies that adhere to principles of good educational practice. These are disseminated to students, faculty, and other interested parties through publications that accurately represent the programmes and services of the institution.

— The institution employs sound and acceptable practices for determining the amount and level of credit awarded for courses, regardless of format or mode of delivery.

— The institution ensures the quality of educational programmes/courses offered through consortia relationships or contractual agreements, ensures ongoing compliance with the comprehensive requirements, and evaluates the consortial relationship and/or agreement against the purpose of the institution.

- The institution awards academic credit for course work taken on a non-credit basis only when there is documentation that the non-credit course work is equivalent to a designated credit experience.
- The institution provides appropriate academic support services.
- The institution defines and publishes general education requirements for its undergraduate programmes and major programme requirements for all its programmes. These requirements conform to commonly accepted standards and practices for degree programmes.
- The institution protects the security, confidentiality, and integrity of its student academic records and maintains special security measures to protect and back up data.
- The institution places primary responsibility for the content, quality, and effectiveness of its curriculum with its faculty.
- For each major in a degree programme, the institution assigns responsibility for programme coordination, as well as for curriculum development and review, to persons academically qualified in the field. In those degree programmes for which the institution does not identify a major, this requirement applies to a curricular area or concentration.
- The institution's use of technology enhances student learning, is appropriate for meeting the objectives of its programmes, and ensures that students have access to and training in the use of technology.

• *Educational Programmes*: Undergraduate Programmes:
  - The institution identifies college-level competencies within the general education core and provides evidence that graduates have attained those competencies.

 - The institution awards degrees only to those students who have earned at least 25 percent of the credit hours required for the degree through instruction offered by that institution.
- *Educational Programmes*: Graduate and Post-Baccalaureate Professional Programmes:
 - The institution's post-baccalaureate professional degree programmes, and its master's and doctoral degree programmes, are progressively more advanced in academic content than undergraduate programmes.
 - The institution ensures that its graduate instruction and resources foster independent learning, enabling the graduate to contribute to a profession or field of study.
 - The majority of credits towards a graduate or a post-baccalaureate professional degree is earned through the institution awarding the degree. In the case of graduate and post-baccalaureate professional degree programmes offered through joint, cooperative, or consortia arrangements, the student earns a majority of credits from the participating institutions.
- Faculty:
 - The institution employs competent faculty members qualified to accomplish the mission and goals of the institution. When determining acceptable qualifications of its faculty, an institution gives primary consideration to the highest earned degree in the discipline in accordance with the guidelines listed below. The institution also considers competence, effectiveness, and capacity, including, as appropriate, undergraduate and graduate degrees, related work experiences in the field, professional licensure and certifications, honours and awards, continuous documented excellence in teaching, or other demonstrated competencies and achievements that contribute to

effective teaching and student learning outcomes. For all cases, the institution is responsible for justifying and documenting the qualifications of its faculty.

— Credential Guidelines:

a. Faculty teaching general education courses at the undergraduate level: doctor's or master's degree in the teaching discipline or master's degree with a concentration in the teaching discipline (a minimum of 18 graduate semester hours in the teaching discipline).

b. Faculty teaching associate degree courses designed for transfer to a baccalaureate degree: doctor's or master's degree in the teaching discipline or master's degree with a concentration in the teaching discipline (a minimum of 18 graduate semester hours in the teaching discipline).

c. Faculty teaching associate degree courses not designed for transfer to the baccalaureate degree: bachelor's degree in the teaching discipline, or associate's degree and demonstrated competencies in the teaching discipline.

d. Faculty teaching baccalaureate courses: doctor's or master's degree in the teaching discipline or master's degree with a concentration in the teaching discipline (minimum of 18 graduate semester hours in the teaching discipline). At least 25 per cent of the discipline course hours in each undergraduate major are taught by faculty members holding the terminal degree—usually the earned doctorate—in the discipline.

e. Faculty teaching graduate and post-baccalaureate course work: earned doctorate/terminal degree in the teaching discipline or a related discipline.

f. Graduate teaching assistants: master's in the teaching discipline or 18 graduate semester hours in the teaching discipline, direct supervision by a faculty member experienced in the teaching discipline, regular in-service training, and planned and periodic evaluations.

- The institution regularly evaluates the effectiveness of each faculty member in accord with published criteria, regardless of contractual or tenured status.
- The institution provides evidence of ongoing professional development of faculty as teachers, scholars, and practitioners.
- The institution ensures adequate procedures for safeguarding and protecting academic freedom.
- The institution publishes policies on the responsibility and authority of faculty in academic and governance matters.

• Library and Other Learning Resources:

- The institution provides facilities, services, and learning/information resources that are appropriate to support its teaching, research, and service mission.
- The institution ensures that users have access to regular and timely instruction in the use of the library and other learning/information resources.
- The institution provides a sufficient number of qualified staff—with appropriate education or experiences in library and/or other learning/information resources—to accomplish the mission of the institution.

• Student Affairs and Services:

- The institution publishes a clear and appropriate statement of student rights and responsibilities and disseminates the statement to the campus community.
- The institution protects the security, confidentiality, and integrity of its student records.

— The institution provides services supporting its mission with qualified personnel to ensure the quality and effectiveness of its student affairs programmes.

RESOURCES

- Financial and Physical Resources
  - The institution's recent financial history demonstrates financial stability.
  - The institution provides financial statements and related documents, including multiple measures for determining financial health as requested by the Commission, which accurately and appropriately represent the total operation of the institution.
  - The institution audits financial aid programmes as required by federal and state regulations.
  - The institution exercises appropriate control over all its financial and physical resources.
  - The institution maintains financial control over externally funded or sponsored research and programmes.
  - The institution takes reasonable steps to provide a healthy, safe, and secure environment for all members of the campus community.
  - The institution operates and maintains physical facilities, both on and off campus, that are adequate to serve the needs of the institution's educational programmes, support services, and other mission-related activities.

FEDERAL REQUIREMENTS

- When evaluating success with respect to student achievement in relation to the institution's mission, the institution includes, as appropriate, consideration of course completion, state licensing examinations, and job placement rates.

- The institution maintains a curriculum that is directly related and appropriate to its purpose and goals and to diplomas, certificates, or degrees awarded.
- The institution makes available to students and the public current academic calendars, grading policies, and refund policies.
- The institution demonstrates that programme length is appropriate for each of the degrees offered.
- The institution has adequate procedures for addressing written student complaints and is responsible for demonstrating that it follows those procedures when resolving student complaints.
- Recruitment materials and presentations accurately represent the institution's practices and policies.
- The institution publishes the name of its primary accreditor and its address and phone number. (The publication of this information is presented so that it is clear that enquiries to the Commission should relate only to the accreditation status of the institution, and not to general admission information.)
- The institution is in compliance with its programme responsibilities under Title IV of the *1998 Higher Education Amendments*. (In reviewing the institution's compliance with these programme responsibilities, the Commission relies on documentation forwarded to it by the U.S. Secretary of Education.)

5

Understanding and Assessing Quality

UNDERSTANDING QUALITY

DIFFERENT UNDERSTANDINGS OF QUALITY

Many sectors have debated how to define quality. A commonly quoted remark in discussions about quality is: 'Quality...you know what it is, yet you don't know what it is'. Another common quote is: 'Some things are better than others; that is, they have more quality. But when you try to say what the quality is, apart from the things that have it, it all goes poof'. Chambers dictionary defines quality both as 'grade of goodness' and as 'excellence'. This indicates the ambiguity in its meaning: namely, that it can mean both 'good' and 'how good'. Similarly, among other things, *Webster's* dictionary describes quality, as a 'degree of excellence' and 'superiority in kind'.

The Oxford English Dictionary (OED) gives similar definitions – the 'degree of excellence of a thing', 'general excellence' and 'of high quality'. 'Degree of excellence' implies that you can talk about something of good quality or poor in quality. The other definitions imply that 'quality' itself means excellence (as in 'quality product' or 'their work has quality'). Such ambiguity leads to many interpretations. It is therefore necessary to describe what is meant by the term in any particular context. Historically, the concept of quality assurance evolved from the manufacturing sector. In this sector, quality is about minimizing variability and ensuring that manufactured products conform to clear specifications. The essence of this concern is that customers could expect the product to perform reliably. Quality therefore means 'zero defects'. While manufacturing companies focus on controlling product variability, service businesses have a more comprehensive view of quality.

They are concerned not only with minimizing defects, but also with managing emotions, expectations and experiences. Service businesses are now shifting the focus from 'zero defects' in products to 'zero defections' of customers. In the service view of quality, businesses must recognise that specifications are not just set by a manufacturer who tells the consumer what to expect. Instead, consumers may also participate in setting specifications. Here, quality means 'consumer satisfaction'. In software and information products, the concept of quality usually incorporates both the conformity and service views of quality. On the one hand, there are a basic set of features that must always work. On the other hand, when customers have problems using a software package, they define quality according to the technical support they experience.

The idea of quality in software products has yet another dimension. Software users expect a continuous stream of novel features: upgrades; high performance and reliability; and ease of installation, use and maintenance. Their perception of quality consists of a synthesis of conformity, adaptability, innovation and continuous improvement. In many ways, this is the way quality is perceived in higher education—as a synthesis of a range of expectations of many stakeholders.

QUALITY IN HIGHER EDUCATION

Many stakeholders in higher education would find it difficult to define quality precisely. In reality, it is a relative concept that means different things to different people. For instance, while discussing the quality of an HEI, students may focus on the facilities provided and the perceived usefulness of education for future employment. Teachers, on the other hand, may pay attention to the teaching-learning process. Management may give importance to the institution's achievements. Parents may consider the achievements of their children. Finally, employers may consider the competence of the institution's graduates. Each stakeholder has a different approach to defining quality.

It is not possible, therefore, to talk about quality as a single concept. Any definition of quality must be defined in terms of the context in which it is used. In the case of HEIs, we should bear in mind that an institution may be of high quality in relation to one factor or in the perspective of a category of stakeholders, but of low quality in relation to another. Considering these factors, Harvey and Green and Green have identified many approaches to the viewing of quality. Green lists five different approaches to quality in the field of higher education.

She considers that it can be viewed:

- In terms of the exceptional (highest standards);
- In terms of conformity to standards;
- As fitness for purpose;
- As effectiveness in achieving institutional goals; and
- As meeting customers' stated or implied needs.

Quality as Exceptionality

This is the more traditional concept of quality. It is associated with the notion of providing a product or service that is distinctive and special, and which confers status on the owner or user. In higher education, an institution that demonstrates exceptionally high standards is seen as a quality institution. This approach may be applicable for 'excellence awards' or to identify a very few highlevel institutions. But it poses a practical problem for QA agencies. A QA agency may commend institutions that demonstrate exceptional standards. However, it is not possible for the agency to condemn all other institutions. That would not serve accountability or self-improvement purposes. Therefore, a 'quality as exceptionality' approach is not generally in vogue among QA agencies. However, there may be areas in higher education where this approach is necessary. This could include, for example, evaluating doctoral programmes or cutting-edge research. There may even be some institutions within a system which choose to be assessed against criteria of excellence (such as flagship universities). Thus, while it cannot be used across the higher education system, excellence cannot be dismissed as one of the ways in which quality is defined.

Quality as Conformance to Standards

This view has its origins in the quality control approach of the manufacturing industry. Here, the word 'standard' is used to indicate pre-determined specifications or expectations. As long as an institution meets the pre-determined standards, it can be considered a quality institution fit for a particular status. This is the approach followed by most regulatory bodies for ensuring that institutions or programmes meet certain threshold levels.

Conformity to standards may result in approval to start programmes or recognition for a particular status or funding depending on the context. Of course, the issue of standards becomes crucial here. Sometimes they are defined in a formal way. This could be, for example, the number of full-time professors, the percentage of them with final degrees, or the number of articles published per full-time equivalent (FTE) faculty member. While this makes assessment fairly easy, it may also make it irrelevant. Indeed, it is usually possible to comply with formal requirements without paying attention to the substantive issues they are meant to safeguard.

Quality as Fitness for Purpose

This approach is based on the view that quality has no meaning except in relation to the purpose of the product or service. Obviously one does not need a super computer to do basic multiplications. What may be considered a quality system for basic computation is different from what is required for scientific experiments. However, this approach begs the questions: 'Who will determine the purpose?' and 'What are appropriate purposes?'. The answers to these questions depend on the context in which quality is viewed. The purposes may be determined by the institution itself, by the government, or by a group of stakeholders.

Quality as Effectiveness in Achieving Institutional Goals

This is one version of the 'fitness-for–purpose' approach, in which the purposes are determined by the institution. In this approach, a high quality institution is one that clearly states its mission (purpose) and is efficient in achieving it. This approach may raise issues such as the way in which the institution might set its goals (high, moderate or low), and how appropriate those goals could be.

Quality as Meeting Customers' Stated or Implied Needs

This is also a variation of the fitness-for-purpose approach. This is where the purpose is customer needs and satisfaction. The issue here is whether customer satisfaction can be equated with what is good for the customer. Are 'needs' the same as `wants'? In higher education, this would mean that what students want may not be the same as what is actually good for them.

It is more reliable to consider different groups such as government, students and parents in determining 'customer needs' and 'customer satisfaction', rather than a single category of customers, such as students. Phrases or notions such as 'value for money', 'added value' and 'transformative process' are also used to define quality in higher education. In the 'value for money' point of view, something has quality when it meets the expectations of consumers in relation to the amount they pay for it. Quality therefore corresponds to the satisfaction of consumers.

These consumers may be students (who are direct consumers and invest their active time in learning), parents (who pay for the educational services of their children) or the government (that sets national policies and invests public money for educational services). From the 'added value' point of view, an institution that enables a student to enhance his/her knowledge, competence and employability is seen as successful in its efforts and therefore in generating quality. The transformative process considers how higher education plays a role in developing a variety of generic competences in students, apart from providing them with a body of academic knowledge.

While Harvey and Green and Green have explored and differentiated every possible definition of quality, there has been criticism that the ramifications of so many definitions of the term might be unhelpful. For example, the 'transformation', 'value added', and 'value for money' definitions of quality prompt criticism that they are all characteristics 'expected as outcomes' of processes. If one does not pay attention to 'what is expected', the definitions will coil back, rendering them meaningless. It is here that 'fitness for purpose' FFP is seen by some quality assurance experts as a meaningful way of defining quality.

It is important to note that there is no one right definition for quality. All the concepts (and others) are valuable. However, when a QA agency chooses a particular definition, it must be clearly specified. When we discuss different approaches to quality assurance in the latter part of this module, we will see that no one perspective of quality may be good by itself. Indeed, agencies must synthesise different understandings to suit their purposes.

DEFINING THE BASIC TERMS

QA agencies develop their procedures for quality assurance from the notion of quality. To do so, they use a variety of terms, such as statistics, indicators, criteria, standards and benchmarks. Agencies use the terms 'indicators', 'performance indicators' and 'indicators of quality' rather loosely. The same is true of the terms 'criteria', 'standards' and 'benchmarks'. Often, the same term is used by different bodies to denote different understandings and measures.

This module may be more useful to readers if we are consistent in using terms. An attempt is made to define the terms distinctly as well as in relation to one another. Most of the definitions are drawn from the background note prepared by the author for the APQN project on 'Indicators of Quality'.

Statistics and Indicators

We know that 'statistics' is a branch of mathematics that deals with the systematic collection, organisation and analysis of data. Statistical data relates to facts and items treated statistically, or collected and organised systematically that can be analysed. Simple forms of statistics have been used since, the beginning of civilization, when pictorial representations or other symbols were used to record numbers of people, animals and inanimate objects on skins, slabs, sticks of wood, or the walls of caves.

Before 3000 BC, the Babylonians used small clay tablets to record tabulations of agricultural yields and of commodities bartered or sold. The Roman Empire was the first government to gather extensive data about the population, area, and wealth of the territories that it controlled. During the Middle Ages in Europe, some comprehensive censuses were taken. These are all examples of systematic collection and organisation of data. From those simple beginnings, statistics has grown in significance to become a reliable means of systematically collecting data on various aspects of economic, political and sociological importance.

Moreover, it serves as a tool to correlate and analyse such data. Very often, the term statistics is used to denote statistical data. In this module, statistics means statistical data. QA agencies collect data on many aspects of institutional functioning or programme delivery. Data collected systematically—primary and derived—are called 'statistics' with or without any value-addition.

They are the building blocks of all the value-added specific terms we will come across later, such as performance indicators. For example, details like student enrolment, the academic calendar and fee structure are statistics. When they are interpreted and used to indicate something, they become indicators. Statistics by themselves are insufficient to make judgements. They must be analysed within a specific context, or against a specific norm. This is what turns them into indicators. Indicators can be either qualitative or quantitative. They can be measures of many aspects of quality of an institution or programme.

While an indicator is a statistic, not all statistics are indicators. Indicators are value-added statistics about something that is being measured. Moreover, there is a reference point against which to interpret the indicator. In other words, indicators differ from statistics in that they are measures of aspects under review. Some QA agencies distinguish between Input Indicators, Process Indicators and Output Indicators. They thus assume that the education process resembles a production process that transforms inputs with processes into outputs and outcomes. Input indicators relate to the resources and factors employed to produce an institution's outputs (financial resources, physical facilities, and student and staff profiles).

Process indicators relate to the ways in which resources and factors are combined and used in order to produce an institution's output (management of teaching, research and services). Output indicators describe the outputs produced by institutions (products of teaching, research and services). To these may be added Throughput Indicators and Outcome Indicators. Outcome indicators are the effects of outputs, (*e.g.*, employment rates). Performance indicators provide measures of performance aspects.

Performance Indicators (PIs)

The indicators used to evaluate an institution, or to judge the effectiveness of a programme, are often referred to as 'performance indicators'. The idea of performance evaluation in higher education has been borrowed from economics. In this sense, the success of a system or institution is related to its productivity in terms of effectiveness and efficiency.

As a result, one may often come across Effectiveness Indicators and Efficiency Indicators in discussions on performance indicators. Effectiveness indicators deal with the extent to which an activity fulfils its intended purpose or function. This could include completion rates, graduate employment rates and student satisfaction, among others. Efficiency indicators deal with the extent to which an activity achieves its goal while minimizing resource usage. This could include, for example, staff-student ratios, unit costs, space utilisation, or time to graduation.

The publication of the Jarratt Report by the Committee of Vice-Chancellors and Principals in the UK generated considerable interest across the world in the use of indicators in evaluating different aspects of higher education. A very large number of such indicators have been identified. Most of them are related to the performance of institutions. As many as 264 were listed by Bottrill and Borden in 1994 (by now, many more may have been added). The basic purpose of a PI is obviously to evaluate the performance of a system, institution or organisational structure.

The indicator may be used for various purposes: to monitor, support decisions, compare, evaluate and improve. PIs help to identify problems. However, they are not able to establish causal relationships. For instance, the HEFCE uses the PIs for funding decisions. An institution may like to use PIs to compare its performance on certain aspects with a similar institution. A QA agency with an 'improvement' agenda may like to draw the attention of the institution or the government to areas needing further improvement. Depending on the use to which PIs would be put, QA agencies use a combination of approaches. Using performance indicators for quality assurance is complex. We will discuss this further in the latter part of this module.

Standards

This is also a term that came from industry. Standards are sets of characteristics or quantities that describe the features of a product, process, service, interface or material. 'Standards New Zealand' defines standards as specifications that define materials, methods, processes or practices. In industry, standards provide a basis for determining consistent and acceptable minimum levels of quality, performance, safety and reliability. For example, the format of credit cards that enables them to be used anywhere in the world is defined by international standards. In higher education and quality assurance, 'standard' denotes a principle (or measure) to which one conforms (or should conform), and by which one's quality (or fitness) is judged.

It also has other meanings, such as the 'degree of excellence required for a particular purpose', and 'a thing recognised as a model for imitation'. There are also contexts in which standard means 'basic', without any value-addition features, or 'average quality' or minimum requirements. Standards can be expressed in many ways—quantitatively and qualitatively. In this module, standards refer to 'the specification of aspects, elements or principles to which one should conform or by which quality is judged'.

Criteria

A criterion is an aspect or element by which a thing is judged. The INQAAHE defines criteria as 'the specifications or elements against which a judgement is made'. While the criteria indicate the elements or aspects, the standards set the level. The AUQA indicates that a 'function of standards is to measure the criteria by which quality may be judged'. In practice, the terms criteria and standards are used interchangeably by QA agencies. The National Assessment and Accreditation Council (NAAC) of India differentiates between criteria and criterion statements.

This may be worth considering. In the NAAC's framework, criteria are the broad aspects on which the quality of the institution is assessed. The Council has identified seven criteria. The criterion statements are similar to the standard statements used by the regional accrediting agencies of the USA. These statements set the level or standards to be achieved under the criteria.

You will notice that the criteria spelt out by the NAAC are related to aspects, while the criteria spelt out by the Higher Education Quality Committee of South Africa are in the form of statements. You will also notice that the standard statements of the regional accrediting agencies of the USA are similar to the criteria of the HEQC and the criterion statements of the NAAC. Agencies vary in the use of the terms 'criteria' and 'standards'. However, they all mean aspects—with or without the levels or specifications—that should be considered in assessing quality.

Benchmarks

A benchmark is a point of reference to make comparisons. A benchmark was originally a surveyor's mark on a wall, pillar, or building used as a reference point in measuring altitudes. Today, the term is used in all activities that involve comparisons. The INQAAHE gives the following definition: "A benchmark is a point of reference against which something may be measured. In the simplest definition, benchmarking is the process of learning by making comparisons. For centuries, comparisons have been made in many informal ways.

Today, benchmarking has come to mean a formal process of comparison as a way of generating ideas for improvement; preferably improvements of a major nature. The American Society for Quality defines benchmarking as an improvement process in which an organisation is able to measure its performance against that of the best-in-class organisations, determine how those organisations achieved their performance levels and use the information to improve its own performance. The INQAAHE defines benchmarking as "a process that enables comparison of inputs, processes or outputs between institutions (or parts of institutions) or within a single institution over time" There are many ways of benchmarking that serve different purposes. To understand the differences, the options available in the different types of benchmarking and methodologies should be considered.

The Commonwealth Higher Education Management Service in its publication *Benchmarking in higher education: an international review*. London: CHEMS.

The following classification:

- *Internal benchmarks* for comparing different units within a single system without necessarily having an external standard against which to compare the results;

- *External competitive benchmarks* for comparing performance in key areas based on information from institutions seen as competitors;
- *External collaborative benchmarks* for comparisons with a larger group of institutions who are not immediate competitors; and
- *External transindustry (best in-class) benchmarks* that look across multiple industries in search of new and innovative practices, no matter what their source.

There are many more types in the litreature on benchmarking. There are also many methodologies that can be adopted to develop these benchmarks. For example, the 'ideal type standards' (or 'golden standards') approach creates a model based on idealised best practice. It is then used to assess institutions on the extent to which they fit that model. On the other hand, vertical benchmarking is an approach that seeks to quantify the costs, workloads, productivity and performance of a defined functional area. *Activity* 2 will familiarise you with more developments regarding benchmarking. The discussions indicate that benchmarks can be in many forms. They can be quantitative (such as ratios) or qualitative (such as successful practices). They can be expressed as 'practices', 'statements' or 'specifications of outcomes', all of which may overlap. In particular, benchmarks can be either 'practices' or 'metrics'. Metrics are the expression of the quantified effects reached once practices have been implemented. For the purposes of this module, we will not go beyond these details.

Keeping in mind the discussions, we will use the following definitions in this module:

- *Statistics*: statistical data or data collected in a systematic way
- *Indicator*: Data or statistic that indicates or signals something
- *Performance Indicator*: Data that signals some aspect of performance

- *Criterion*: Aspect or element against which a judgement is made
- *Standard*: Specification of aspects or elements or principles to which one should conform or by which quality is judged
- *Benchmark*: A point of reference to make comparisons

APPROACHES TO QUALITY ASSURANCE

Based on the various understandings of quality and the context, QA agencies adopt a particular definition of quality to develop their procedures. We will discuss two sets of different understandings of quality that may be adopted by QA agencies.

STANDARDS-BASED *VS.* FITNESS-FOR-PURPOSE

Some QA agencies build their understanding of quality taking the 'self-defined' goals and objectives of the institution or programme as the starting point. Other agencies determine quality with reference to a set of standards, specifications or expectations set externally. The agencies of the latter group define quality externally. They may not care what an institution means to do. Rather, they demand that at the very least it does A, B or C, which are set as external requirements. There are also differences in the levels set by the agencies to demonstrate quality—whether these are minimum requirements or high standards.

Standards-based Understanding of Quality

In the 'standards-based' understanding of quality, institutions must demonstrate their quality against a set of pre-determined standards. Adherence to standards developed externally by a reference group is seen as a threshold level of quality. Compliance to norms, accountability, adherence to rules and regulations and adopting codes of practice are predominant here. This is also the practice where the outcomes and competencies acquired are important, as in the case of licensing for professional practice. It may be noted that standards are not necessarily quantitative. To judge whether standards are met, some level must be agreed on or set. This level may be quantitative, (*e.g.*, student-teacher ratio) or qualitative (adequate, competent and qualified faculty). From the examples given within brackets, it is clear that issues perceived to be quantitative can have a qualitative basis. Most qualitative aspects can be given a quantitative expression.

We talk about the student-teacher ratio based on the assumption that a particular ratio is necessary for good teaching and learning. Similarly, competent and qualified faculty can be expressed in terms of academic qualification, years of experience, publications record, student evaluation of faculty, etc. However, quality assurance today has changed. While in the past quantitative criteria was enough to demonstrate that a standard had been met, more qualitative criteria is now incorporated and institutions are encouraged to maintain their individuality. Standards may also be qualitative statements, such as in the case of the regional accreditation agencies of the USA.

Some agencies develop standards based on good practices required in quality institutions or programmes. There are also agencies that spell out detailed specifications to be fulfilled. These rely more on quantitative specifications. The set of standards developed by the Commission on Institutions of Higher Education, New England Association of Schools and Colleges, USA is an example of the former. The standards developed by the All India Council for Technical Education (AICTE) is an example of the latter.

AICTE has a set of standards that must be fulfilled for the establishment of new institutions wishing to offer undergraduate degrees in engineering and related areas. The standards set by AICTE are meant to check whether institutions have the potential and adequate facilities to offer quality programmes. For certain aspects, AICTE has spelt out quantitative standards.

In the case of the standards-based understanding, the examples show that whether something is of quality depends on whether it conforms to externally-derived standards. Contrary to this perspective, the 'fitness-for-purpose' understanding of quality begins with the institution's purposes.

Fitness-for-purpose (FFP) Understanding of Quality

In the 'fitness-for-purpose' approach to quality, an organisation or object is 'fit for purpose' if:

- There are procedures in place that are appropriate for the specified purpose(s); and
- There is evidence that these procedures are in fact achieving the specified purpose(s).

In this sense, an institution that achieves the goals and objectives it has set for itself is considered a quality institution. The goals and objectives of the institution or programme become the lens through which the QA agency analyses the quality of the institution or programme.

Whether the purpose of the institution may be mandated from outside-by the government or by other stakeholders-is debatable. This is what would be called the 'fitness-of-purpose' approach. In this approach, a person determines which purposes are acceptable. These purposes are then measured against external standards. But 'fitness-for-purpose' implies that we are talking about the purposes set out by the institution itself. Once the institution incorporates the mandate into its purposes, they all become 'self-defined' purposes of the institution. This is true even in cases where the mandate of the institution is given by external stakeholders. The institution is then measured against those purposes. This is suitable in systems where other mechanisms ensure that pre-determined or threshold-level standards are met by the institutions or programmes.

It is also effective in systems with good self-regulation mechanisms, where institutional diversity is promoted (as against conformity to standards) and where institutions of higher education are granted a high level of autonomy. The Australian Universities Quality Agency (AUQA) is specific about its 'fitness-for-purpose approach'. The AUQA does not impose an externally prescribed set of standards upon auditees. Instead it uses each organisation's own objectives as its primary starting point for audit. This approach recognises the auditee's autonomy in setting its objectives and in implementing processes to achieve them. The core task of AUQA audit panels is to consider the auditee's performance against these objectives.

Within the same country, different QA agencies might have a different understanding of quality depending on their mandate. For example, professional bodies that look into the quality of professional areas of studies build their understanding of quality around the competence of the graduates to practice the profession. In the same country, the agency responsible for monitoring the establishment of new institutions would have different expectations. Very often, QA agencies use a combination of these understandings as required by the context in which they have to operate. They then develop their quality assurance practices around this. The 'fitness-for-purpose' *vs.* 'standards-based understanding' determines the broader approach followed by the QA agency. For example, audit is more naturally based on 'fitness-for-purpose' and accreditation is 'standards-based'.

The fitness-for-purpose approach has been criticised because it undermines the 'fitness of purpose'. For instance, when evaluating performance against aims and objectives defined by the institution itself, the review team may find that the self-defined aims and objectives have been fully met. However, this tells us nothing about the academic worth of the aims and objectives. Indeed, these may have been pitched, deliberately, at a modest level. This has led to criticisms on 'set aims and objectives' and measuring standards against these. However, one can argue that it is difficult to separate the two definitions. Practically, it is not possible to have an absolute 'fitness-for-purpose' understanding of quality.

Some amount of what is 'acceptable and appropriate' to be considered as quality can be found in all understandings of quality. There are certain non-negotiable national development requirements within which HEIs must determine their mission. This takes care of the appropriateness of purposes, even if the QA agency chooses 'fitness-forpurpose' as its focus. For example, the University of Western Sydney defines quality in its Quality Assurance Framework as 'fitness for moral purpose'. This recognises that purposes should be appropriate.

Although the national quality agency of Australia, the AUQA, follows the fitness-for-purpose approach for its audit scheme, all Australian HEIs are subject to the provisions of a broad quality assurance system that consists of the following actors (in addition to the AUQA):

- The Federal Government, through the Department of Employment, Science and Training (DEST);
- The Ministerial Council of Employment, Education, Training and Youth Affairs (MCEETYA);
- The Australian Qualifications Framework (AQF);
- The National Protocols, devised by MCEETYA and enacted by each state and territory; and
- The Australian Vice Chancellor's Committee (AVCC).

In other words, appropriateness of purposes is well regulated by the other mechanisms in the higher education sector. This makes it possible for the AUQA to focus on fitness for purpose. Looking at this issue from another point of view, all HEIs function under certain regulations and guidelines. They get their approval to function by agreeing to follow certain rules and codes of practice.

To the extent that the regulations and recommendations are accepted by institutions, they become part of the institution's policies (and implicitly, therefore, part of an institution's objectives). The AUQA may thus consider whether an institution has adopted or adapted such guidelines, and investigate the extent to which the institution's objectives are being met in this regard. The Chilean QA agency uses a definition of quality that combines both aspects and highlights the need for HEIs to take responsibility for their quality.

MINIMUM REQUIREMENTS *VS.* STANDARDS OF HIGH QUALITY (OR GOOD PRACTICE)

Some quality assurance models ensure only that the minimum requirements are fulfilled for a particular status. Such models are generally meant for compliance purposes. The outcome has implications for approvals and sanctions. Within the context of diversification and privatisation, most developing countries are confronted with many low level providers and have no system in place for dealing with them. Thus, minimum standards are now frequently the priority. Complementing the approach, within the same country other initiatives emphasising 'improving institutions' do not follow this regulatory approach. Sometimes, the same agency may have two different approaches.

One ensures minimum requirements, while the other pays attention to high standards. Depending on the stage of development of the higher education system, QA agencies may set standards of high quality. Moreover, the frame of reference for assessment may be 'excellence' and not just fulfilment of minimum requirements. The Middle States Commission on Higher Education, USA calls its standards for accreditation 'characteristics of excellence of higher education'. This discussion may appear to present contradictory approaches to quality assurance. But it should be remembered that quality assurance deals with institutions and programmes of varying levels of quality. Moreover, the quality concerns of countries vary greatly. Within the same country, many mechanisms may co-exist to address different quality concerns.

There should be co-ordination between these various quality assurance efforts. In general, those QA agencies that look into minimum standards and those that go beyond the minimum requirements in the same system complement each other. Mechanisms are required to ensure a threshold level of quality as well as to enhance quality among institutions having crossed the threshold level.

AREAS OF QUALITY ASSESSMENT

Areas or aspects considered by QA agencies have a lot in common. Indeed, while they may have different names, or follow different organisational structures, most quality assurance agencies look at the same things. Certainly, they may have different emphases. Certain areas are key to assessing quality. This is true in all agencies, regardless of differences in the country context in which they operate and the unit of quality assurance, In August 2002, the UNESCO Asia-Pacific Regional Bureau of Education, Bangkok sponsored an experts meeting on 'Indicators of Quality and Facilitating Academic Mobility Through Quality Assurance Agencies' for the Asia-Pacific region.

The meeting was well attended by quality assurance and higher education experts from eight countries. Participants at the meeting agreed that the following areas are key to quality:

- Integrity and mission;
- Governance and management;
- Human resources;
- Learning resources and infrastructure;
- Financial management;
- Student profile and support services;
- Curricular aspects;
- Teaching-learning and evaluation;
- Research, consultancy and extension; and
- Quality assurance.

Participants also identified the areas to be considered under the key areas.

These were:

- Integrity and mission: honesty and transparency in policies and procedures; interaction with the community and stakeholders; a clearly formulated realistic mission; aims and objectives known to all constituents of the institution; equity and reservation for disadvantaged groups;
- Governance and management: autonomy of governance; organisational structure; delegation of powers; institutional effectiveness; strategic plan; documentation; modernisation of administration;
- Human resources: recruitment procedures; adequacy, qualification and competence of staff; awards, honours, membership, prises, medals of learned societies of staff; retention; staff development; recognition and reward; staff workloads; welfare schemes; grievance redressal;

- Learning resources and infrastructure: land and buildings; ownership; labs and lecture halls; library and information technology facilities; library spending per student; spending on computing facilities per student; health services, sports and physical education and halls of residence; campus maintenance; optimal usage; community use of institutional facilities; commercial use of institutional facilities;
- Financial management: funding sources; ownership of resources; sustainability of funding; resource mobilisation; resource allocation; accountability; liquidity; budget for academic and developmental plans; unit cost of education; strategic asset management; matching of receipts and expenditure.
- Student profile and support services: admission procedures; student profile—gender, age, social strata, geographical distribution, foreign students, enrolment by levels of study, age ratio, staff/student ratio, out-of-state enrolment, distribution of entry grade; drop out and success rate; progression to employment and further studies; student achievement; student satisfaction; personal and academic counselling; participation of staff in advising students; merit-based scholarships; other scholarships and fellowships; informal and formal mechanisms for student feedback; student representation; student complaints and academic appeals; student mobility; recreational activities for students; placement rate of graduates; employer satisfaction with graduates; graduate earning by field of study; alumni association and alumni profile;
- Curricular aspects: conformity to goals and objectives; relevance to social needs; integration of local context; initiation, review and redesign of programmes; programme options; feedback mechanism on programme quality; interaction with employers and academic peers; demand for various course combinations;

- Teaching-learning and evaluation: teaching innovations; use of new media and methods; co-curricular activities; skill and competence development; projects and other avenues of learning; linkage with institutions, industries and commerce for teaching; linkage for field training; monitoring student progress; continuous internal assessment; use of external examiners; examination schedule, holding of examinations, evaluation, declaration of results; remedial and enrichment programmes;
- Research, consultancy and extension: institutional support for research; staff active in research; research students by field of study; number of PhDs awarded per academic staff; number of research projects per academic staff; research projects sponsored by industry; public sector research funding; ratios of research expenditure and income; research assistantships and fellowships; staff supported by external research grants; existing research equipment; usefulness of research results for education; social merits of research; interdisciplinary research; student involvement in faculty research; research quality—citation of publications, impact factors, patents and licenses; benefits of consultancy to industry and the public; communityoriented activities; and
- Quality assurance: internal quality assurance; institutional research on quality management; co-ordination between the academic and administrative functions; outcomes of external quality assessments; academic ambience; educational reforms.

These areas indicate how a group of QA agencies have identified key areas with a bearing on the quality of institutions. You will notice that some of them could be linked to quantitative expressions while some are qualitative. The examples indicate that the areas of assessment overlap for institutional and programme accreditation. However, there are differences in terms of focus and scope. While the curricular aspects under institutional accreditation may be more concerned with the overall policies and practices of the institution, programme accreditation would look more closely into the quality of the curriculum of the programme under review. Institutional accreditation might also look at the quality of one or more programmes to seek evidence for the evaluations. However, the purpose is not to pass judgement about the quality of the curriculum of that programme. Rather, it aims to make inferences about the overall curricular aspects of the institution.

QUALITY ASSURANCE DECISION-MAKING

QA agencies must build up a framework for translating their notion of quality into 'quality assurance decisions'. Indeed, evaluative guidelines or a framework against which the agency can make decisions are a critical element in quality assurance.

A quality assurance process may examine many academic and administrative aspects of the institution or programme being reviewed and collect data on those aspects. However, the information gathered does not speak for itself. An evaluative judgement must be made, and the evidence gathered must be interpreted in light of some prior questions. This may be done in a rather explicit fashion, where both quantitative and qualitative benchmarks are set for desirable achievements and the reviewer simply establishes the evidence. However, there are also systems in which the assessment is based on the professional judgement of the reviewer.

This use of evidence, judged against a quality assurance framework, leads to decisions with important consequences. Agencies do this in many ways. Some develop standards. Others agree on a set of indicators, while yet others define benchmarks. While some agencies develop specific indicators, others develop broad standard statements against which quality is assessed by experts.

DIFFERENT APPROACHES TO USING STANDARDS

QA agencies adopt different ways of developing and using standards. The standards prescribed by the AICTE mostly relate to 'inputs' to the institution required to offer a quality programme. Some agencies have shifted their focus to 'outcomes'. In most programme accreditation in professional areas of studies, standards relate to good institutional procedures and practices. A practice-focused perspective is adopted in these cases.

These agencies interpret quality in terms of how effectively new entrants to the profession have been prepared for their responsibilities. In recent years, this has resulted in many professional bodies paying attention to competency-based standards. These focus on the appropriate and effective application of knowledge, skills and attitudes. They emphasise the relationship between formal education and work outcomes. This means that they are concerned with the ability to apply relevant knowledge appropriately and effectively in the profession.

The agencies that adopt this understanding of quality generally require institutions and programmes to demonstrate the 'output' of the programme rather than the 'input'. The focus is therefore on developing competence among students to become good professionals, rather than on the number of hours of tutorials or hands-on experience provided. Professional regulation bodies develop their methodologies based on competencybased standards in many ways. For example, the Canadian Institute of Chartered Accountants (CICA) has developed 'The CA Candidate's Competency Map' for its qualification (recognition or registration) process of Chartered Accountants (CAs). CICA together, with the CA institutes, represents approximately 68,000 CAs and 8,000 students in Canada and Bermuda.

It has identified two types of competencies: pervasive qualities and skills (that all CAs are expected to bring to all tasks); and specific competencies. The specific competencies are grouped into six categories. In addition to different ways of using standards, the decision-making process allows for varying levels of professional judgement. Most QA agencies have some level of specifications and reliance on quantification. In some quality assurance frameworks, peers are more free to make judgements against a broad framework. In most other systems, peer judgement is guided by explicit considerations, such as quantitative specifications and indicators.

RELIANCE ON QUANTITATIVE ASSESSMENT

QA agencies may rely on quantification at various levels. Some of the ways are: requiring institutions to demonstrate that they fulfil certain quantitative norms; requiring peers to assess whether the norms are fulfilled; requiring peer assessment to be recorded on a quantitative scale; and requiring the final outcome to be expressed on a quantitative scale.

This raises the question: 'Can quality be assessed against quantitative measures?' Several points of view exist on this fundamental question. Indeed, quality assessment is necessary and inevitable for several human activities. However, the techniques employed may be quite subjective. For instance, we depend to a large extent on human sensory perceptions for assessing aspects such as beauty, music, tea, comfort levels in air-conditioning and perfumes. It is also well recognised that we do not have clear measures for measuring many things in life such as feelings, intellect and emotion. It is widely believed that quality, like beauty, is an elusive characteristic. Earlier, we discussed quality as an idea that is complex and multi-dimensional. There is no doubt that there are many other things of significance.

These include, for example, development, growth, excellence, democracy and religion. We have learnt to deal with these. In this sense, there have been many efforts to assess quality. Some of these efforts rely more on quantitative methods, while others depend on qualitative ones. Some agencies base their decisions mostly on quantitative data. Mexico's accreditation agency for engineering is a case in point. When there is an emphasis on consistency, compliance or agreement on expected levels of performance, QA agencies tend to develop quantitative norms. They then use them as the frame of reference for quality assurance. The AICTE's standards are an example. At the same time, some agencies seek to ensure minimum standards that are not expressed quantitatively. The set of eligibility criteria of the accreditation agencies of the USA is an example. On the other hand, some agencies rely on quantification to consider the excellence of institutions. For example, the National Council of Accreditation in Colombia (NCAC) has 'excellence' as its focus. It defines quality as the integration of 66 characteristics. For each characteristic, a series of qualitative and quantitative variables have been spelt out.

In other words, quantification can be relied on irrespective of whether the agency seeks to ensure minimum standards or standards of high quality. QA agencies that seek to ensure objectivity and reduce subjectivity of peer assessment, especially in systems where identifying competent peers might be challenging, opt to rely on quantitative measures. They claim that quantitative measures help to ensure that the quality assurance process is transparent. A predominant way of carrying out quantitative assessment is using performance indicators.

Use of Performance Indicators

Using PIs in quality assurance is still debated. However, it has gained acceptance in some accountability-related decision-making. In the UK, it came as a response to market forces demanding better products from universities. In Australia, PIs were developed so that education institutions could respond more positively to government priorities. In the Netherlands, PIs have been used to impose fiscal responsiveness and discipline. And in the USA, its use enabled institutions to obtain more autonomy from state legislatures.

Proponents of performance indicators argue that they help in the following ways:

- PIs may be useful to check accountability concerns.
- PIs help in comparing performances of similar institutions.
- PIs can provide a range of information about performance to steer selfimprovement and effective management strategies.

- PIs can provide simple public information about the health of the institution in several areas of functioning.
- PIs can shape policy formulations

In other words, PIs are seen to help HEIs in planning and managing for selfimprovement, in providing public information, and in making comparisons and setting benchmarks. It might help the government as a measure of accountability and for policy formulations. While many are willing to accept PIs for the purposes of self-improvement, they are afraid that it may be used to control institutions. Davis sums up the situation in this way: "Where performance indicators become most controversial is, where the emphasis shifts from their use as one of many inputs into effective decisionmaking to using them as a ranking device, to allocate esteem and funding differentially".

Those who do not support PIs in quality assurance point to the fact that institutions' performance or the quality of programme delivery may be influenced by a variety of factors. Moreover, assessing the institution or programme considering all those factors is not easy. It also indicates how assessing quality is a complex task that must be balanced with peer assessment.

Quantification to Guide Peer Assessment

Reviewers may be required to follow certain guidelines related to quantitative measures within which the qualitative judgement must be made. For example, the accreditation methodology of the NBA (India) requires reviewers to express their judgement in terms of indicators, with the maximum score for each indicator being predetermined by the NBA. This is despite the NBA's methodology being oriented towards peer assessment.

Quantification in Reporting the Outcome

In the case of the NAAC, the scores given by the reviewers are used to calculate the institutional scores in percentage form. The institution's score determines its grade on a nine-point scale: Grade C denotes the score range 55-60; C+ denotes 60-65; C++ denotes 65-70; B is 70-75; B+ is 75-80; B++ is 80-85; A is 85-90; A+ is 90-95; and A++ is 95-100. Institutions that do not get the minimum 55 per cent are not accredited. Some more recent systems follow this approach to establish credibility and ensure objectivity.

This is especially true in the absence of a well-established corps of assessors or in big systems with a lot of inter-team variance. However, the relationship between numbers and objectivity is questionable. Numbers only help when certain assumptions operate. That is, they operate when you can be sure that the difference between 50 per cent and 60 per cent is the same as the difference between 75 per cent and 85 per cent, for example. This is not usually the case in practice. Quantitative measures give a misleading sense of objectivity, hiding the real subjectivity involved in setting the scores. Reliance on quantification has been debated by different stakeholders for various reasons. It may help an agency to ensure consistency in its approach and minimize inter-team variance among the review panels. It might also be very useful in emerging systems to assure transparency.

However, it may encourage HEIs to report simple quantitative measures that benefit them instead of truthful qualitative assessments. Or, it may encourage them to chase the measures themselves, rather than what they represent. Fears have also been expressed regarding the relevance, accuracy and efficacy of many measures that have been, or are likely to be, employed by the QA agencies. Reliance on quantification and quantitative indicators becomes most controversial when the emphasis shifts from their use as an input in decision-making, to their use as a ranking device. Much depends on how the reliance on quantifications is balanced with peer assessment.

RELIANCE ON PROFESSIONAL JUDGEMENT

Some QA agencies do not provide explicit norms and quantitative targets because they feel that once the norms are made explicit, they might become counter-productive to 'institutional diversity' and the 'fitness-for-purpose approach'. This does not mean that compliance to standards is not important. However, other mechanisms may ensure compliance. Once the threshold level is already ensured, the agency checks how well the HEIs are performing in their own way to achieve their goals and objectives. Considering diversity is important here and relying on quantitative assessment may not help.

Professional judgement adhering to the quality assurance framework of the agency is central here. Agencies that do not want to be very prescriptive do not require institutions to comply with specific quantitative targets. But they may provide detailed guidelines (or standards) on issues such as demonstrating adequacy and efficiency. For example, an agency may not insist that there be a teacher for every 10 students. Similarly, it might not insist that postgraduate programmes be handled only by doctoral degree holders. But it might say in general language that it should have adequate and competent faculty to run the programme under review. For example, the AUQA gives only the indicative areas to be covered.

It is the professional judgement of peers that is important. Agencies that rely more on the professional judgement of a review team must be aware of the subjectivity that might creep into the quality assurance process. QA agencies handle this concern by developing manuals and guidelines to guide peer assessment. As discussed in earlier modules, a rigourous training strategy is key to ensuring reliable peer assessment. An interesting strategy that helps enhance the objectivity of a peer review team's judgements is the requirement that they reach their conclusions by consensus, not by vote. Thus, objectivity is ensured through a measure of intersubjectivity, as extreme views are dismissed. What prevails is what all the members of the team agree on.

The composition of teams, and the way in which they cover different views and disciplinary approaches, are also important factors in making sound decisions. QA agencies generally rely both on quantification and on peer assessment.

To suit the context and their mandate, they must choose an appropriate stand. The options are not to be seen as clear-cut options. Rather, they are approaches that may be used in combination, because they bring different strengths and weaknesses to the fore.

FLEXIBILITY TO SUIT THE CONTEXT

QA agencies should also address the issue of flexibility in the appreciation of quality in both self-assessment and the review framework. The fitness-for-purpose approach is one way of introducing flexibility to take into account specific missions relating to local circumstances. Basically, the agency must ask itself whether it can use the same set of standards and criteria for different types of institutions and different types of programmes.

Flexible Approaches to Self-assessment

The QA agency may initially develop a general framework for self-assessment of the institutions or programmes. As the methodology develops, however, it must consider fine-tuning its approaches. One of the issues it might consider is awareness of 'institutional diversity'. It must also make self-assessment more relevant and useful to institutions. In any system of higher education, institutions have varying characteristics. For example, they may be research-intensive, teaching-oriented, young, old, specialised and/or multi-faculty. Whether the same set of guidelines, criteria and expectations for self-assessment are adequate is an issue in these systems.

In general, agencies provide very limited flexibility in planning and organising self-assessment. Some agencies provide different sets of guidelines and manuals to help different categories of institutions. In some cases, innovative approaches have been tried to introduce flexibility. In the USA, where accreditation has a long history, there are many examples of flexible approaches to self-assessment. This is partly in response to the growing diversity of institutions. It also partly relates to complaints from institutions about the burden of repeated accreditation visits. Some regional accrediting agencies offer different options for conducting a self-study (self-assessment). For example, the Middle States Commission on Higher Education (MSCHE) has four major models for self-study: the comprehensive model; the comprehensive model with special focus; the selected topics model; and the alternate self-study model.

The New England Association is also flexible in its approach to self-study. Some regional accrediting agencies have introduced projects to lead to accreditation being continued. These may be seen as variations of flexibility in the approach to selfstudy. However, they would require more concerted effort and serious commitment to the project. The AQIP discussed in *Module 3* is an example of this. With the AQIP, an institution has the opportunity to demonstrate that it meets the Higher Learning Commission's accreditation standards and expectations. It can do so through sequences of events which naturally align with ongoing activities that characterise organisations striving to improve their performance.

Flexibility in the Definition of Standards and the Self-Assessment Exercise

Perhaps the most common and effective way of being flexible is the use of qualitative descriptions of standards. Many standards require institutions to provide evidence that they have *sufficient* resources for doing something. Or, they may require institutions to provide *adequate* facilities, develop a *significant* level of research, or use *appropriate* teaching methodologies. It is then the responsibility of the institution to show that what they have is sufficient, adequate, significant, and/or appropriate to carry out their work well.

This helps institutions really think about what they are actually doing. In particular, it forces them to consider whether the resources they have, or the way in which they do their work, is really what they need. Of course, in order for this approach to be effective, institutions must provide relevant quantitative and qualitative supporting information. This will enable them to demonstrate, to the satisfaction of the external review team and of the agency, that what they are doing is right. What is adequate for a law programme, in terms of the number of faculty members or percentage hired on a full-time basis, may be totally inadequate for an architecture programme or a dentistry programme. On the other hand, what is sufficient for a teaching institution may be quite insufficient for a research institution.

Flexibility in the Assessment Framework

When institutions of different types fall under the purview of an agency, the quality debate often raises this question: 'How can the same set of standards apply to all institutions or programmes?' Some agencies rely on peer assessment to take note of institutional diversity. Some have successfully addressed this issue by developing differential frameworks.

Role of Peers in Contextualising the Assessment

Each entity has a unique characteristic. Indeed, the agency cannot possibly cater to all the differences by developing differential frameworks. But agencies consider this an important issue to which the reviewers are sensitised or oriented. Training programmes and orientations usually discuss contextualising the assessment. Furthermore, agencies facing the issue of 'institutional diversity' and 'contextualisation' constitute review teams carefully. They do so by choosing reviewers who will bring relevant experience and expertise to the team. This helps the team to understand the context without compromising the quality assurance framework and agency's consistency of approach.

If reviewers do not differentiate between 'understanding the context' and 'excuses for non-performance', the credibility of the agency and objectivity of the assessment will be damaged. QA agencies must have appropriate training programmes and safeguards in place if they wish to introduce flexibility through peer assessment. The considered the various approaches to quality assurance. Each method has its advantages and disadvantages, depending on where it is used, how it is implemented and for what purposes. It is essential to carefully analyse the various factors in order to make an appropriate choice. The discussions and case studies illustrated above may be useful to broaden the understanding of the various options available. But no one approach will offer a perfect solution to the problems of your country. Indeed, any strategy must be aware of the context. However, when the quality assurance strategy is being developed, the experiences of other countries are always useful. The discussions in this module should be viewed with this understanding.

6

Academic Library Environment

THE LIBRARY ENVIRONMENT

The library resource centre should provide a dynamic, stimulating and motivational environment for students and teachers.

To ensure the library resource centre supports the learning environment for students, consideration should be given to:

- Resources
- Furniture
- Signposting
- Access policies
- Accessories
- Information technology
- Space for resources, users, work area and service provision

Effective use of each of these aspects will enhance the quality of the library service provided.

DISPLAYS

Displays are an integral part of any school activity or situation and are well suited to the library resource centre environment due to the availability of both space and resources.

A good display is the result of careful thought and planning.

- Why have displays?

- Who can help with displays?
- Display Formats
- Display Strategies
- Display Photo Gallery
- Display Planner

WHY HAVE DISPLAYS

Displays can:

- Develop understandings of curriculum or learning area content
- Inform and explain
- Enhance the appearance of the LRC and create an atmosphere conducive to learning
- Publicise resources
- motivate users
- Highlight school and community activities
- Provide a showplace for students. work, and
- Direct users.

WHO CAN HELP WITH DISPLAYS

- Class teachers
- Library Officer
- Students
- Parent helpers
- Community members
- Children with special interests
- Community agencies/groups
- Commercial providers
- Movie theatres
- Other resource teachers

Student Involvement:

- Whole ClassClass roster
- Voluntary
- Coordinated by resource teacher with class input, *e.g.*.Meet our Year 1s.. May include photos, pieces of art/craft, interests, hobbies, favourite toys, etc.
- Every class or class member contributes a piece of work

- Assignments completed

Individual/Group:

- Children with special interests, *e.g.*, rock collecting. includes samples, information and supplement with library resources
- Library Monitors plan, locate resources and set up displays
- Students create a display in answering a focus question
- Set task of creating a display as an assignment
- Allocate Learning Area displays to teachers with responsibility for the respective curriculum area.

Parent/Community:

- Allocate volunteers to take on responsibility for one section of the library
- Invite different community members to contribute to displays for special events, *e.g.*, school's anniversary
- Organise to rotate displays with other libraries
- Join organisations which provide displays, e.g. One World Centre
- Organise a workshop to design letter banks, signs, pictures, etc., for future use.

DISPLAY STRATEGIES

Select labels/headings:

- Relate headings to students. interests. may include: a catch phrase, quotation, saying, proverb, slogan, statement or date
- Focus questions, keywords and explosion charts / concept maps help add interest, poems, songs, extracts from resources
- Store all letters created in a.letter bank
- Create large letters/labels using the Overhead Projector
- Have letter templates that are used to create letters of different colours and textures

Select resources:

- Use students to help locate resources

- Discard old, unappealing resources keep pictures from these discarded resources if they can be used for displays
- Include a variety of formats; book, non-book, equipment, realia, moving items
- Use old calendars, postcards etc to add colour
- Household items e.g boxes, chairs, tubs, pots

Locate area:

- Small displays. bookshelf, window ledge, empty corner, table top, cabinets
- Large displays. walls, central floor area, mobile and /or fixed display boards, hang from ceiling
- Regularly shift/relocate display areasDisplay backdrops
- *Fabric*: use large pieces of hessian, velvet, cotton or felt, curtains, sheets or tablecloths
- Paper and Card-crepe paper, wallpaper, alfoil, corrugated card, brenex paper
- *Props*: screens, boxes, tables, polystyrene, trellis, fishing net, bamboo etc
- *Stands*: wire book stands, pegboard
- *Fasteners*: double-sided tape, plastic sleeves, rubber bands, Pins, plastic strips with Velcro
- Pictures from old calendars

Display Borders:

- Commercial borders:
  - Wide ribbon
  - Lengths of calico, chiffon or other fabric
  - Stems of leaves, branches etc
  - Coloured/patterned cardboard or origami paper
  - Twisted crepe paper or streamers
  - Repetitive patterns
  - Laminated napkins
  - Circular paper
  - Any thematic shape
  - Paper plates

USEFUL AIDS

It is always handy to have a ready supply of items available to ensure the quick and effective creation of displays. The following items could be considered your.First Aid Kit. for quick and easy displays!A letter bank

- Self sticking Velcro
- Large dressmaking pins
- Double-sided adhesive tape
- Glue sticks
- PVA glue
- Blutac
- Staple Gun
- Nylon Fishing Line
- Bookstands

KEEPING RECORDS

- Displays take time and effort to create so where ever possible you should try to retain / preserve your efforts
- Materials used for one display can often be kept and recycled for future displays
- Take photos of your displays. these photos are not just a visual record but a trigger of ideas for other displays
- Any lettering that you use should be kept and used again. Keep in a.letter bank
- Display planners. help you to plan your displays and can then be kept as a record for future reference

ACADEMIC LIBRARIES' EXTERNAL ENVIRONMENT AND ENVIRONMENTAL SCANNING BY MANAGERS

Academic libraries just like other libraries, information centers and similar organisations operate within the context of two environments - internal and external. Both of these environments are interconnected. Whilst, the library's internal context consists of organisational structure and of its functions and the way they are configured in pursuit of specified organisational objectives; each library operates in complex and changing external environments, which frequently produce new challenges which must be controlled to ensure the library's future survival and success.

Their impact is a two-way process. Changes in the external environment affect the organisation's internal environment, whilst decisions made at managerial level will impact upon both the external and internal environment. Finally, one of the major and important tasks of a manager is the environmental scanning to acquire information and use it to determine the role of the library in its environment, its influence and image, and the services it provides. The external environment of an organisation may be viewed as a source of information, resources, or variation. External environment is not a collection of other systems and organisations, but it is an active environment. Changes, events and trends in the environment continually create signals and messages. Organisations detect or receive these cues and use the information to adapt to new conditions.

Dill views the environment as a source of information, and suggests that the best way for analysing the environment is to treat the environment as information which becomes available to the organisation, or the organisation may get access via search activity. Because information allows management to improve its strategic planning, tactical implementation of programme and it's monitoring and control; in messy environments, having access to timely and relevant information can give a firm competitive advantage. Information perspective indicates that, when managers suppose that. the environment is unpredictable, they feel uncertainty, and this situation occurs, when they feel that they have no information for accurate decision-making.

Another perspective views the environment as a source of resources upon which the organisation is dependent. Munificence; concentration, and inter-connectedness are three structural characteristics of the environment that affect resource dependence. Organisations require resources to survive. Typically, acquiring resources means that the organisation must interact with others who control those resources. The third perspective, based on ecological view in organisation studies, developed principally by Hannan and Freeman, and Aldrich.

This point of view tries to explain why certain forms of organisations survive and thrive, while others languish and perish by using evolutionary biology rules. A firm's competitive position, financial success, and even survival depend on its ability to scan, understand and adapt to environmental conditions. In many of related studies, the external environment serves as a great source of strategic information. In order to succeed in formulating the strategy for future, managers and decision-makers need to collect, interpret and utilise information from the external environment.

A manager achieves this factor of importance by environmental scanning. Environmental scanning is the activity of gaining information about events and relationships in the organisation's environment, the knowledge of which would assist management in planning future courses of action; and has been the subject of extensive research. Hosseini define environmental scanning as monitoring, evaluation and dissemination of information about environment of organisation to important personnel of organisation.

This object reports on how managers of academic libraries of IAU perceive environmental sectors as "important, variable and complex"; and how they scan environment. We examined how their perceptions of environmental uncertainty and how their perceived strategic uncertainty affect the amount of scanning activity.

CONCEPTUAL FRAMEWORK AND RESEARCH QUESTIONS

In the most general sense, an environment can be defined as everything which surrounds a system. Duncan, defines the environment as "the totality of physical and social factors that are taken directly into consideration in the decision-making behaviour of individuals in the organisation". The external environment comprises all of those forces and events outside the organisation that impinge on its activities. One of the research found that perceived importance is itself the most important predictor of scanning activity.

Kefalas and Schoderbek found that executives in a dynamic environment did more scanning than those in a stable environment; and they concluded that executives' hierarchical level was not related to the focus of scanning and there was considerable scanning of the market sector by executives of all functional specialties. Burns and Stalker indicated that when the external environment was stable, the internal environment of the organisation was generally characterised rules, procedures and clear hierarchy of authority - a typical bureaucratic structure.

Uncertainty is inherent in the environment and Duncan found that the level of perceived uncertainty increases with the complexity and the rate of environment change. The amount of scanning measured was based on Hambrick's study, by analysing the manager's level of interest in keeping abreast of trends; the frequency with which information comes to the manager's attention. In this study we measured the perceived importance (PI), variability or rate of changes (PV) and complexity of academic libraries environment from the managers' viewpoints.

Then Daft, Sormunen and Parks' definition of environmental sectors was accepted, and thus the external environment of academic libraries at IAU were divided into six sectors as was applied by Choo: Customer, Competitor, Technological, Regulatory, Economic, and Socio-cultural.

RESEARCH OBJECTIVES

This study attempts to achieve the following objectives:

- To determine "important, variable and complex" sectors in the external environments of libraries as perceived by managers.
- To determine the amount of scanning that managers do on each of the environmental sectors of the target libraries.

- To determine the PSU and PEU of each of the environmental sectors and their relation with the amount of scanning.

RESEARCH QUESTIONS

- *Q1:* Which sectors of the external environment of academic libraries of IAU are perceived to be important by respondents?
- *Q2:* Which sectors of the external environment of academic libraries of IAU are perceived to be variable by respondents?
- *Q3:* Which sectors of the external environment of academic libraries of IAU are perceived to be complex by respondents?
- *Q4:* Which sectors of the external environment of academic libraries of IAU are scanned mostly by respondents?
- *Q5:* What is the rank of each sector of the external environment of academic libraries of IAU by applying *perceived strategic uncertainty* (PSU)?
- *Q6:* What is the rank of each sector of the external environment of academic libraries of IAU by applying *perceived environmental uncertainty* (PEU)?

RESEARCH HYPOTHESES

The Perceived Strategic Uncertainty (PSU) for each sector was calculated by adding the Perceived Variability (PV) and Perceived Complexity (PC) values of each environmental sector and multiplying the sum by the perceived importance value of that sector for formulating the hypothesis.

This study hypothesised that:

- *H1:* Perceived Strategic Uncertainty (PSU) of an environmental sector positively correlates with the Amount of Scanning (AMS) in that sector.

Then, Perceived Environmental Uncertainty (PEU) was measured by summing the variability and complexity values across the six environmental sectors and the second hypothesis was formulated as follows:

- *H2*: Perceived Uncertainty (PEU) of an environmental sector positively correlates with the Amount of Scanning (AMS) in that sector.

METHODOLOGY

In the context of this research, the following analytical survey method and face to face interview is used to explore the relationship between variables and recognise the managers of point of view.

POPULATION AND DATA COLLECTION

The study population consists of managers of library and information centers of large and very large units of IAU. The units of IAU are located in different groups based on. All units of IAU are more than 232 units in total. Foe homogeneous of research population and delete impact of organisation size we select the large and very large units as populations of this study. Of the 94 selected units, 33 were large and 61 very large, where library and information center managers composed the population of this study.

DATA COLLECTION INSTRUMENT

Data were collected by mail questionnaires which were sent to the managers of libraries and information center of study populations; and personal interviews were performed via telephone to check validity of results from the mail questionnaires. From the population of 94 managers, 85 returned questionnaires, giving a response rate of 90.42 per cent. Chronbach's alpha was accounted for examining the reliability of questionnaire, that was equal to.922, and therefore the reliability of the questionnaire was confirmed.

Based on Saaty and Shih approaches, it was confirmed that "no matter how a structure is validated, group participation with knowledgeable people is a good way to ensure its logicality and completeness". Thus, the questionnaires were reviewed by fifteen experts in the field of Library and Information Science and Management. In order to prepare the items in the questionnaires, the items in the previous researches were used as a valid pattern.

MEASUREMENT OF VARIABLES

Environmental Sectors

In order to measure perceived environmental uncertainty, the external environment is divided to six sectors, as defined by Daft, Sormunen and Parks, and Choo.

Customer, Competition, Technology, Regulatory, Economic, and Socio-cultural Sectors.

- Customer sector refers to those companies or individuals that use the services offered by the respondent's library and information centre, and include companies that acquire information materials and products of library.
- Competition sector includes the companies, products and services, and competitive tactics: companies that offer substitute services and compete with respondent's library, and competitive actions between the respondent's library and other organisations in the same industry.
- Technological sector includes the development of new techniques, innovation and methods in offering information services to customers, and general trends in research and science relevant to the respondent of library.
- Regulatory sector includes governmental legislation and regulations, community policies and political developments at all levels of government.
- Economic sector includes economic factors such as rate of income for individuals, rate of inflation, unemployment rate, and economic growth rate.
- Socio-cultural sector comprises social values in the general population, work ethics, Islamic-based ethics, and other demographic and cultural trends.

Environmental Uncertainty

In organisational research, perceived environmental uncertainty is often analysed using Duncans of two dimensions of environmental complexity and variability. A complex environment requires that numerous environmental factors be taken into account in decision-making.

A variable environment is one in which these factors change frequently and rapidly. In this study the measurement of perceived environmental uncertainty is based on Duncan's two dimensional model: The Simple complex dimension is the number of environmental factors taken into consideration in decision-making; the static-dynamic dimension is the degree to which these factors remain the same or change continually over time.

Following Duncan's model, Daft, Sormunen and Parks, and also Choo used complexity and variability and Revilla, Prieto, and Prado, used dynamism and complexity to measure the perceived environmental uncertainty of chief executives. The perceived importance of environmental sectors were used to formulate the perceived strategic uncertainty. Finally, the perceived environmental uncertainty and perceived strategic uncertainty were measured by the following formulas:

- PEU= PV+PC
- PSU= PI* (PV+PC)

The following questions are asked for taking respondent approach about perceived importance, perceived variability and perceived complexity: Respondents assessed the relative importance, variability and complexity of each of the six defined environmental sectors by answering the following questions:

- *Q1:* How important to your organisations (libraries) are trends and events in each environmental sectors?
- *Q2:* What is the rate of change taking place in each environmental sector?
- *Q3:* What is the complexity level of each environmental sector?

By using a five-point likert scale labeled from 1= Not important to 5= Very important, for Q1; using a five-point scale labeled from 1= Low to 5= High, for Q2; and using a fivepoint scale labeled from 1= Low to 5= High, for Q3 respondents answered.

Amount of Scanning

Although Hambrick measured environmental scanning using frequency, level of interest, and hours spent scanning, this study similar to Choo used only frequency and level of interest such as: How frequently does information about each environmental sector come to your attention? To what extant do you keep yourself informed about developments in each environmental sector?

RESULTS

Both descriptive profiles of respondent managers' statistics were applied to reach valid findings. The nature and application of these statistical tests and methods are detailed out where results are offered. Data collected were analysed using the statistical software package Statistical Product and Service Solutions (SPSS).

Of the 94 managers of Library and Information Centers of IAU, 85 managers returned completed questionnaires. The distribution of respondents is similar to that of the study population: 30 respondents from large units and 55 from very large units.

As for their educational backgrounds, approximately 40 per cent have bachelor, 40 per cent master, and 10 per cent have Ph.D. degrees. On the whole, 85 per cent of respondents' educational field was library and information science and 15 per cent was in other fields.

PERCEIVED IMPORTANCE, VARIABILITY AND COMPLEXITY

Answering the Research Questions

For answering the questions 1 to 3, the mean responses and their standard deviations are calculated and shown in table 6.1.

As a group the respondents perceive the customer sector to be the most important (mean= 4.67), variable (mean= 4.32) and complex (mean= 4.26), followed by the technological sector respectively (mean= 4.14 for (PI), 4.08 for (PV) and 3.99 for (PC)). The socio-cultural sector is placed next in importance (mean=3.99) and variability (mean=3.95), followed by economic sector (mean=3.89 for PI and 3.8 for PV); and the competition sector (mean=3.88) is placed next in complexity and is followed by socio-cultural (mean=3.81) and then economic sector (mean=3.75).

In importance approach, the regulatory and competition sectors are perceived less important (mean=3.59 & 3.52). In variability approach, also competition and regulatory sectors are perceived less variable (mean=3.73 & 3.52). In complexity approach, regulatory sector is perceived less complex (mean=3.58).

Table 6.1 PI, PV, and PC of Environmental Sectors, and Calculated PSU and PEU (Mean Response Scores and Standard Deviations

Environmental Sectors	Perceived Importance		Perceived Variability		Perceived Complexity		Perceived Strategic Uncertainty	Perceived Environmental Uncertainty
	Mena	SD	Mean	SD	Mean	SD	Mean	Mean
Customer Sec.	4.67	0.564	4.32	0.680	4.26	0.657	40.07	8.58
Competition Sec.	3.52	0.717	3.73	0.713	3.88	0.808	26.78	7.61
Technological Sec.	4.14	0.742	4.08	0.774	3.99	0.732	33.41	8.07
Regulatory Sec.	3.59	0.660	3.52	0.647	3.58	0.713	25.49	7.1
Economic Sec.	3.89	0.724	3.8	0.768	3.75	0.705	29.37	7.55
Socio Cultural Sec.	3.99	0.732	3.95	0.770	3.81	0.748	30.96	7.76

Amount of Scanning

In answering the 4th question the mean responses are calculated and shown in figure, which shows the mean amount of scanning of each environmental sector by the managers. As discussed earlier, two measures of the amount of scanning are used: the frequency with which information comes to their attention, and their level of interest in keeping informed about that sector.

By both the frequency and interest measures, the customer (mean=4.32 & 4.29), technological (mean=4.07 & 3.89) and socio-cultural sector (mean=3.95 & 3.88) are scanned most frequently, followed by economic (mean=3.8 & 3.68), competition (mean=3.71 & 3.78) and regulatory sectors (3.51 & 3.48).

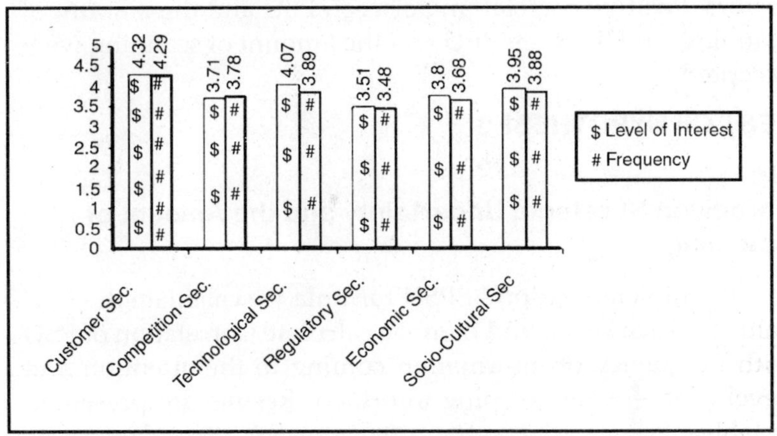

Fig. *6.1* Amount of Scanning of Environmental Sectors

Rank of Each Sector of External Environment by Applying PSU and PEU

For answering questions 5 & 6, by applying PSU and PEU formulas the mean was accounted. As a result, the customer (mean=40.07 for PSU and 8.58 for PEU), technological (mean=33.41 for PSU and 8.07 for PEU) and socio-cultural (mean=30.96 for PSU and 7.76 for PEU) sectors are seen to be the most important, and uncertain by two accounted items (PSU & PEU); the economic (mean=29.37), competition (mean=26.78) and regulatory (mean=25.49) sectors are seen to be less important and uncertain by PSU, and the competition (Mean=7.61), economic (Mean=7.55), and regulatory (Mean=7.1) sectors are seen to be less important and uncertain by PEU.

FINDINGS

Findings of this research indicate that library managers scan the external environment. Customer, technological and socio-cultural sectors are seen to be the most important and also uncertain areas as conceived by respondents.

On the other hand, customer and technological sectors are determined to be as importance, variable and complex sectors. Positive correlation between PSU and the amount of scanning, and between PEU and the amount of scanning were accepted.

TEST OF HYPOTHESES

H1

Perceived St rategic Uncertainty and the Amount of Scanning

By implementation of PSU formula we calculate the PSU value for each sector and then we calculate Correlation of PSU with Frequency of information coming to the attention and Level of interest in keeping informed. Results are presented in table 6.2.

All the correlation coefficients are positive and statistically significant. The correlation coefficients between PSU and Frequency of information coming to the attention range from 0.339 to 0.745, with an average value of 0.574.

The correlation coefficients between PSU and Level of interest in keeping informed range from 0.648 to 0.796, with an average of 0.727.

Table 6.2 Correlations Between PSU and Amount of Scanning (Pearson's Correlation Coefficients)

Environmental Sector	Amount of Scanning	
	Frequency of information coming to Attention	Level of interest in keeping informed
Customer Sector	.559 *•	.757*•
Competition Sector	.339 *•	.706**
Technological Sector	.540 *•	.683**
Regulatory Sector	.644*•	.648**
Economic Sector	.619 *•	.776**
Socio-cultural Sector	.745*•	.796**

Note: ** *Correlation is significant at the 0.01 level (2-tailed).*

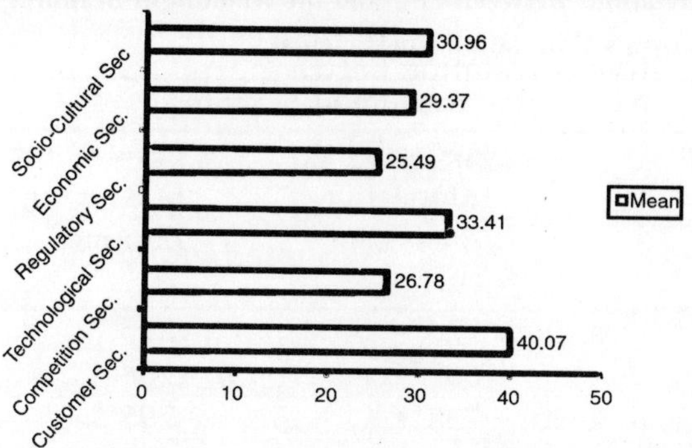

Fig. 6.2 Perceived Strategic Uncertainty (PSU) of Environmental Sectors

H2

Perceived Environmental Uncertainty and the Amount of Scanning

By implementation of PEU formula based on previous research and Duncan's definition, first PEU value and then Correlation of PEU were calculated using information frequency and the level of interest in keeping informed. Results are presented in table. All the correlation coefficients are positive and statistically significant.

The correlation coefficients between PEU and Frequency of information coming to attention range from 0.607 to 0.770, with an average value of 0.682. The correlation coefficients between PEU and Level of interest in keeping informed range from 0.650 to 0.811, with an average of 0.758.

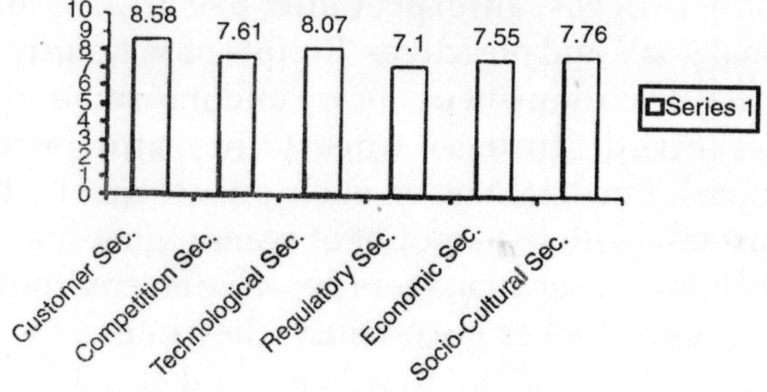

Fig. 6.3 Perceived Environmental Uncertainty (PEU) of Environmental Sectors

Table 6.3 Correlations Between PEU and the Amount of Scanning (Pearson's Correlation Coefficients)

	Amount of Scanning	
Environmental Sector	Frequency of Information Coming to Attention	Level of Interest in Keeping Informed
Customer Sector	.770*•	.725**
Competition Sector	.607*•	.758**
Technological Sector	.738*•	.795**
Regulatory Sector	.613*•	.650**
Economic Sector	.691*•	.811**
Socio-cultural Sector	.675*•	.808**

Note: ** Correlation is significant at the 0.01 level (2-tailed).

DISCUSSION

Today's managers face a business environment that is increasingly complex and turbulent. Findings of previous researches approve this, and indicate that change is a fundamental part of corporate life everywhere, and corporate should foster closer relationships with environmental elements to be able to remain and survive.

From an information perspective, every change and development in the external environment creates signals and messages that managers may need to heed. Some of the signals would be weak, many would be confusing, and others would be spurious.

Manager's act as a processing system that give these signals, then process, interpret,and use it as a base of organisational goals and objectives. Results of this study shows that in external environment of library and information center of IAU, perceived strategic uncertainty and perceived environmental uncertainty of each environment sector, strongly correlate with the amount of scanning on that sector. On the other hand, when managers perceive an environmental sector with a high level of uncertainty, they interest to aware themselves from events about that sector; and also information about that sector come with a high frequent to their attention.

Table 6.4 Compare of Results About PI, PV and PC with Some Previous Research

Variable	Babalhavaeji And Farhadpoor (2011)	Hosseini (2010)	Popoola (2000)	Kefalas and Schoderbeck (1973)	Daft Sormunen And Parks D. (1988)	Choo (1993)
	Environmental Sec.	**Environmental Sec.**	**Environmental Sec.**	**Environmental Sec.**	**Environmental Sec.**	**Environmental Sec.**
Perceived Importance	Customer Sec.	Economic Sec.	Customer Sec.	Dynamic Environment	Customer Sec.	Technological Sec.
Perceived Variability	Customer Sec.	Economic Sec.	Customer Sec.	Dynamic Environment	Customer Sec.	Technological Sec.
Perceived Complexity	Customer Sec.	Economic Sec.	Customer Sec.	Dynamic Environment	Customer Sec.	Technological Sec.

In the field of, library and information center that act as a service base organisation, managers who scan the environment, customer, and technologic sector are perceived Important, variable and complex. The great mean value of competition sector in the field of complexity shows the complexity of this sector and numerous factors in the field of information services. Prior research has shown that environmental uncertainty has important implications for the firm's environmental scanning efforts, and result of this study also approve the previous research's results. Table compares the result of this study about PI, PV and PC with some previous researches.

Finally, environmental scanning is an important organisational effort aimed at understanding, accurately interpreting, and predicting the firm•fs external environment, and this is true when environment is uncertain as is the case today in library and information center of IAU. This study has presented a test of the linkage and correlation between selected dimensions of the external environment and environmental scanning behaviour. And the results show that customer and technological sector are uncertain sectors, and managers need to focus more on them.

ACADEMIC LIBRARY IN CHANGING ENVIRONMENT

Information technologies are impacting the university library's collections, services and spaces. Learning and research are dependent on the availability of a mechanism or system that stores, transfers and transmits knowledge. No effective learning or research can take place without this mechanism. This is because learning and research are cumulative activities.

Progress in learning and research depends on prior progress made and the knowledge transfer mechanism is necessary for cumulative knowledge to be used effectively. Our future libraries must include the latest in information technology, wireless access, production and multimedia software and workstations for users, these are now combined with the expertise of librarians and IT staff, and often focussed in a learning commons area. As well, print collections of books, journals, government reports, special collections and archives are essential resources to access the past and present.

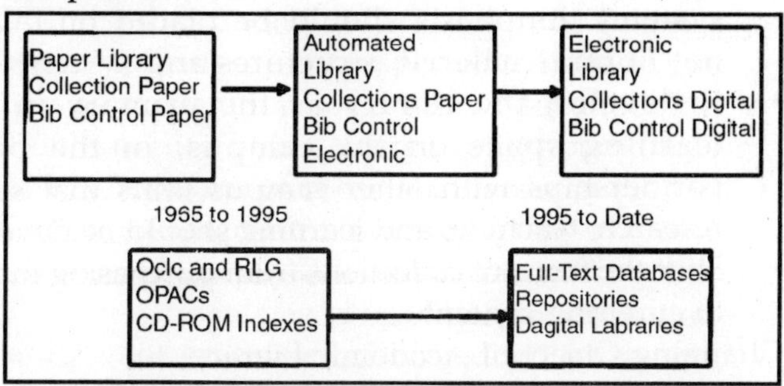

THE NEW LEARNING ENVIRONMENT AND ITS IMPACT ON LIBRARIES

The future of academic libraries is dependent on the future of universities. The information and communication revolution in the last decade have created many new scenarios for universities to ponder. E-learning, open learning, digital libraries, collaborations and strategic alliances are some of the buzzwords we hear today. However, whatever the future scenario, it is likely that the role of universities in learning and research will remain fundamental to their mission. What will probably change will be the mode, scale and ways in which we engage in learning, teaching and research.

ACADEMIC LIBRARY IN TOMORROW

Five Parts of a Strategy

There are five parts of a strategy for maintaining the library as a vibrant enterprise worthy of support from our campuses:

- Complete the migration from print to electronic collections and capture the efficiencies made possible by this change.
- Retire legacy print collections in a way that efficiently provides for its long-term preservation and makes access to this material available when required. This will free space that can be repurposed.

- Reposition library and information tools, resources, and expertise so it is embedded into the teaching, learning, and research enterprises. This includes both human and, increasingly, computer-mediated systems. Emphasis should be placed on external, not library-centered, structures and systems.
- Redevelop the library as the primary informal learning space on the campus. In the process partnerships with other campus units that support research, teaching, and learning should be developed.
- Shift the focus of collections from purchasing materials to curetting content.

Changing Object of Academic Library:

- Is changing 'L' school to 'I' school a solution?
- 'L' or 'I' knowledge *vs.* domain knowledge

Changing Roles of Academic Library:

- Libraries as Educators
- Libraries as R&D Organisations
- Creating Metadata
- Offering Virtual Reference Services
- Maintaining Digital Repositories
- Collaborators in research, teaching

Changing Role of Librarians:

- Knowledge Resources for Community
- Promoters of Open Strategies
- Researchers and Developers of Open Capabilities
- Enablers of Open Digital Education
- Interact more with the users and have better understanding of their information seeking and problem solving behaviour.

Changing of User Expectation:

- Perfect collection
- Excellent services
- Beautiful and lively place
- Physical and virtual accessibilities
- Friendly and helpful library staff
- Modern technology, Etc.

Institutional Expectation:

- Teaching and learning support
- Effective budget management
- Efficient library staff
- And compared with other libraries, *'We Are Better Or The Best'*

Advancing the Repository Movement:

- National Repositories
- Institutional Repositories
- Discipline Repositories
- Consortium Repositories
- Individual Repositories
- Virtual Repositories

Group Membership:

- National Libraries
- University Presses
- University Libraries
- Book Publishers
- Software Companies
- Electronic Publishers
- Library Associations
- Museums

Library Cooperation:

- Library Systems
- Local and Regional Cooperation
- National Consortia
- International Partnerships
- Researcher Collaboration
- Publisher Collaboration
- Collaboration with Technology Organisations

Advantages of Digital Information:

- Accessibility
- Availability
- Searchability
- Dynamism
- Researchability
- Interdisciplinary
- Multimedia Aspects
- Linkability

Digital Library what is needed:

- Building the Infrastructure
- Open Web Content
- Institutional Content
- Multimedia Content
- Integrated Services
- Software Tools
- Creating Metadata

Education in Cyberspace:

- Land Rush/Web Rush
- Electronic Commerce
- Online Education Entrepreneurs

Network Development what is needed:

- Connectivity
- Performance
- Reliability
- Capacity/Bandwidth
- Interoperability
- New Applications

Academic libraries provide services that help students and academics reduce, or at least deal with such complexities more effectively. The future of academic libraries is dependent on the future of universities. The information and communication revolution in the last decade have created many new scenarios for universities to ponder. E-learning, open learning, virtual libraries, digital libraries, collaboratories and strategic alliances are some of the buzzwords we hear today. If we cannot or will not do this, our campuses will invest in other priorities and the libraries will slowly, but surely, atrophy and become a little used museum of the book.

7

Transfer and Reward of Academic Credit

This statement is directed to institutions of higher education and others concerned with the transfer of academic credit among institutions and award of academic credit for extra-institutional learning. Basic to this statement is the principle that each institution is responsible for determining its own policies and practices with regard to the transfer and award of credit.

Institutions are urged to review their policies and practices periodically to ensure that they accomplish the institution's goals and that they function in a manner that is fair and equitable to students. Any statements, this one or others referred to, should be used as guides, not as substitutes, for institutional policies and practices. Transfer of credit is a concept that now involves transfer between dissimilar institutions and curricula and recognition of extra-institutional learning, as well as transfer between institutions and curricula of similar characteristics.

As their personal circumstances and educational objectives change, students seek to have their learning, wherever and however attained, recognised by institutions where they enroll for further study. It is important for reasons of social equity and educational effectiveness, as well as for the wise use of resources, for all institutions to develop reasonable and definitive policies and procedures for acceptance of transfer of credit. Such policies and procedures should provide maximum consideration for the individual student who has changed institutions or objectives. It is the receiving institution's responsibility to provide reasonable and definitive policies and procedures for determining a student's knowledge in required subject areas. All institutions have a responsibility to furnish transcripts and other documents necessary for a receiving institution to judge the quality and quantity of the work. Institutions also have the responsibility to advise the students that the work reflected on the transcript may or may not be accepted by a receiving institution.

INTERINSTITUTIONAL TRANSFER OF CREDIT

Transfer of credit from one institution to another involves at least three considerations:

- The educational quality of the institution from which the student transfers.
- The comparability of the nature, content, and level of credit earned to that offered by the receiving institution.
- The appropriateness and applicability of the credit earned to the programmes offered by the receiving institution, in light of the student's educational goals.

ACCREDITED INSTITUTIONS

Accreditation speaks primarily to the first of these considerations, serving as the basic indicator that an institution meets certain minimum standards. Users of accreditation are urged to give careful attention to the accreditation conferred by accrediting bodies recognised by the Council for Higher Education Accreditation (CHEA). CHEA has a formal process of recognition which requires that any accrediting body so recognised must meet the same standards.

Under these standards CHEA has recognised a number of accrediting bodies, including:

- Regional accrediting commissions which accredit total institutions.
- Certain national accrediting bodies that accredit various kinds of specialised institutions.

- Certain specialised organisations that accredit free-standing professional schools, in addition to programmes within multi-purpose institutions.

The American Council on Education annually publishes for CHEA a list of recognised accrediting bodies, as well as a directory of institutions accredited by these organisations. Although accrediting agencies vary in the ways they are organised and in their statements of scope and mission, all accrediting bodies that meet CHEA's standards for recognition function to ensure that the institutions or programmes they accredit have met generally accepted minimum standards for accreditation.

Accreditation affords reason for confidence in an institution's or a programme's purposes, in the appropriateness of its resources and plans for carrying out these purposes, and in its effectiveness in accomplishing its goals, insofar as these things can be judged. Accreditation speaks to the probability but does not guarantee that students have met acceptable standards of educational accomplishment.

COMPARABILITY AND APPLICABILITY

Comparability of the nature, content, and level of transfer credit and the appropriateness and applicability of the credit earned in programmes offered by the receiving institution are as important in the evaluation process as the accreditation status of the institution at which the transfer credit was awarded.

Since, accreditation does not address these questions, this information must be obtained from catalogues and other materials and from direct contact between knowledgeable and experienced faculty and staff at both the receiving and sending institutions. When such considerations as comparability and appropriateness of credit are satisfied, however, the receiving institution should have reasonable confidence that students from accredited institutions are qualified to undertake the receiving institution's educational programme.

ADMISSIONS AND DEGREE PURPOSES

At some institutions there may be differences between the acceptance of credit for admission purposes and the applicability of credit for degree purposes. A receiving institution may accept previous work, place a credit value on it, and enter it on the transcript.

However, because of its nature and not its inherent quality, may be determined to have no applicability to a specific degree to be pursued by the student. Institutions have a responsibility to make this distinction and its implications clear to students before they enroll. This should be a matter of full disclosure, with the best interests of the student in mind. Institutions also should make every reasonable effort to reduce the gap between credits accepted and credits applied towards an educational credential.

UNACCREDITED INSTITUTIONS

Higher education Institutions that are not accredited by CHEA-recognised accrediting bodies may lack that status for reasons unrelated to questions of quality. Such institutions, however, cannot provide a reliable, third-party assurance that they meet or exceed minimum standards.

That being the case, students transferring from such institutions may encounter special problems in gaining admission and in transferring credits to accredited institutions. Institutions admitting students from unaccredited institutions should take special steps to validate credits previously earned.

FOREIGN INSTITUTIONS

In most cases, foreign institutions are chartered and authorised by their national governments, usually through a ministry of education or head of state. Although this provides for a standardisation within a country, it does not produce useful information about comparability from one country to another.

Two organisations assist institutions by providing information or guidelines on admissions and course placement of international students: the Foreign Educational Credential Service of the American Association of Collegiate Registrars and Admissions Officers (AACRAO) and the National Association of Foreign Student Affairs (NAFSA) Association of International Educators. Equivalency or placement recommendations are to be evaluated in terms of programmes and policies of the individual receiving institution.

VALIDATION OF EXTRA-INSTITUTIONAL AND EXPERIENTIAL LEARNING FOR TRANSFER PURPOSES

Transfer-of-credit policies should encompass educational accomplishment attained in extra-institutional settings as well as at accredited higher education institutions. In deciding on the award of credit for extra-institutional learning, institutions will find the services of the American Council on Education's College Credit Recommendation Service (CREDIT) helpful. One of the Office's functions is to operate and foster programmes to determine credit equivalencies for various modes of extra-institutional learning. CREDIT maintains evaluation programmes for formally structured courses offered by the military and civilian non-collegiate sponsors such as business, corporations, government agencies, and labour unions.

Evaluation services are also available for examination programmes for occupations with validated job proficiency evaluation systems, and for correspondence courses offered by schools accredited by the Distance Education and Training Council. The results are published in a Guide series. Another resource is the General Education Development (GED) Testing Programme, which provides a means for assessing high school equivalency.

For learning that has not been validated through the ACE formal credit recommendation process or through credit-by-examination programmes, institutions are urged to explore the Council for Adult and Experiential Learning (CAEL) procedures and processes. Pertinent CAEL publications designed for this purpose are available.

USES OF THIS STATEMENT

This statement has been endorsed by the national associations most concerned with practices in the area of transfer and award of credit-the American Association of Collegiate Registrars and Admissions Officers, the American Council on Education/Commission on Adult Learning and Educational Credentials, and the Council for Higher Education Accreditation.

Institutions are encouraged to use this statement as a basis for discussions in developing or reviewing institutional policies with regard to transfer. If the statement reflects an institution's policies, that institution might want to use this publication to inform faculty, staff, and students.

DISTANCE DELIVERY OF COURSES, CERTIFICATE, AND DEGREE PROGRAMMES

This policy is intended to apply to the broadest possible definition of distance delivery of instruction, including telecommunications technologies—audio, video, and computer-based technologies—used for instruction in either live or stored modes.

The degree programme and credit courses may or may not be delivered exclusively via telecommunications; for example, the course may include a print component and a degree programme may include an on-campus requirement. The existence of these requirements for instruction via telecommunications does not relieve an accredited institution of the obligation to meet the *Eligibility Requirements*, standards, and policies of the Northwest Commission on Colleges and Universities.

The institution's programmes with specialised accreditation meet the same requirements when offered through distance delivery. Applicable institutional accreditation standards and the Commission's substantive change policy apply regardless of when, where, or how instruction takes place, or by whom taught.

APPLICATION OF REQUIREMENTS

These requirements are to be addressed in the periodic review—self-study and peer evaluation—conducted for reaffirmation of accreditation by every accredited institution that engages in distance delivery through telecommunications. For the institution that proposes to initiate distance learning through telecommunications, these requirements will form the framework for a substantive change review by the Commission.

DEFINITION

Distance education is defined, for the purposes of accreditation review, as a formal educational process in which the majority of the instruction occurs when student and instructor are not in the same place. Instruction may be synchronous or asynchronous.

Distance education may employ correspondence study, or audio, video or electronically mediated technologies. Institutions offering courses, certificate and degree programmes at a distance for academic credit are expected to address in their self-studies and/or proposals for institutional change. The following requirements will be reviewed as appropriate by the Commission.

8

Service Quality in Academic Libraries

BACKGROUND

Libraries exist to collect the record of human experience and to provide intellectual and physical access to that record. For academic libraries in particular, there is a responsibility to preserve scholarly communications as well as the primary resources upon which scholarship often depends.

During the past two decades, myriad challenges and opportunities for libraries have been presented as a result of the rapid development and deployment of information technologies. This environment has spurred librarians to reconsider and redefine collections, services, organisational structure, the skill sets required of library staff, and the attributes of library facilities.

A task force of the University of California Libraries recognised this state of change in libraries.

- The continuing proliferation of formats, tools, services, and technologies has upended how we arrange, retrieve, and present our holdings. Our users expect simplicity and immediate reward and Amazon, Google, and iTunes are the standards against which we are judged.

Library decision makers must therefore determine how to meet new and evolving expectations for library services and materials. Clearly, libraries are operating from vastly different assumptions about the ways in which they might best carry out their responsibilities than they did a few, short years ago. While library practice is changing, it remains based in a commitment to service. Collections of books and other information resources without accompanying access tools, instruction, or other library services are mere warehouses, not libraries. Librarians in all types of libraries work to ensure that their organisations provide high quality service in support of the goals of the library's parent institution.

It would be rare indeed to discover an academic library, for example, that did not consider service quality an important aspect of carrying out its mission to support teaching, learning, and research in the college or university in which it operates. But how do library administrators know whether their libraries are meeting the new expectations of users or providing high quality service?

CUSTOMER SATISFACTION AND SERVICE QUALITY

In the for-profit sector, customer satisfaction measurement and management has long been a common practice, and contemporary service quality assessment has its roots in customer satisfaction measurement. During the past 40 years, the concept of customer satisfaction has changed a number of times. From the corporate image studies of the 1960s to the total quality approach in Western economies in the late 1980s, several approaches to customer satisfaction led to the contemporary conceptual model of service quality.

The first phase of customer satisfaction measurement took the form of corporate image studies in the 1960s. Customer satisfaction and perception of quality were often included indirectly in image surveys as questions about company characteristics such as progressiveness or involvement in the community.

The second phase saw the birth of product quality studies beginning in the late 1960s. The primary measurement was the adequacy-importance model that created an index of satisfaction to explain customer attitudes. The index was created by "summing measures of satisfaction with product performance multiplied by measures of feature importance". Beginning in the 1970s, a new phase was evidenced by some early customer satisfaction studies that were implemented in regulated industries, notably by AT&T.

Without market-based performance indicators, monopolies sought to justify rate increases by garnering favourable customer satisfaction measures. The 1980s marked the next major evolution in thinking about customer satisfaction. The increased competition in the American automobile market from foreign companies gave rise to syndicated automotive studies, such as the J. D. Powers and Associates studies.

The current focus of customer satisfaction measurement can be traced most directly to the 1980s, when the total quality movement captured the attention of businesses in Western economies and businesses recognised the need for a model that addressed the fundamental shift to a service-based, rather than product-based, economy. There was no longer a specific, tangible product to assess, and businesses turned to customer perceptions of whether their expectations were being met or exceeded.

THE GAPS MODEL OF SERVICE QUALITY

The marketing research group of Parasuraman, Zeithaml, and Berry developed an approach to customer satisfaction measurement in the 1980s called the Gaps Model of Service Quality. The Gaps Model assessed customer satisfaction by identifying the differences, or gaps, between customer expectations and customer perceptions of service.

In this model, Customer expectations are established by the customer, who defines the minimum acceptable and the desired levels of service.

The customer then describes his or her perception of the level of service he or she received and the gap is thereby defined by the difference between perceived level of service and desired level of service. Hernon and Nitecki noted that service quality definitions vary across the litreature and are based on four underlying perspectives. 1. Excellence, which is often externally defined. 2. Value, which incorporates multiple attributes and is focused on benefit to the recipient. 3. Conformance to specifications, which enables precise measurement, but customers may not know or care about internal specifications. 4. Meeting or exceeding expectations, which is all-encompassing and applies to all service industries. Most marketing and library science researchers, however, have focused on the fourth perspective and the Gaps Model of Service Quality uses that perspective as a framework to identify the gaps created when performance either exceeds or falls short of meeting customer expectations. In fact, the Gaps Model expands the fourth perspective to five, with the addition of "gaps that may hinder an organisation from providing high quality service".

In the Gaps Model customer expectations are viewed as subjective and based on the extent to which customers believe a particular attribute is essential for an excellent service provider. Customer perceptions are judgements about service performance. Furthermore, expectations are not viewed as static; they are expected to change and evolve over time.

Hernon wrote that:

- The confirmation/disconfirmation process, which influences the Gaps Model, suggests that expectations provide a frame of reference against which customers' experiences can be measured . . . customers form their expectations prior to purchasing or using a product or service. These expectations become a basis against which to compare actual performance.

The measurement of service quality using the Gaps Model, therefore, focuses on the interaction between customers and service providers and the difference, or gap, between expectations about service provision and perceptions about how the service was actually provided.

The difference between the minimum acceptable and the perceived levels of service is the adequacy gap; larger adequacy gaps indicate better performance. The difference between the desired and perceived levels of service is the superiority gap; ideally, these scores would be identical so a perfect score is zero. As the superiority gap score gets further from zero, either positive or negative, it indicates poorer performance.

MEASURING LIBRARY QUALITY

The recent emphasis on assessment in higher education has affected every facet of post-secondary institutions. Administrators in college and university libraries are no exception; they need assessment tools that provide data for continuous improvement, documentation of assessment, and evidence of the thoughtful use of assessment data for accreditation organisations.

The traditional measure of academic library quality has been collection size. In fact, many institutions still organise special events to commemorate the acquisition of a library's millionth volume.

Rather than providing a census of its collections, however, the Middle States Commission on Higher Education now requires the institution to demonstrate the "availability and accessibility of adequate learning resources, such as library and information technology support services, staffed by professionals who are qualified by education, training, and experience to support relevant academic activities. Colleges and universities are therefore required to determine adequacy without prescriptive measures such as volume counts or numbers of professional staff.

The other regional associations have similarly broad statements, leaving librarians and institutional effectiveness staff to figure out a new approach. This shift in the assessment of libraries has been described as a "move beyond the rearview mirror approach" of simply reporting what libraries acquired or how many users walked through the front gates in a given year.

This emphasis on assessment for accountability has motivated librarians to seek out more meaningful measures of quality. Rather than focusing solely on inputs such as collection size or staffing level, the first new library measures were output measures that sought to describe what libraries produced with their inputs. That is, in the 1990s librarians began to report outputs such as the number of items borrowed or the number of reference questions answered. Those measures alone, however, still fell short of addressing whether library services were sufficient.

As colleges and universities created student learning outcomes beginning in the late 1990s, librarians also created measures that were based on outcomes, or the extent to which student and faculty contact with libraries affected them and contributed to the mission of the university. New instruments and protocols, however, were needed for libraries to meet demands for accountability, measure service quality, and generate data for effective library management.

LIBQUAL+™

Service-based industries in the private sector began using an instrument called SERVQUAL for assessing customer perceptions of service quality in the 1980s. SERVQUAL was developed by Parasuraman and grounded in their Gaps Model of Service Quality. In 1995, 1997, and 1999, the Texas A&M University Libraries, seeking a useful model for assessment, used a modified SERVQUAL instrument.

Their experience revealed the need for an adapted tool that would use the Gaps Theory underlying SERVQUAL and better address the particular requirements of libraries. In 1999 the Association of Research Libraries (ARL) partnered with Texas A&M University to develop, test, and refine the adapted instrument. As a result of their collaboration, LibQUAL+™ was "initiated in 2000 as an experimental project for benchmarking perceptions of library service quality across 13 libraries". During 2006 the LibQUAL+™ survey was administered in 298 institutions.

This study analysed data collected from the two administrations of LibQUAL+™ during 2006. A description of the instrument will facilitate an understanding of the investigation. With each administration, the LibQUAL+™ instrument was improved and it is currently composed of 22 questions and a comment box. The results for each library include three dimension scores derived from responses to the 22 questions. There is also an overall, weighted score.

Table 8.1 LibQUAL+™ Dimensions and their Component Items

Dimension	Components
Service Affect	1. Employees who instill confidence in users 2. Giving users individual attention 3. Employees who are consistentlycourteous 4. Readiness to respond to users' questions 5. Employees who have the knowledge to answer user questions 6. Employees who deal with users in a caring fashion 7. Employees who understand the needs of their users 8. Willingness to help users 9. Dependability in handling users' service problems
Information Control	1. Making electronic resources accessible from my home or office 2. A library Web site enabling me to locate information on my own 3. The printed library materials I need for my work 4. The electronic information resources I need 5. Modern equipment that lets me easily access needed information 6. Easy-to-useaccess tools that allow me to find things on my own 7. Making information easily accessible for independent use 8. Print and/or electronic journal collections I require for my work
Library as Place	1. Library space that inspires study and learning 2. Quiet space for individual activities 3. A comfortable and inviting location 4. A getaway for study, learning or research 5. Community space for group learning and group study

The three dimensions measured by LibQUAL+™ are service affect, information control, and library as place. The perceptions of customers about library staff competency and helpfulness are derived from nine questions that compose the service affect dimension score.

The information control dimension is derived from eight questions and focuses on whether the library's collections are adequate to meet customer needs and whether the collections are organised in a manner that enables self-reliance for library users.

Finally, the library as place dimension is derived from five questions that address user perceptions regarding the facility's functionality and adequacy for academic activities. All of the scores are scaled from 1 to 9 with 9 being the highest rating, so that scores can be compared.

RELIABILITY AND VALIDITY

A number of studies have examined the LibQUAL+™ instrument for score reliability and validity. In a key study by Heath, Cook, Kyrillidou, and Thompson, validity coefficients replicated closely across different types of post-secondary libraries, leading them to conclude that *'LibQUAL+™ scores may be valid in reasonably diverse library settings'*.

This study explored that conclusion as it relates to institutional size, institutional type, and level of investment by the institution in its library.

Since, 2000 LibQUAL+™ has been administered in every state except Alaska and South Dakota, and... in various language variations in Canada, Australia, Egypt, England, France, Ireland, Scotland, Sweden, the Netherlands, and the United Arab Emirates.

The 2005 cycle saw administration in several South African universities. And the summer of 2005 brought training in Greece. The instrument has consistently tested as psychometrically valid and the protocol has "a universality that crosses language and cultural boundaries at the settings where LibQUAL+™ has been implemented to date'.

REVIEW OF THE LITERATURE

CUSTOMER SATISFACTION AND SERVICE QUALITY

Consumer satisfaction research 'matured into a respectable research stream' in the mid-1960s. Several approaches to customer satisfaction have emerged since, then that contributed to the conceptual model of service quality used in contemporary measurement efforts.

From the corporate image studies and product quality studies beginning in the late 1960s, measurement approaches emerged based on customer expectations or values.

The adequacy–importance model, for example, was one such measurement that moved from just measuring consumer satisfaction with product performance to enriching those product performance measures with consumer values. It added ratings of the importance of each product feature. The level of satisfaction with performance was then multiplied by the product feature importance to create an index of consumer satisfaction.

Expectancy Disconfirmation Theory

One of the primary areas of exploration in the emerging field of consumer satisfaction research in the 1960s was from the perspective of expectancy disconfirmation theory. Expectancy disconfirmation is a process theory that creates a framework for examining the formation of customer expectations and the subsequent confirmation or disconfirmation of those expectations through comparisons with product performance.

Consumers are thought to compare post-purchase performance to their expectations prior to purchase 'using a 'better-than, worse-than heuristic' to arrive at a judgement of simple confirmation if the product performs as expected.

If performance is better than anticipated, there is a positive disconfirmation of the consumer's expectations; if the performance is worse than anticipated, there is a negative disconfirmation.

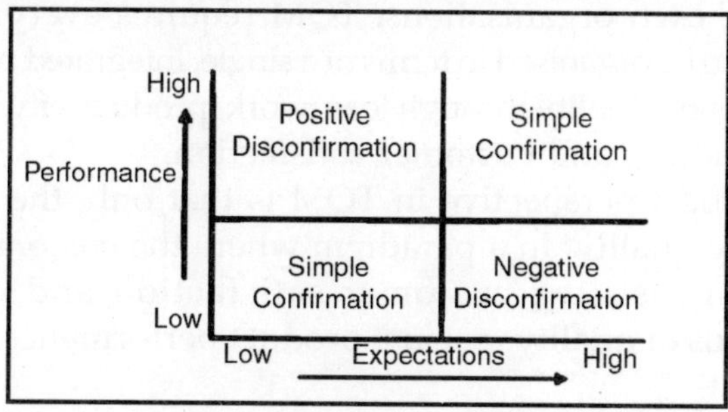

Fig. 8.1 Expectancy Disconfirmation Theory

THE SERVICE-BASED ECONOMY

In the 1980s, consumer satisfaction theorists and businesses alike began to realise that, in terms of the gross national product and employment statistics, the economy in the United States had become dominated by service industries. For the purposes of customer satisfaction measurement, there was no longer just a physical product to assess in terms of durability or number of defects.

The commercial sector was beginning to recognise the need for a new customer satisfaction model that addressed the fundamental shift to a service-based economy and it turned to examining customer perceptions of whether their expectations were being met.

Total Quality Management

Crosby contends that the contemporary emphasis on quality is 'largely attributable to the quality movement in business' that took hold in the United States in the mid-1980s. The success of foreign companies in the American market in the late 1970s and the 1980s was unprecedented.

The success of Japanese companies in particular, such as Toyota and SONY, led many American companies to look at how the Japanese had become so successful. Since, the end of World War II, Japanese companies had focussed on quality and embraced Total Quality Management (TQM). American companies subsequently looked for ways to integrate TQM into their own organisations. TQM requires every part of a company to be organised in terms of a single, integrated philosophy encompassing quality through teamwork, productivity, customer understanding, and customer satisfaction.

A critical perspective in TQM is that only the customer may judge quality. In a paradigm where the customer judges quality, measuring customer satisfaction and customer perceptions of quality, not just product performance, becomes significant.

THE GAPS MODEL OF SERVICE QUALITY

As TQM became popular in the United States, the marketing researchers Parasuraman developed the Gaps Model of Service Quality. The Gaps Model is based on the expectancy disconfirmation perspective with a focus on service quality rather than product quality.

In his review of quality assessment, Hernon wrote that:

- "The confirmation/disconfirmation process, which influences the Gaps Model, suggests that expectations provide a frame of reference against which customers' experiences can be measured.... customers form their expectations prior to purchasing or using a product or service. These expectations become a basis against which to compare actual performance'.

The Gaps Model is described by Hernon as a way to measure customer perceptions of service quality by identifying gaps, or differences, between customer expectations and customer perceptions of service.

In the Gaps Model, customer expectations are viewed as subjective judgements based on the extent to which customers believe a particular attribute is essential for an excellent service provider. Expectations are affected by experience and are not expected to remain the same over time.

In this model, customer perceptions are the judgements about how well service was performed. To deploy the Gaps Model, a survey instrument is used and customers are asked to define the minimum level of service they will accept and the level of service they desire. Customers are then asked to describe their perceptions of the service that was actually provided.

The gaps between perceived performance level and customer-defined desires or expectations can be used to identify and target areas for improvement.

Hernon's examination of the Gaps Model identifies five types of gaps created by discrepancies between:

- Customer expectations of service and management's perspective on these expectations;
- Service quality specifications and management's perspective of customer expectations;
- Service quality specifications and service delivery;
- Service delivery and external communication to customers about that delivery; and
- Customers' expectation of service and perceived service delivery.

The fifth type of gap, between customers' expectation of service and perceived service delivery, is the one used by Parasuraman in defining the framework for SERVQUAL, the instrument they created to assess service quality in the for-profit sector.

SERVQUAL

The SERVQUAL instrument is a multi-item scale that was developed to assess customer perceptions of service quality in retail businesses. It is based in the Gaps Model of Service Quality, which is grounded in expectancy disconfirmation theory.

Customers Define Quality

The SERVQUAL instrument was designed from data gathered in an exploratory customer study by Parasuraman. The exploratory customer study conducted focus-group interviews of customers in four distinct markets: retail banking, credit cards, securities brokerage, and product repair and maintenance. The focus-groups were designed to discover the elements that form the concept of service quality from the customers' perspective. Using a focus-group methodology reflects the TQM focus on quality as well as the precept that 'only customers judge quality; all other judgements are essentially irrelevant'. The definition of service quality that emerged from the customer focus groups was 'the extent of discrepancy between customers' expectations or desires and their perceptions'.

The investigators also found that 'the criteria used by consumers in assessing service quality fit into 10 potentially overlapping dimensions... tangibles, reliability, responsiveness, communication, credibility, security, competence, courtesy, understanding/knowing the consumer, and access".

Refining Serqual

The first version of the SERVQUAL instrument was composed of 97 scale items designed by Parasuraman to gather data that would address those 10 dimensions. In the next phase of development, SERVQUAL was administered and data were collected for the 97 items.

The investigators performed a factor analysis and applied reliability testing. Using Cronbach's alpha coefficient, with alpha values ranging from.72 to.83 across the 10 dimensions, the instrument was refined to 54 items.

Factor analysis of the resulting 54 items changed the factor loadings, suggesting reassignment of some items and deletion of others. Each time the factors were changed, the factor analysis was repeated and this iterative process ultimately resulted in 22 items loading on five dimensions.

SERVQUAL Dimensions and their Components Dimension Components Tangibles Physical facilities, equipment, and appearance of personnel Reliability Ability to perform the promised service dependably and accurately Responsiveness Willingness to help customers and provide prompt service.

Assurance Knowledge and courtesy of employees and their ability to inspire trust and confidence Empathy Caring, individualised attention the firm provides to customers

Table 8.2 Servqual Dimensions and their Components

Dimension	Components
Tangibles	Physical facilities, equipment, and appearance of personnel
Reliability	Ability to perform the promised service dependably and accurately
Responsiveness	Willingness to help customers and provide prompt service
Assurance	Knowledge and courtesy of employees and their ability to inspire trust and confidence
Empathy	Caring, Individualised attention the firm provides to customers

The final five dimensions in SERVQUAL included three of the initial dimensions: tangibles, reliability, and responsiveness, as well as two new, combined dimensions: assurance and empathy.

LIBRARY QUALITY ASSESSMENT

Historically, academic library quality has been expressed in terms of collection size. The "ultimate goal of bringing together a perfectly customised collection of books for the purposes of fulfilling users' needs' drove collection sizes higher and led to assessing a library's quality by the 'magnitude of its resources'. In this environment, libraries relied upon collecting statistics and analysing input measures. Input measures, the financial, human, and material resources available to the library organisation, have been measured in some form by research libraries since, 1908. With the increasing emphasis on assessment and accountability, coupled with the changes in libraries and library collections made possible by information technology, librarians began to seek new measures of quality that would be more meaningful.

From Inputs to Outcomes

In the first phase of seeking out new measures, librarians shifted from focussing solely on what libraries had acquired, and developed measurement models beyond simple inputs.

In the 1990s, library measurement expanded to include output measures: the activities that libraries produced from inputs, such as the number of items borrowed or questions answered. Library professional associations, including the Association of Research Libraries (ARL) and the Association of College and Research Libraries (ACRL), as well as the National Center for Education Statistics (NCES) continue to collect collection- and activity-based data from academic libraries.

NCES maintains an academic library comparison tool on its web site for the purpose of comparing such data among institutions in the United States. Input and output measures are useful yardsticks, but they do not capture the full extent of the impact a library has on its institution. In its 1998 report, the ACRL Task Force on Academic Library Outcomes Assessment captured the limitations of such measures, noting that "measurement of inputs, or the specification of quantities of them by standards, is viewed by some as a primitive, or at least insufficient way' of assessing libraries.

The Task Force argued for libraries to develop outcomes-based measures. In the late 1990s the movement to hold schools, colleges, and universities accountable for establishing and meeting outcomes was becoming formalised by accreditation requirements and pressure from State legislatures for accountability. Educators had been using learning outcome measures for about 15 years at that time, but until the 1990s, most of them had not been required to use formal outcome measures in accreditation reports or legislative budget requests. Libraries tapped into this activity on campus and began to develop outcomes and outcomes-based performance measures. Library outcomes were intended to measure "the ways in which library users are changed as a result of their contact with the library's resources and programmes' as well as document how libraries contribute to meeting institutional outcomes.

Service Quality from the User Perspective

It is only since, the beginning of the 21st century that libraries have engaged in directly measuring service quality from a user perspective. As recently as 2001 the library assessment litreature did not, for the most part, consider direct measurement of quality. For example, as late as 2001, Shim, McClure, and Bertot observed, in a report on measures and statistics for ARL, that "to accurately indicate the success or quality of an academic library, measurement should be implemented at three key levels: outcome level, use/capacity level, and resources level.

In other words, prominent library science researchers were still relying on measures that assessed quality indirectly. Of the measurement methods Shim, McClure, and Bertot identified, there was no instrument or protocol for directly measuring service quality in a library, and there was certainly no instrument to measure service quality across libraries for benchmarking purposes.

Pritchard offers a cogent description of the measurement challenge that faced librarians.

- The difficulty lies in trying to find a single model or set of simple indicators that can be used by different institutions, and that will compare something across large groups that is by definition only locally applicable—, *i.e.,* how well a library meets the needs of its institution. Librarians have either made do with oversimplified national data or have undertaken customised local evaluations of effectiveness, but there has not been devised an effective way to link the two.

As library practitioners and scholars worked to develop meaningful measures for libraries, the need for reliable and meaningful assessment instruments intensified. In their quest to discover better measures, the Texas A&M University Libraries turned to marketing research in the 1990s to identify instruments for measuring library service quality. At that time the SERVQUAL instrument had been widely used in the private sector for about 10 years; moreover, SERVQUAL's creators, Parasuraman, were members of the Texas A&M University faculty. The Texas A&M University Libraries used SERVQUAL three times, in 1995, 1997, and 1999, to track perceptions of library service quality from samples of its library users. Through that experience, the assessment team recognised that the instrument could be improved for libraries by adapting it to address the concepts most critical to library service and removing "items not considered relevant by some library users.

The Texas A&M University group approached ARL about working jointly to adapt SERVQUAL for libraries and they collaborated to apply for a grant from the Fund for the Improvement of Post-Secondary Education (FIPSE). The FIPSE award funded the effort to develop a modified protocol, which they called LibQUAL+™.

VALIDITY AND RELIABILITY

The LibQUAL+™ survey is the first assessment instrument that is claimed to produce reliable and valid national benchmarks for library service quality. A number of studies have supported the instrument's score reliability. LibQUAL+™ has also consistently tested as psychometrically valid. Roszkowsli, Baky, and Jones criticised one aspect of validity by examining LibQUAL+™ scores from a slightly different perspective. In a 2005 investigation, they analysed data from 709 respondents at one institution that participated in LibQUAL+™ during 2003. The study found that the perceived performance rating was a more valid indicator of user satisfaction than the superiority gap score.

This criticism of the LibQUAL+™ protocol focused on the validity of the superiority gap score, which is the difference between users' perceived and desired levels of performance. The investigators argued that user-defined desired levels of performance are irrelevant and only user perceptions of actual performance are valid measures of library service. In a study by Heath, Cook, Kyrillidou, and Thompson, validity coefficients replicated closely across different types of post-secondary libraries, from which they concluded that LibQUAL+™ scores may be valid in different types of library settings.

The study described in this report investigates that conclusion by exploring whether and to what extent there are relations between LibQUAL+™ scores and the following key characteristics: institutional size, institutional type, and level of investment by the institution in its library. Only one study was identified in the litreature review that specifically explored potential relationships between LibQUAL+™ scores and institutional characteristics. However, this study used an earlier version of the LibQUAL+™ instrument with four dimensions and used a different set of institutional characteristics for the independent variables than those in the present study.

Kyrillidou and Heath found a "moderate negative relation of the ARL Membership Criteria Index with LibQUAL+™ scores". The ARL Membership Criteria Index is composed of volumes held, gross volumes added, current serials, total staff, and expenditures. In other words, the Index is composed of traditional input and output measures of library quality. Kyrillidou and Heath concluded that students and faculty members in libraries at large research institutions have higher expectations for library collections, which results in lower LibQUAL+™ scores. The negative relationship found between the ARL Membership Criteria Index and LibQUAL+™ scores occurred, they asserted, because such library users "are highly skilled, have specialised and diverse information needs . . . are clearly more demanding and harder to please" than library users at other types of institutions.

CONCEPTUAL FRAMEWORK

This litreature review served as the basis for the conceptual framework underlying this study. It is clear that demands for assessment are directed at post-secondary institutions and their libraries by internal and external constituencies including governing boards, state and federal agencies, accreditation organisations, and administrators who need data for decision making.

In addition, library users bring expectations to the library about services and resources based on their understanding of the institution as well as their experience and skill in using libraries.

Figure illustrates the relationships among several concepts that constitute the factors relevant to evaluating academic library service quality with the LibQUAL+™ survey.

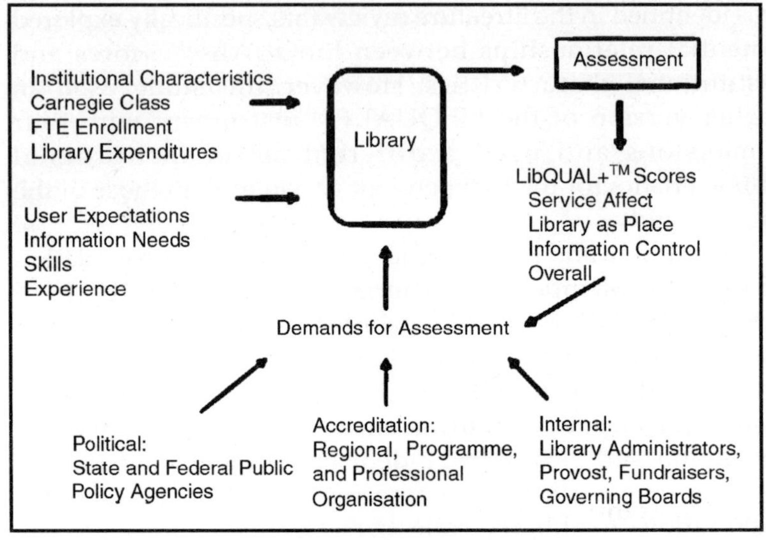

Fig. 8.2 LibQUAL+™ Service Quality Assessment Factors

METHODOLOGY

The purpose of this study was to explore and expand on the current understanding of the meaning of LibQUAL+™ scores in college and university libraries. Specifically, this study addressed whether the scores were related to characteristics that express institutional mission, institutional size, or level of investment in libraries.

The definition of service quality that underlies the LibQUAL+™ protocol is the definition that was used in the present study. Service quality was defined as 'the result of the consumer's comparison of expected service with perceived service'.

VARIABLES

The independent variables that were investigated for potential relationships with LibQUAL+™ scores were institutional type, institutional size, and investment in libraries. For this investigation, institutional type was defined as the classification assigned by the Carnegie basic classification, institutional size was defined as 12-month FTE enrollment, and institutional investment in libraries was defined as total annual library expenditures.

The dependent variables in this investigation were the mean perceived scores for the three dimensions of LibQUAL+™ and the overall, weighted LibQUAL+™ score.

SAMPLE AND POPULATION

This study investigated potential relationships between institutional characteristics and LibQUAL+™ scores in American colleges and universities. According to the *National Centre for Education Statistics.*

(NCES), the population of post-secondary, degree-granting institutions that confer at least four-year degrees is 2,217. The sample of institutions for this investigation was a non-random, convenience sample.

Selecting the Sample

The sample was limited to an existing group of American college and university libraries that opted to participate in the LibQUAL+™ survey during 2006.

Furthermore, institutional score reports were included in the sample only if all of the following conditions were met.

- The institution agreed to share its results.
- The institution used the American English version of the survey.
- The institution placed itself in the 'Colleges and Universities' category.

Selection of institutions for the sample began with institutional type. Of the 298 institutions, 216 institutions had self-identified as College or University libraries.

Table (8.3) 2006 LibQUAL+™ Participants by Library Type Institution Type No. Academic Health Sciences 10 Academic Law 6 College or University 216 Community

College 29 European Business 16 Family History 1 Hospital 1 National Health Service (England) 10 Public 4 Research Centres Libraries 1 State 3 University/TAFE 1 Total 298

Table 8.3 2006 LibQUAL+™ Participants by Library Type

Institution	No
Academic Health Sciences	10
Academic Law	6
College or University	216
Community College	29
European Business	16
Family History	1
Hospital	1
National Health Service (England)	10
Public	4
Research Centers Libraries	1
State	3
University/TAFE	1
Total	**298**

In the next step, 55 participating institutions were removed from the sample because they were from countries other than the United States.

Table (8.4) 2006 LibQUAL+™ Participants by Country Country No. Australia 2 Canada 11 Denmark 2 Finland 4 France 2 Ireland 2 Netherlands 5 Norway 2 South Africa 8 Sweden 2 Switzerland 2 UK 34 USA 222 Total 298

Table 8.4 2006 LibQUAL+TM Participants by Country

Country	No.
Australia	2
Canada	11
Denmark	2
Finland	4
France	2
Ireland	2
Netherlands	5

(Contd...)

Norway	2
South Africa	8
Sweden	2
Swizerland	2
UK	34
USA	222
Total	**298**

Finally, two more libraries were removed from the sample because complete data for this study could not be obtained. In both cases, the libraries participated in LibQUAL+TM as single institutions but did not report individual institutional statistics to the NCES Academic Library Survey; NCES data were subsumed in the reports of a parent institution.

Size and Representativeness

Of the 298 institutions that participated in the 2006 administration of LibQUAL+™, the sample was composed of 159 institutions that met all of the selection criteria.

The resulting sample of 159 institutions is an adequate sample size since, it is generally considered acceptable to have a minimum of 30 cases in each group for a correlational study. For an exploratory, goodness-of-fit analysis, a one-sample Kolmogorov-Smirnov test was computed for the independent variables: library expenditures, FTE enrollment, Carnegie basic classification, and library expenditures per FTE.

The test results were significant for all of the independent variables, which indicated that the distribution was significantly different from a normal distribution. Since, the distribution did not meet the assumption of normality, the data analysis required non-parametric procedures. The one-sample Kolmogorov-Smirnov test was also computed for the dependent variables, which had distributions that were not significantly different from a normal distribution.

LIMITATIONS AND DELIMITATIONS

Since, the sample of score reports included in the study is a convenience rather than a random sample from a self-selected group of institutions, it may not be representative of all academic libraries.

In addition, the findings of this investigation cannot be generalised to institutions that administered the survey in other languages, including British English. Finally, since, the study analysed data related to college and university libraries, findings cannot be generalised to other types of libraries.

DATA ACQUISITION

The data analysed in this study were originally collected and published by the Association of Research Libraries (ARL), the Carnegie Foundation for the Advancement of Teaching, and the National Centre for Education Statistics (NCES). A number of validity and reliability tests have confirmed the integrity of the LibQUAL+™ protocol.

Data were retrieved from the publications of these organisations to enable an analysis designed to address whether, and to what extent, there were relationships between LibQUAL+™ scores and the following characteristics of colleges and universities: institutional type, institutional size, or level of investment in libraries.

The following research questions were posed as a framework for the study.

- What were the 2006 LibQUAL+™ scores for American college and university libraries?
- What were the characteristics of the American college and university libraries that administered LibQUAL+™ 2006?
- To what extent, if any, were scores for the information control dimension related to institutional type as expressed by the Carnegie basic classification?
- To what extent, if any, were scores for the library as place dimension related to library expenditures per FTE student?
- To what extent, if any, were scores for service affect related to institutional size as expressed by FTE enrollment?
- To what extent, if any, was institutional investment

in the library, as expressed by library expenditures, related to scores for each of the three dimensions, or to overall LibQUAL+™ scores?

The data for the dependent variables were LibQUAL+™ scores that were collected for this study from the LibQUAL+™ score reports of libraries in the sample. The data for the independent variable, 'institutional type' were collected from the Carnegie Foundation's published basic classification of each institution. The library expenditures and 12-month FTE enrollment data were obtained from the NCES publication, *Academic libraries: 2004*.

STATISTICAL ANALYSIS

The first two questions were addressed by conducting descriptive statistics procedures that summarised the distribution of LibQUAL+™ scores and institutional characteristics for the libraries in the sample.

Frequencies for all values of each variable were determined; mean and median scores were calculated as measures of central tendency.

Variability was described by variance and standard deviation calculations, and outliers were identified. For the remaining four questions, correlations and regressions were performed to discover whether, and to what extent, the relationships existed.

Simple linear correlation, non-parametric correlation and bivariate linear regression were used to assess the potential relationships of the independent variables with the dependent variables.

DATA ANALYSIS

PROBLEM AND APPROACH

The recent emphasis on assessment in higher education has prompted university administrators, including library administrators, to develop new ways of evaluating services and programmes. Libraries are service-oriented organisations, yet the traditional measure of academic library quality has been collection size. The emphasis on formal assessment in recent years has motivated librarians to seek out more meaningful measures of service quality. There is a need for assessment tools that produce data that can be used to inform improvement, as well as document assessment practices for accreditation organisations, funding agencies, and governing boards.

The LibQUAL+™ Instrument

In the 1990s, the Texas A&M University Libraries began using a survey instrument called SERVQUAL, which had been designed to measure customer perceptions of service quality in the private sector.

After administering the instrument three times to assess library service quality, the Texas A&M University Libraries entered into a partnership with the Association of Research Libraries (ARL) to develop, test, and adapt the instrument for academic libraries. That collaboration created the LibQUAL+™ survey, which was first administered in 2000 by the ARL across 13 research libraries as an experimental project for benchmarking perceptions of service quality. Since, that first administration, the LibQUAL+™ survey has become an increasingly popular tool. In 2006, there were 298 libraries that participated in LibQUAL+™. The instrument has been improved and refined and it is currently composed of 22 questions and a comment box. Each question is answered on a scale from 1 to 9, with 9 being the highest rating. Table shows how the responses to the 22 questions are grouped to measure three dimensions of library service quality: service affect, information control, and library as place.

Table 8.5 LibQUAL+™ Dimensions and Corresponding Survey Questions

Dimension	Components (Item #)
Service Affect	Employees who instill confidence in users (1)
	Giving users individual attention (4)
	Employees who are consistently courteous (6)

(Contd...)

	Readiness to respond to users' questions (9) Employees who have the knowledge to answer user questions (11) Employees who deal with users in a caring fashion (13) Employees who understand the needs of their users (15) Willingness to help users (18) Dependability in handling users' service problems (22)
Information Control	Making electronic resources accessible from my home or office (2) A library Web site enabling me to locate information on my own (5) The printed library materials I need for my work (7) The electronic information resources I need (10) Modern equipment that lets me easily access needed information (14) Easy-to-use access tools that allow me to find things on my own (16) Making information easily accessible for independent use (19) Print and/or electronic journal collections I require for my work (20)
Library as Place	Library space that inspires study and learning (3) Quiet space for individual activities (8) A comfortable and inviting locatio (12) A getaway for study, learning or research (17) Community space for group learning and group study (21)

The *service affect dimension* is concerned with the perceptions of customers about library staff competency and helpfulness; the *information control dimension* is concerned with whether the library's collections are adequate to meet customer needs and organised in a manner that enables self-reliance for library users; and the *library as place dimension* is concerned with the library facility's functionality and adequacy for academic activities.

PURPOSE AND DESIGN OF THE STUDY

Considering the increasing level of participation in the LibQUAL+™ survey, and the relatively small body of research about the meaning of LibQUAL+™ results, this study was completed for the purpose of adding to the library profession's understanding of the meaning of LibQUAL+™ scores.

Research found that validity coefficients for LibQUAL+™ replicated closely across different types of post-secondary libraries in one study, leading the authors to conclude that '*LibQUAL+™ scores may be valid in reasonably diverse library settings*'. This study explored an aspect of that conclusion by seeking to determine whether institutional characteristics would impact LibQUAL+™ scores.

The data analysis was designed to address whether, and to what extent, there were relationships between LibQUAL+™ scores and selected institutional characteristics of American colleges and universities.

Specifically, this study examined the following institutional characteristics for potential relationships with the 2006 LibQUAL+™ scores.

- Institutional type as defined by the Carnegie basic classification;
- Institutional size as defined by 12-month FTE enrollment; and
- Institutional investment in libraries, as defined by annual library expenditures.

METHOD

The sample was composed of libraries in American colleges and universities that conferred at least 4-year degrees and participated in LibQUAL+™ during 2006. This was a sample of convenience that included a total of 298 participating libraries.

Initially, 82 libraries were removed from the total sample of 298 libraries because they did not identify themselves as libraries in colleges or universities. From the remaining 216 institutions in the sample, 55 additional participating institutions were removed because they were from countries other than the United States.

The remaining 161 libraries became the initial sample. During the data collection phase of the study, two additional institutions were removed from the sample because complete data required for this study could not be obtained. In both cases, the libraries had participated in the LibQUAL+TM survey as independent institutions. However, during data collection it was discovered that neither library reported statistics as an independent institution to the Academic Library Survey administered by the *National Center for Education Statistics* (NCES). NCES data for both of the libraries were subsumed in the reports provided to NCES by their parent institutions.

The remaining 159 libraries formed the final sample that was used in this study. The research questions that framed the study were addressed by using SPSS for Windows to analyse the data. The calculations produced descriptive statistics, calculations of bivariate correlations, and bivariate regression analyses. The independent or predictor variables were annual library expenditures, FTE enrollment, Carnegie basic classification, and library expenditures per FTE. The design of this study employed an approach that required multiple calculations using the same set of variables. For this reason, the Bonferroni adjustment was applied to the significance levels to reduce the chance of a Type I error.

The conventional.05 significance level was divided by four to account for the four questions that were addressed. Subsequently, data were accepted and interpreted as statistically significant at the.013 level or lower.

9

Code Practices in Academic and Research Libraries

GENERAL POINTS ABOUT THE PRINCIPLES

This code of best practices identifies eight sets of common current practices in the use of copyrighted materials in and around academic and research libraries, to which the doctrine of fair use can be applied. It articulates principles describing generally how and why fair use applies to each such practice or situation.

Each principle is accompanied by a list of considerations that the library community believes should inform or qualify it: limitations that should be observed to assure that the case for fair use is strong, and enhancements that could further strengthen that case. Please note that enhancements represent what the community believes are additional practices that demonstrate 'above and beyond' efforts to add value to existing material or accommodate the interests of other stakeholders; such measures are laudable when they will not cause undue hardship but are not prerequisite to support a strong fair use rationale.

Some of the limitations and suggested enhancements involve the use of Technical Protection Measures (TPMs) to help ensure that material intended for a particular institutional audience is confined to that audience. In some circumstances, the use of TPMs may be a meaningful demonstration of 'good faith' on the part of the library in question. However, TPMs come in many varieties; for a library's purposes, less obtrusive ones may be as or more appropriate than, for example, encryption. Because, in the opinion of some courts, fair use is sensitive to whether a use is undertaken in good faith, some of the principles include limitations or enhancements that address broader ethical concerns.

While issues such as respecting privacy and including proper attribution may seem unrelated to copyright at first, they show good faith and serve the same overarching goals of responsible stewardship of library collections. These values are central to academic and research libraries, of course, but it is worth noting that by doing what comes naturally, libraries are also strengthening their fair use case. In addition, the code refers at several points to providing copyright holders an opportunity to register concerns or complaints about a library's decision to employ fair use.

The library community believes that engaging in such a process should not necessarily lead to automatic removal of content. Rather, it would trigger a conversation between the library and the rights holder, which would inform the institution's decision about whether to remove or maintain the material. Welcoming this interaction with a rights holder shows the library's good faith and provides an opportunity to develop voluntary arrangements that benefit all parties. The fair use doctrine draws no blanket distinctions among different media or among different formats. Librarians felt strongly that except in narrow, specific instances, all kinds of content should be subject to the same principles.

Likewise, they did not distinguish generally between uses in various media. So, except as otherwise indicated, a digital copy should be considered on the same footing as an analog one for purposes of fair use. The situations below concern the fair use of copyrighted materials, not the way the user acquires the copy from which she works.

When a user's copy was obtained illegally or in bad faith, that fact may negatively affect fair use analysis; similarly, special contractual restrictions may circumscribe fair use. The principles therefore assume the library or user has obtained a copy in good faith and that it is not subject to conflicting licence or contract restrictions.

While the principles address separate situations, in practice these areas are sure to overlap from time to time; some special collections will need digitising for both scholarly access and preservation, for example, implicating both the third and fourth principles. Libraries should feel free to consult multiple principles to determine the best fair use rationale to apply to their specific situations.

SUPPORTING TEACHING AND LEARNING WITH ACCESS TO LIBRARY MATERIALS VIA DIGITAL TECHNOLOGIES

DESCRIPTION

Academic and research libraries have a long, and largely non-controversial, history of supporting classroom instruction by providing students with access to reading materials, especially via physical on-site reserves. Teachers, in turn, have depended on libraries to provide this important service.

Today, students and teachers alike strongly prefer electronic equivalents to the old-media approaches to course support. *Section 110(2) of the Copyright Act* provides specific protection for some streaming and other uses, but it does not cover the entire variety of digital uses that are becoming increasingly important to twenty-first-century instruction. Over time, a set of practices has grown up around the related but distinct practice of providing students with physical 'course packs,' which typically occurs outside the library setting.

The following principle is not intended to address that activity, but rather to focus on emerging digital uses in the library context. Fair use will play an important role in making these uses possible. There are multiple bases on which these library uses can be considered fair ones. These modes of course support occur in a non-profit educational environment, can be persuasively analogised to activities specifically authorised by Congress in Section 110 of the Copyright Act, may be supported by a 'place-shifting' argument,12 and are susceptible to a compelling transformativeness rationale.

Most of the information objects made available to students, in whatever format, are not originally intended for educational use. For example, works intended for consumption as popular entertainment present a case for transformative repurposing when an instructor uses them as the objects of commentary and criticism, or for purposes of illustration.

Amounts of material used for online course support should be tailored to the educational purpose, though it will not infrequently be the case that access to the entire work will be necessary to fulfill the instructor's pedagogical purpose. It is also reasonable for works to be posted repeatedly from semester to semester to the extent that they are the most appropriate, relevant, and still timely materials for the course.

PRINCIPLE

It is fair use to make appropriately tailored course-related content available to enrolled students via digital networks.

LIMITATIONS

- Closer scrutiny should be applied to uses of content created and marketed primarily for use in courses such as the one at issue. Use of more than a brief excerpt from such works on digital networks is unlikely to be transformative and therefore unlikely to be a fair use.
- The availability of materials should be coextensive with the duration of the course or other time-limited use for which they have been made available at an instructor's direction.
- Only eligible students and other qualified persons should have access to materials.
- Materials should be made available only when, and only to the extent that, there is a clear articulable nexus between the instructor's pedagogical purpose and the kind and amount of content involved.

- Libraries should provide instructors with useful information about the nature and the scope of fair use, in order to help them make informed requests.
- When appropriate, the number of students with simultaneous access to online materials may be limited.
- Students should also be given information about their rights and responsibilities regarding their own use of course materials.
- Full attribution, in a form satisfactory to scholars in the field, should be provided for each work included or excerpted.

ENHANCEMENTS

- The case for fair use is enhanced when libraries prompt instructors, who are most likely to understand the educational purpose and transformative nature of the use, to indicate briefly in writing why particular material is requested, and why the amount requested is appropriate to that pedagogical purpose. An instructor's justification can be expressed via standardised forms that provide a balanced menu of common or recurring fair use rationales.
- In order to assure the continuing relevance of those materials to course content, libraries should require instructors of recurrently offered courses to review posted materials and make updates as appropriate.

USING SELECTIONS FROM COLLECTION MATERIALS TO PUBLICISE A LIBRARY'S ACTIVITIES, OR TO CREATE PHYSICAL AND VIRTUAL EXHIBITIONS

DESCRIPTION

Academic and research libraries have always sought publicity of a certain kind—in order to introduce themselves, their services, and their valuable holdings to potential students, scholars, and others, as well as to attract donors of materials and to assure administrators and funders of their fidelity to mission. Just as libraries have chosen in the past to display their holdings through on-site exhibitions, or through in-house publications ranging from simple newsletters to glossy magazines, they now use the Internet as a tool for making themselves known.

Library web sites have become extremely important modes of access for library patrons, and most temporary physical exhibitions now have permanent virtual counterparts. While the lawfulness of past practices has been widely assumed, the use of new technology adds a new dimension to the issue. The wider audience that online exhibits reach, and the possibility of downstream misuse, could lead librarians to avoid online uses, but in fact these uses can be just as fair as their physical counterparts.

Section 109(c) of the Copyright Act provides a safe harbour for certain on-site exhibits. However, exhibition and related illustrative uses, whether physical or virtual, can also be transformative. They highlight and publicise library collections and stimulate interest in the individual original works of which they are comprised.

Exhibits place original works in a new context to convey information and illustrate themes and ideas that can be quite different from those of the single work. Curation, in-line commentary, and juxtaposition add to the transformative nature of exhibits, displays, and other illustrative uses.

PRINCIPLE

It is fair use for a library to use appropriate selections from collection materials to increase public awareness and engagement with these collections and to promote new scholarship drawing on them.

LIMITATIONS

- Full attribution, in a form satisfactory to scholars in the field, should be provided for each work included or excerpted in an exhibit, to the extent it can be determined with reasonable effort.

- The amount of any particular work used and the format in which it is displayed should be appropriate to the illustrative purpose, *i.e.*, tailored to support the goals of the exhibit or other illustrative project. The use of a work in its entirety is likely to require a special level of justification. Similarly, larger-scale, high-resolution images should be displayed only when appropriate to the pedagogical or illustrative purpose of the exhibit.
- This principle does not apply to the sale of souvenirs and other non-print merchandise in connection with an exhibit.

ENHANCEMENTS

- For publications such as catalogs of exhibitions, the case for fair use will be stronger when the material is offered to the public without charge, or on a cost-recovery basis.
- Where library web sites are concerned, fair use claims will be enhanced when libraries take technological steps, reasonable in light of both the nature of the material and of institutional capabilities, to discourage downloading.
- Fair use claims will be further enhanced when libraries provide copyright owners a simple tool for registering objections to use of copyrighted works, such as an e-mail address associated with a full-time employee.
- Fair use arguments will be enhanced when curation is overt and visible rather than implicit—for instance, when commentary is being provided on the illustrative objects, whether by means of express written or spoken commentary by critics or curators, through selection and juxtaposition of works in a larger context, or both. For example, when exhibited works and excerpts are viewable online in isolation from the larger exhibit or display, it may be helpful to use graphical cues or navigational elements to

ensure that visitors who find the item via a deep link can perceive and easily move to the larger exhibit of which the item is a part.

DIGITISING TO PRESERVE AT-RISK ITEMS

DESCRIPTION

Preservation is a core function of academic and research libraries. It involves not only rescuing items from physical decay, but also coping with the rapid pace of change in media formats and reading technologies. Even when libraries retain the originals of preserved items, digital surrogates can spare the original items the wear and tear that access necessarily inflicts.

Section 108 of the Copyright Act authorises some preservation activities, but does not address some of today's most pressing needs: the pre-emptive preservation of physical materials that have not yet begun to deteriorate but are critically at risk of doing so, and the transfer to new formats of materials whose original formats are not yet obsolete but have become increasingly difficult for contemporary users to consult.

The primary purpose of preservation is indubitably beneficial and arguably strongly transformative: ensuring access to aspects of our cultural heritage for future generations, well past the limited term of copyright protection. Furthermore, responsible preservation is a necessary precursor for future scholarly use in a variety of transformative contexts, including criticism, commentary, and teaching.

A broader, four-factor analysis further supports digital preservation: Its purpose is non-commercial and educational, the amount of the work used is appropriate to the purpose, the nature of the works will in many cases be scholarly non-fiction and preservation in the absence of a suitable replacement copy has no negative effect on the potential market of the preserved work. To justify the effort and expense of digital preservation, the works preserved will typically be unique, rare, or, in any event, out-of-commerce, and the library's activities therefore will not be mere substitutes for acquisition of a new digital copy of the work.

Works in obscure, near-obsolete formats present access challenges as well as preservation ones, but the same fair use rationales will apply. Works trapped in decaying and increasingly obscure formats will disappear completely without diligent work from librarians to migrate them to usable formats.

PRINCIPLE

It is fair use to make digital copies of collection items that are likely to deteriorate, or that exist only in difficult-to-access formats, for purposes of preservation, and to make those copies available as surrogates for fragile or otherwise inaccessible materials.

LIMITATIONS

- Preservation copies should not be made when a fully equivalent digital copy is commercially available at a reasonable cost.
- Libraries should not provide access to or circulate original and preservation copies simultaneously.
- Off-premises access to preservation copies circulated as substitutes for original copies should be limited to authenticated members of a library's patron community, *e.g.,* students, faculty, staff, affiliated scholars, and other accredited users.
- Full attribution, in a form satisfactory to scholars in the field, should be provided for all items made available online, to the extent it can be determined with reasonable effort.

ENHANCEMENTS

- Fair use claims will be enhanced when libraries take technological steps to limit further redistribution of digital surrogates, *e.g.,* by streaming audiovisual media, using appropriately lower-resolution versions, or using watermarks on textual materials and images.

- Fair use claims will be further enhanced when libraries provide copyright owners a simple tool for registering objections to use of digital surrogates, such as an e-mail address associated with a full-time employee.

CREATING DIGITAL COLLECTIONS OF ARCHIVAL AND SPECIAL COLLECTIONS MATERIALS

DESCRIPTION

Many libraries hold special collections and archives of rare or unusual text and non-text materials that do not circulate on the same terms as the general collection. The copyright status of materials in these collections is often unclear. Despite the investments that have been made in acquiring and preserving such collections, they frequently are of limited general utility because they typically can be consulted only on-site, and in some cases using only limited analog research aids.

The research value of these collections typically resides not only in the individual items they contain but also in the unique assemblage or aggregation they represent. Special collections can have a shared provenance or be organised around a key topic, era, or theme. Libraries and their patrons would benefit significantly from digitisation and off-site availability of these valuable collections.

While institutions must abide by any donor restrictions applicable to their donated collections, and they will inevitably consider practical and political concerns such as maintaining good relations with donor communities, librarians will benefit significantly from knowing their rights under fair use.

Presenting these unique collections as a digital aggregate, especially with commentary, criticism, and other curation, can be highly transformative. Works held in these collections and archives will serve a host of transformative scholarly and educational purposes relative to their typically narrower original purposes. Materials in special collections typically include significant amounts of primary sources and artifacts whose value as historical objects for scholarly research is significantly different from their original purpose. The new value created by aggregating related documents in a single, well-curated collection is also significant. In addition to access for scholarly purposes, digitisation facilitates novel transformative uses of the collection as a whole.

PRINCIPLE

It is fair use to create digital versions of a library's special collections and archives and to make these versions electronically accessible in appropriate contexts.

LIMITATIONS

- Providing access to published works that are available in unused copies on the commercial market at reasonable prices should be undertaken only with careful consideration, if at all. To the extent that the copy of such a work in a particular collection is unique, access to unique aspects of the copy will be supportable under fair use. The presence of non-unique copies in a special collection can be indicated by descriptive entries without implicating copyright.
- Where digitised special collections are posted online, reasonable steps should be taken to limit access to material likely to contain damaging or sensitive private information.
- Full attribution, in a form satisfactory to scholars in the field, should be provided for all special collection items made available online, to the extent it is reasonably possible to do so.

ENHANCEMENTS

- The fair use case will be even stronger where items to be digitised consist largely of works, such as personal photographs, correspondence, or ephemera, whose owners are not exploiting the material commercially and likely could not be located to seek permission for new uses.

- Libraries should consider taking technological steps, reasonable in light of both the nature of the material and of institutional capabilities, to prevent downloading of digital files by users, or else to limit the quality of files to what is appropriate to the use.
- Libraries should also provide copyright owners with a simple tool for registering objections to online use, and respond to such objections promptly.
- Subject to the considerations outlined above, a special collection should be digitised in its entirety, and presented as a cohesive collection whenever possible.
- Adding criticism, commentary, rich metadata, and other additional value and context to the collection will strengthen the fair use case.
- The fair use case will be stronger when the availability of the material is appropriately publicised to scholars in the field and other persons likely to be especially interested.

REPRODUCING MATERIAL FOR USE BY DISABLED STUDENTS, FACULTY, STAFF, AND OTHER APPROPRIATE USERS

DESCRIPTION

Print-disabled academic and research library patrons require access to readable text in order to function as full members of an academic community; likewise, hearing-disabled patrons require captioned audiovisual materials, while those with physical disabilities may require the electronic delivery of materials outside the library setting. Relatively new electronic technologies make these kinds of accommodations possible at relatively low cost.

True accommodation for these patrons means access to any materials in the library's collection for any reason the patron may have, *i.e.,* access that is equivalent to the access afforded to students without disabilities. In addition to moral and mission-related imperatives to serve all patrons, there are also legal obligations to accommodate scholars and researchers with diverse needs. Although Section 121 of the Copyright Act authorises the reproduction of copyrighted materials to meet these needs under some circumstances, there is continued controversy over its exact scope.

Some stakeholders insist, however unreasonably, that Section 121 does not cover academic libraries' efforts to provide accessible materials to print-disabled members of a college or university community. No specific exception to copyright even arguably addresses the needs of patrons with disabilities related to media other than print.

Making library materials accessible serves the goals of copyright, not to mention the goals of a just and inclusive society, and has no negative consequence for rights holders who have not entered the market to serve these users. Such uses add value to a work by making it available to communities that would otherwise be excluded, presenting the work in a format the rights holder has not provided and to an audience that the rights holder is not serving.

Making this material available to disabled patrons, furthermore, should not penalise other potential constituents, for instance, by removing the original copy for the time that the version for the disabled is available.

PRINCIPLE

When fully accessible copies are not readily available from commercial sources, it is fair use for a library to:

- Reproduce materials in its collection in accessible formats for the disabled upon request; and
- Retain those reproductions for use in meeting subsequent requests from qualified patrons.

LIMITATIONS

- Libraries should provide patrons with information about their own rights and responsibilities regarding works provided to them in this way.
- When appropriate, the requester's use of the materials should be time-limited by analogy to the limits the library imposes on use by other persons.

- Libraries should coordinate their response to requests with the university's disability services office, or the equivalent, and observe standard conventions on the identification of individuals entitled to service.

ENHANCEMENTS

- Claims for fair use may well be further reinforced if technological protection measures are applied to assure that limitations on the use of accessible copies are observed.
- The fair use case will be enhanced by programmes that are well publicised to the affected communities together with policies that are widely and consistently applied.

MAINTAINING THE INTEGRITY OF WORKS DEPOSITED IN INSTITUTIONAL REPOSITORIES

DESCRIPTION

Many libraries that serve postsecondary institutions are developing digital institutional repositories that house and provide access to a variety of different kinds of material directly related to their institutions' activities, including scholarship of faculty and graduate students as well as documentation of institutional histories.

The collection and maintenance of electronic theses and dissertations is a related issue. Access to ETDs and other material in IRs may be restricted to individuals with institutional affiliations, but many libraries aspire to make their contents available to the general public. Many deposited works quote or incorporate third-party material in ways that represent appropriate fair use by the faculty member or student in question.

Librarians can and should respect the integrity of deposited materials that include selections from copyright works incorporated in reliance on fair use. Use of quotations, still frames, illustrative excerpts, and the like is common practice in scholarly writing, and is at the heart of fair use.

Libraries respect the authors' fair use rights when they accept these materials intact into the IR and make them available unchanged to the public.

Libraries that operate IRs can and should respect and maintain the integrity of materials they accept for deposit, rather than insisting on unnecessary permissions or requiring unnecessary deletions.

Fair use makes this possible. Many institutions use vendors to host and maintain ETDs and IRs, and libraries should work to ensure that vendors also respect authors' fair use rights.

PRINCIPLE

It is fair use for a library to receive material for its institutional repository, and make deposited works publicly available in unredacted form, including items that contain copyrighted material that is included on the basis of fair use.

LIMITATIONS

- In the case of publicly accessible IRs, libraries should provide copyright owners outside the institution with a simple tool for registering objections to the use of materials in the IR, and respond to such objections promptly.
- Libraries and their parent institutions should provide depositing authors with useful information about the nature and the scope of fair use, and the proper forms of attribution for incorporated materials, in order to help them make informed uses in their own work. This information should specifically address the fact that fair use is context-specific, and that what is fair use within the academy may not be fair use when a work is more broadly distributed.
- Full attribution, in a form satisfactory to scholars in the field, should be provided for all incorporated third-party materials included in works deposited to the IR, to the extent it is reasonably possible to do so.

ENHANCEMENTS

- The fair use case will be stronger when institutions have developed or adopted a clear institutional policy about appropriate use of quotations, illustrations, etc., in faculty and student scholarship.
- Likewise, libraries may consider providing individualised advice on the appropriate use of copyrighted material in scholarship to members of the community upon request.

CREATING DATABASES TO FACILITATE NON- CONSUMPTIVE RESEARCH USES (INCLUDING SEARCH)

DESCRIPTION

In addition to making specific collection items available to patrons for intensive study, librarians have always played an important role in conducting and supporting scholarship in disciplines that examine trends and changes across broad swaths of information, *e.g.*, information science, linguistics, bibliography, and history of science. Developing indexing systems and finding aids is also a core part of the library mission.

Digital technology offers new possibilities where both of these traditional functions are concerned. Libraries can offer scholars digital databases of collection items on which to perform computerised analyses, and they themselves can employ such databases to develop new and powerful reference tools. Because they do not involve ordinary reading or viewing of the processed works, these uses are often referred to as non-consumptive.

Non-consumptive uses are highly transformative. Digitising and indexing works for purposes such as statistical meta-analysis and search creates a powerful new scholarly resource that is not at all a mere substitute for the original work. The analyses facilitated by scanning for non-consumptive use do not use the works for their original intended purposes; no person ever 'reads' the underlying work or works. Instead, this kind of analysis focuses on the underlying facts about a collection of works rather than the protected expression of any single work.

Courts have found search engines, which copy millions of web pages into their indexed databases in order to help users find relevant sites, to be fair uses for precisely this reason. Non-consumptive uses are an emerging phenomenon at many libraries, and despite their obvious transformative character, there is a risk that the opportunity to make use of these techniques will be lost due to overly restrictive licensing provisions.

If librarians agree to licensing restrictions that prohibit such uses, they lose their ability to exercise or permit others to exercise their fair use rights. Librarians should be mindful of this as they negotiate license agreements and should work to preserve their patrons' rights to conduct non-consumptive research across licensed database materials.

PRINCIPLE

It is fair use for libraries to develop and facilitate the development of digital databases of collection items to enable non-consumptive analysis across the collection for both scholarly and reference purposes.

LIMITATION

- Items in copyright digitised for non-consumptive uses should not be employed in other ways without independent justification, either by a license from the rights holder or pursuant to a statutory exception. Search access to database materials should be limited to portions appropriate to the non-consumptive research purpose.

ENHANCEMENTS

- The case for fair use will be at its strongest when the database includes information such as rich metadata that augments the research or reference value of its contents.

- Assertions of fair use will be particularly persuasive when libraries cooperate with other institutions to build collective databases that enable more extensive scholarship or reference searching.

COLLECTING MATERIAL POSTED ON THE WORLD WIDE WEB AND MAKING IT AVAILABLE

DESCRIPTION

Gathering impressions of ephemeral Internet material such as web pages, online video, and the like is a growth area in academic and research library collection-building, with activities typically focusing on areas in which the institution has an established specialty, or on sites specific to its local area. Such collections represent a unique contribution to knowledge and pose no significant risks for owners of either the sites in question or third-party material to which those sites refer.

In the absence of such collections, important information is likely to be lost to scholarship. Selecting and collecting material from the Internet in this way is highly transformative. The collecting library takes a historical snapshot of a dynamic and ephemeral object and places the collected impression of the site into a new context: a curated historical archive. Material posted to the Internet typically serves a time-limited purpose and targets a distinct network of users, while its library-held counterpart will document the site for a wide variety of patrons over time.

A scholar perusing a collection of archived web pages on the Free Tibet movement, or examining the evolution of educational information on a communicable disease, seeks and encounters that material for a very different purpose than the creators originally intended. Preserving such work can also be considered strongly transformative in itself, separate from any way that future patrons may access it.

Authors of online materials often have a specific objective and a particular audience in mind; libraries that collect this material serve a different and broader purpose and a different and broader network of users. Libraries collect not only for a wide range of purposes today, but also for unanticipated uses by future researchers.

PRINCIPLE

It is fair use to create topically based collections of web sites and other material from the Internet and to make them available for scholarly use.

LIMITATIONS

- Captured material should be represented as it was captured, with appropriate information on mode of harvesting and date.
- To the extent reasonably possible, the legal proprietors of the sites in question should be identified according to the prevailing conventions of attribution.
- Libraries should provide copyright owners with a simple tool for registering objections to making items from such a collection available online, and respond to such objections promptly.

ENHANCEMENTS

- Claims of fair use relating to material posted with 'bot exclusion' headers to ward off automatic harvesting may be stronger when the institution has adopted and follows a consistent policy on this issue, taking into account the possible rationales for collecting Internet material and the nature of the material in question.
- The more comprehensive a collection of web impressions in a given topic area is, the more persuasively the inclusion of any given item can be characterised as fair use.

10

Developing an Accreditation System for LIS

INTRODUCTION

The issue of accreditation of Library and Information Studies (LIS) programmes and degrees in the Southeast Asian region was raised during the 2001 International Conference for Library and Information Science Educators in the Asia Pacific Region held in Kuala Lumpur.

The conference had surveyed LIS education programmes in the region, discussed the core competencies of the profession and examined some of the issues in LIS education. It was felt that an accreditation scheme for the region would be useful in enhancing the quality and acceptability of LIS degrees as well as providing more flexible mobility of library and information professionals in the region.

There was a general consensus that some effort needs to be made in this direction. In 2002, Prof. Shaheen Majid undertook a questionnaire survey of LIS schools in the region to gather views on various issues related to a regional accreditation scheme, including the need for an accreditation scheme, geographical scope of accreditation, coordination, duration, expenses and cost and potential problems. The results were reported in a paper presented at the Library and Information Science Education in Asia (LISEA) Workshop—a post-conference workshop of the 2003 International Conference on Asian Digital Libraries (ICADL) in Singapore. The chapter also proposed an organisational model for the accreditation of LIS education programmes in Southeast Asia under the auspices and oversight of CONSAL.

The issue of accreditation and certification was raised at the recent CONSAL XII conference in Brunei, and a proposal for the development of a regional accreditation and certification scheme was included in the conference resolutions. The outgoing conference chairperson from Brunei and the CONSAL General Secretary highlighted this in their concluding speeches, and expressed the hope that Philippines, now assuming chairmanship of CONSAL, would work hard towards achieving this goal.

This chapter seeks to stimulate further discussion regarding the development and implementation of a regional accreditation system. The education standards and accreditation procedures of the following library associations were examined to identify their main features and to understand the major phases or aspects of the accreditation process:

- American Library Association (ALA);
- Australian Library and Information Association (ALIA);
- Chartered Institute of Library and Information Professionals (CILIP, U.K.);
- International Federation of Library Associations and Institutions (IFLA).

Specifically, we examined the following standards:

- ALA Standards for accreditation of Master's programmes in library and information studies;
- IFLA Guidelines for professional library/information educational programmes - 2000;
- ALIA Education policy statement number 1;
- ALIA The library and information sector: core knowledge, skills and attributes;
- CILIP Accreditation instrument: Procedures for the accreditation of courses.

IFLA chose to call the standards 'guidelines.' ALIA specified the standards as a series of education policy statements. CILIP does not have a separate accreditation standard, but specified the accreditation criteria in its 'accreditation instrument'.

The IFLA *Guidelines for Professional Library/Information Educational Programmes* seem to be the logical choice as a basis to develop a regional standard for Southeast Asia, since, international feedback was taken into consideration in developing the Guidelines. The discussion in this chapter focuses on the IFLA Guidelines, with additional features found in the other standards highlighted where appropriate.

We outline the main features and content of the standards, and discuss in some detail four major aspects or activities in the accreditation process—dialogue, self-evaluation, documentation and external review. We then summarise the results of the 2002 Majid Survey and discuss the regional issues raised in the survey. The organisational model for regional accreditation proposed by Majid is outlined and further steps towards implementing an accreditation system is suggested.

FEATURES OF THE ACCREDITATION STANDARDS

What is *accreditation*? Majid defined it as "a process which assures that education institutions and their programmes meet appropriate standards of quality and integrity.

It is a collegial process based on self-evaluation and peerassessment for the improvement of academic quality and public accountability.' The ALA accreditation standards defined it in greater detail:

- Accreditation assures the educational community, the general public, and other agencies or organisations that an institution or programme;
  - Has clearly defined and educationally appropriate objectives;
  - Maintains conditions under which their achievement can reasonably be expected;
  - Is in fact accomplishing them substantially; and
  - Can be expected to continue to do so. Accreditation serves as a mechanism for quality assessment and quality enhancement with

quality defined as the effective utilisation of resources to achieve appropriate educational objectives.

All the accreditation standards are fairly general, broad and open to interpretation in the context of the individual LIS programme. This is to accommodate different kinds of LIS programmes and specialisations, different contexts and different national and regional needs.

All the standards reflect a consciousness of the breadth of the LIS field, the varied roles information professionals play, and the variety of information services, organisations and contexts in which information professionals work. The IFLA Guidelines state in the preamble that "Today...the concentration is on information provision in a variety of contexts.'

The ALA Standards point out that the standards "are indicative, not prescriptive, with the intent to foster excellence through the development of criteria for evaluating educational effectiveness."

The CILIP Accreditation Instrument said that "in view of the wide range of skills and expertise now needed for the efficient provision of information and the effective management of library and information services, the professional body does not seek to stipulate precise requirements for course content." The standards are specified relative to the context of the LIS programme being accredited.

The context are specified at three levels:

- The standards and objectives of the parent institution, *i.e.,* a university (institutional context);
- The requirements for professional education in the country (national context);
- The objectives of the programme (local context).

The IFLA Guidelines state that the programme should be responsive to the needs of the country, and meet the educational and professional accreditation requirements as are the norm in the country. However, the LIS programme should be part of a degree-granting institution, (*i.e.,* university).

The evaluation of an LIS programme is performed largely with respect to the stated objectives of the programme:

- Programme goals and objectives are fundamental to all aspects of master's degree programmes and form the basis on which educational programmes are to be designed and developed and upon which they are evaluated.

The accreditation standards of the four library associations cover the following areas:

- The context of the programme, institutional support, and relationship with the parent institution;
- Mission, goals and objectives;
- The curriculum;
- Faculty and staff;
- Students, and policy and procedures relating to students;
- Administration and financial support;
- Instructional resources and facilities;
- Regular review of the programme, the curriculum, and the employment market;
- Documentation.

Even though the main focus of the accreditation evaluation is the objectives of the programme and those of its parent institution, there needs to be some means of determining whether a programme is an 'LIS programme' and whether the programme objectives are appropriate for an LIS programme. The IFLA Guidelines do not attempt to define the LIS field. The ALA Standards define LIS broadly:

- The phrase 'library and information studies' is understood to be concerned with recordable information and knowledge and the services and technologies to facilitate their management and use. Library and information studies encompasses information and knowledge creation, communication, identification, selection, acquisition, organisation and description, storage and retrieval, preservation, analysis, interpretation, evaluation, synthesis, dissemination, and management.

CILIP characterised LIS as:

- The principles and management of the production, organisation, analysis and provision of information and information services. It is concerned with the study of information from its generation to its exploitation, and its transmission in a variety of forms through a variety of channels.

LIS core skills and competencies are specified in a general kind of way in the standards.

IFLA Guidelines listed the following core areas:

- The Information Environment, Information Policy and Ethics, the History of the Field;
- Information Generation, Communication and Use;
- Assessing Information Needs and Designing Responsive Services;
- The Information Transfer Process;
- Organisation, Retrieval, Preservation and Conservation of Information;
- Research, Analysis and Interpretation of Information
- Applications of Information and Communication Technologies to Library and Information Products and Services;
- Information Resource Management and Knowledge Management;
- Management of Information Agencies;
- Quantitative and Qualitative Evaluation of Outcomes of Information and Library Use.

All the standards also specify general transferable skills that the programme should impart. IFLA listed the following skills: communication skills, teamwork, time and task management skills, and analytical and problem-solving skills. ALIA listed the following additional skills: management skills; ability to think critically, reflectively, and creatively; evaluation skills; valuing of professional ethical standards; commitment to life-long learning; IT skills; and information litreacy skills. CILIP added the following skills: human resource management, training and development, financial and budgetary management, statistical analysis, research methods, project management, and language skills. The IFLA Guidelines specify that the programme should cover theory and practice and professional concerns, and suggested having practicum, internship and fieldwork for students.

CILIP requires an individual project or a dissertation for graduation. Students are also expected to have a broad general education as preparation for the LIS education. The general and flexible nature of the accreditation standards make it possible to adopt one of these standards as the basis for an accreditation standard for Southeast Asia.

However, since, the different countries in Southeast Asia have different national needs and different education systems, and we do want graduates of accredited programmes to be able to work in different countries, the different national contexts have to be examined before instituting a regional accreditation system.

The Southeast Asia regional context may have to be taken into consideration when evaluating LIS programmes. It may difficult to decide whether the core areas are adequately covered by an LIS programme for accreditation. Guidelines may need to be drawn up regarding the extent and depth of coverage of the core skills.

ALA and CILIP standards indicate the possibility of accrediting specialised programmes, though the programme should be built on an broader LIS foundation:

- Courses that are submitted may be generalist in nature, designed to provide entry to any part of the profession, or more specialised. In the case of specialised courses the professional body will look for an element that sets the specialism within a broader professional context.

This suggests that a programme may provide in-depth coverage of a few areas, and much less coverage of other areas. The next part discusses the four main aspects or activities in the accreditation process—dialogue, self-evaluation, documentation and external review. Though we consider them part of the accreditation process, they are specified in the standards and are important features of the standards.

MAJOR ACTIVITIES IN THE ACCREDITATION PROCESS

DIALOGUE

'Accreditation' sounds intimidating and evokes in our minds a picture of hostile outsiders, possibly foreign, on a fault-finding mission to uncover the weaknesses of the programme and assess the programme against international norms.

Accreditation can be seen as interference by outsiders. However, a closer examination of the accreditations standards and procedures suggests that the accreditation process need not be a hostile and fear-inspiring activity, and can be a 'collegial' and productive process involving dialogue, consultation and mutual-help. Our perspective is that dialogue and consultation are the most important aspects of the accreditation process.

The LIS school has to engage in dialogue with many different parties, including:

- *Faculty members within the LIS school*: Dialogue within the LIS school is clearly necessary for self-evaluation, planning for improvement and preparing the case for accreditation.
- *The parent institution:* in which the LIS programme resides. The parent institution may need to be approached for financial, administrative and infra-structural support to meet accreditation standards and to continually improve the programme.
- *The profession*: including practising library and information professionals, and employers. The profession needs to be consulted regarding employment prospects, skills needed and adequacy of the training provided by the programme.
- *Students and alumni:* for feedback on the programme.
- *The accreditation body*. Documentation and information have to be provided to the accreditation committee for assessment. The committee can also provide

advice and suggestions for improving the accreditation case as well as for improving the programme to meet the standards.

- *Other library schools:* can be consulted on putting up the accreditation case and also for help to strengthen various aspects of the programme.
- *Other related programmes:* in the university, and other related professions. The LIS field is multi-disciplinary, and LIS professionals play many different roles in industry. It is thus important for the LIS schools to interact with and possibly collaborate with other departments and programmes in the university and also related fields and professions in industry.

Dialogue among LIS schools is possibly the most beneficial side-effect of a regional accreditation scheme. This dialogue is necessary to formulate regional accreditation standards and procedures that are acceptable to most LIS schools. Dialogue is needed to improve understanding of each other's unique context, history and objectives.

This understanding is important since, LIS faculty members will probably be serving in accreditation panels for other LIS programmes. An LIS school undergoing an accreditation process can seek advice and consultancy from faculty members in other LIS schools in preparing the accreditation case as well as improving the programme itself. Indeed, the ALA accreditation procedure specifically advises the LIS school seeking accreditation to "seek advice from individuals within the profession who have experience with accreditation".

The accreditation process can help to identify the particular strengths and best practices of individual LIS programmes, so that LIS schools know who to approach for assistance in particular areas of LIS education.

LIS schools seeking accreditation also need to have more dialogue with the profession. Dialogue with the profession is a two-way communication. On one hand, it involves feedback from professionals and employers on employment opportunities, skills needed, the adequacy of the programme in preparing graduates for professional work, and trends and developments in the profession.

On the other hand, the LIS schools also needs to:

- Explain to the profession the objectives, content, approach and rationale of the programme;
- Disseminate research results and new ideas, and inform the profession of trends and developments reported in the litreature;
- Provide continuing education and consultancy to the profession;
- Provide leadership to the profession.

Indeed providing continuing education and consultancy to the profession, and membership and service of faculty members in professional associations are part of the IFLA Guidelines.

IFLA guidelines state that "in order to assist practising librarians and information specialists to maintain competence in a changing society and to keep educators aware of issues and trends in practice, the programme should either conduct suitable workshops and short courses ..." Furthermore "the programme's staff should have the opportunity of offering consulting to libraries and information agencies to develop further interplay between the educational institution and practice." Dialogue with other university departments in related disciplines and dialogue with related professions are also important.

The IFLA Guidelines specify that the LIS programme should demonstrate awareness of related disciplines, and that "the administrators, faculty and staff of the library/information educational programme should be aware of, and in communication with other related professions and disciplines within and outside the educational establishment."

The ALA Standard also specifies that faculty members should interact with faculty of other disciplines. This makes sense considering the multidisciplinary nature of the LIS field and the convergence and growing overlap between LIS, computer science, information systems, communication studies, and other disciplines. LIS schools should also be an active participant in the university community and participate in the intellectual dialogue across the university, and forge partnerships and collaborations. Otherwise the LIS schools may become isolated entities in the university, and seen as redundant and not contributing to the mission of the university.

SELF-EVALUATION

Although we can expect all LIS schools to do a certain amount of self-evaluation and self-reflection, the accreditation process requires the LIS schools to do this self-evaluation systematically and regularly:

- The programme should have a clearly developed, regular planning and evaluation process. The process should include an ongoing review of policies and procedures in light of anticipated changes in the library/information field and in the larger society. Faculty, staff, and students should be involved in the planning and evaluation activities. Employers and practitioners should be consulted as well.

The ALA accreditation procedures emphasise the use of qualitative and quantitative 'outcomes assessment':

- Each school and programme will have its own ways of expressing its goals, determining desired outcomes, and measuring its accomplishments. The results of developing and evaluating outcomes assessments will be a unique set of measures of what constitutes success for that school and programme. ... Not all outcomes measures need to be objective or easily quantifiable; they must, however, be verifiable. The first places to look for outcomes measures are in existing documents about the programme, its resources, and its external environment. Examples of sources of data for demonstrating attainment of objectives include student achievements, alumni surveys, faculty accomplishments, employer feedback, and departmental or programme evaluations. Assessment measures for the curriculum come from testing for success in attaining course and

> programme objectives, school objectives, or institutional objectives for basic skills, thinking and practice in the discipline, and preparations for lifelong learning. The development of measures for teaching might begin with answering questions such as: What methods of presentation accommodate various learning styles? How are students encouraged to practice and apply their learning? ... The plan should include and describe plans for data-collection efforts that are necessary for the review; for example, will the school conduct focus groups, structured interviews, mail or telephone surveys with its constituent groups and/or students and alumni?

The accreditation procedures thus call for a fairly extensive and detailed evaluation study of the programme—a daunting task requiring substantial manpower and financial resources and research skills.

We have doubts that such an extensive evaluation is necessary to assess whether standards are met and to identify areas for improvement. Simpler accreditation procedures will need to be developed for use in the Southeast Asian context. Perhaps the ALIA and CILIP accreditation procedures can be taken as starting points. A few model programme evaluations will have to be developed to provide LIS schools guidance on what is expected.

DOCUMENTATION

Extensive documentation has to be done by the LIS schools to show that the programme complies substantially with the accreditation standards and also to present the evaluation study and results. The IFLA Guidelines emphasise transparency and detailed documentation in publicly available documents.

Policies and procedures to be documented and made publicly available include:

- The programme's mission, goals and objectives;
- Philosophy, principles and methods of the programme;
- Areas of specialisation;
- Level of preparation provided;

- Teaching, service and research values;
- Role of library and information services in society;
- Curriculum, including the aims, prerequisites, content, learning outcomes, and assessment methods for each course;
- Student recruitment, admission, financial aid, placement, and other academic and administrative policies for students;
- Criteria for selection of students, including interest, aptitude, intellectual and educational backgrounds and diversity.

ALA has more details about what is to be included in the programme objectives:

- Definition of LIS;
- The philosophy, principles, and ethics of the field;
- Appropriate principles of specialisation;
- The value of teaching and service to the advancement of the field;
- The importance of research to the advancement of the field's knowledge base;
- The importance of contributions of library and information studies to other fields of knowledge;
- The importance of contributions of other fields of knowledge to library and information studies;
- The role of library and information services in a rapidly changing multicultural, multiethnic, multilingual society, including the role of serving the needs of underserved groups;
- The role of library and information services in a rapidly changing technological and global society;
- The needs of the constituencies that a programme seeks to serve.

Policies and procedures to be documented:

- Faculty appointment, review and promotion policies;
- Faculty continuing education and professional development;
- Policy for reviewing the currency and relevance of courses and teaching methods.

The accreditation standards and procedures developed for Southeast Asia will need to specify what LIS schools need to document and make public, and the amount of documentation.

EXTERNAL REVIEW

Finally, an accreditation review panel will be formed by the accrediting agency to review the documents and the accreditation case presented by the school, and assess whether the programme substantially meets the 'standards'.

This would involve a site visit by the accreditation panel to review aspects of the programme that cannot be assessed fairly from documentation alone, and to meet with the various constituencies of the programme.

SURVEY OF LIS SCHOOLS

Prof. Shaheen Majid carried out a questionnaire survey of LIS schools in Southeast Asia in January and February 2002, to explore the perceptions of the LIS schools about a regional accreditation scheme for the LIS degrees.

A summary of the results is provided here. Fourteen LIS schools from five Southeast Asian countries participated in the study. No LIS programmes could be identified in four countries: Brunei, Cambodia, Laos and Myanmar. The highest number of participants was from Thailand, followed by the Philippines with 4 schools. Two schools each from Singapore and Malaysia participated in this study.

Twelve of the 14 schools agreed there is a need for developing an accreditation scheme for LIS degrees awarded in Southeast Asian countries. One school from Thailand was unsure, and one school from Malaysia disagreed pointing out that 'the process of accreditation by concerned authorities at national level ... is effective and good enough'.

Thirteen schools expressed interest in participating in an accreditation scheme developed for Southeast Asian countries. The Malaysian school, which earlier disagreed, expressed its inability to join since, government authorities would not accept such an exercise undertaken by a body not authorised by them. Most of the schools agreed that implementation of an accreditation scheme would result in better coordination among LIS programmes in the region, result in wider acceptance, higher creditability and recognition of LIS degrees, better job prospects for LIS graduates, and better quality of LIS programmes and their graduates.

Eleven schools agreed while three were not sure that such a scheme would enhance the mobility of LIS graduates in the region.

Regarding the implementation and coordination of accreditation activities, a majority of the respondents agreed that a joint committee of representatives from CONSAL and LIS schools should be responsible for developing rules and procedures as well as for coordination of the proposed regional accreditation scheme.

The following factors were considered very important in the accreditation criteria by at least 10 LIS schools:

- Relevance of curriculum to market needs;
- Faculty educational/ professional qualifications;
- Number of faculty members;
- Faculty areas of specialisation and diversity in background;
- Total credit hours/workload for graduation;
- Funds for developing resources and facilities;
- Physical Resources and Facilities;
- Computer hardware/software/networking;
- Access to the Internet;
- Instructional equipment;
- Library Resources.

The main problems to developing and implementing a regional accreditation scheme were identified as:

- Non-availability of funds;
- Limited understanding and appreciation for such a scheme;
- Lack of expertise and procedural difficulties.

Four schools feared that there might be some resistance from LIS programmes in implementing this scheme.

AN ORGANISATIONAL MODEL FOR A REGIONAL ACCREDITATION SYSTEM

Majid also outlined a model for developing and implementing an accreditation scheme. They proposed that in the first phase of implementation only Master's degrees will be accredited, and extended to Bachelor's degree in the second phase. They proposed that a regional accreditation scheme be developed under the auspices and oversight of CONSAL.

They proposed a CONSAL Special Committee on Accreditation with representatives from LIS schools, National Libraries, professional associations, library and information practitioners, etc., to draft rules, procedures and accreditation standards, and submit the report to the CONSAL Executive Board (EB) for implementation.

CONSAL will then form a *CONSAL* Advisory Committee on Accreditation (CACA) with 14 members for coordinating and implementing the proposed accreditation scheme, representing CONSAL, LIS schools, National Libraries, LIS professional associations, and practitioners.

To accredit a particular LIS programme, CACA will nominate an Accreditation Review Panel (ARP) in consultation with the CONSAL Executive Board, to visit candidate schools and assess their eligibility by using the approved *Accreditation Standards*.

For this purpose, a pool of experts would be developed with appropriate qualifications, experience and interest in LIS education. Each ARP would consist of four members, two academicians and one representative each from library associations and National Libraries of ASEAN member countries. Based on the recommendations of the Accreditation Review Panel, the CONSAL Advisory Committee on Accreditation (CACA) would decide whether or not to grant accredited status to the candidate school.

Table 10.1 Proposed Composition of the CONSAL Advisory Committee on Accreditation.

Agency	Number of Representatives	Duration	Remarks
CONSAL	1	Two years	-
LIS Schools	6	Three years	No more than two persons from each countryon staggered-
		rotation basis	
National Libraries	2	Two years	On staggered-rotation basis
Library Associations	2	One year	On staggered-rotation basis – to be nominated by National Library of the respective country on rotation basis
LIS Practitioners	3	One year	Representing different specialisations – not more than one person from each country

STEPS TOWARDS ESTABLISHING A REGIONAL ACCREDITATION SYSTEM

Clearly, for an accreditation scheme to be developed and accepted by LIS schools in the region, extensive dialogue among the LIS schools need to take place to draft the accreditation standards and procedures.

The schools will then have to perform self-evaluation, and apply the draft standards and procedures to their own programmes to identify problems and assess to what extent their programmes meet the draft standards. LIS faculty may also need to visit other schools to understand the problems encountered by other schools and to simulate accreditation panel site visits. The CONSAL Special Committee on Accreditation proposed by Majid could be the coordinating body for these efforts. Once the accreditation standards and procedures have been agreed on, a CONSAL Advisory Committee on Accreditation (CACA) could coordinate and implement the accreditation scheme.

Initially, the accreditation committee will have to spend a substantial amount of time clarifying the standards and procedures. The committee will have to provide guidance to LIS schools to prepare the required documents, carry out the evaluation study, and prepare the case for accreditation. A consultant with extensive experience of the accreditation process in Australia, UK or the US will probably need to be engaged to advise the accreditation committee, and to ensure that the accreditation process is performed properly. Nearly two-thirds of the respondents of Majid's survey indicated non-availability of funds as a major problem.

To reduce the financial burden of the candidate schools, it is suggested that members of the Review Panel be encouraged to seek travel funds from their parent organisations. Alternatively, CONSAL could approach appropriate international donors for grants to cover costs for the initial implementation of this scheme.

The respective national library associations will also need to set up a Standards and Accreditation Committee to represent the interests of the profession and the association, and to liaise with the CONSAL Advisory Committee on Accreditation.

The Library Association of Singapore has set up a Standards and Professional Sub-Committee with the objectives:

- To develop standards and guidelines for LIS professional and paraprofessional education;
- To develop standards and guidelines for library and information services;
- To develop library and information industry competency standards;
- To develop accreditation and certification guidelines and procedures;

- To liaise with LIS-related standards and accreditation bodies in Singapore and other countries.

The sub-committee has set up a Web site to gather resource materials on standardisation, accreditation and certification.

CONCLUSION

We have examined some of the issues involved in developing accreditation standards and procedures for LIS professional education programmes in Southeast Asia.

The accreditation standards of the ALA, ALIA, CILIP (UK) and IFLA were examined, and their main features identified and discussed with respect to the Southeast Asian context.

The main advantages of a regional accreditation scheme were identified as:

- Assuring students and employers of the quality of the programme;
- Encouraging commitment to continual improvement;
- Improving the mobility of graduates;
- Encouraging interaction, dialogue, collaboration and cooperation between LIS schools;
- Encouraging dialogue between LIS schools and their constituencies, as well as with other disciplines and professions;
- Greater transparency and more documentation of policies and procedures;
- Helping the region to negotiate mutual recognition of professional qualifications with the library associations of other countries.

We identified *dialogue* with different parties and *self-evaluation* as very beneficial aspects of the accreditation process, as well as point out the enormous amount of *documentation* that might be needed. We have also proposed a organisational model for regional accreditation and steps that may need to be taken to develop the system. It is hoped that the analysis and proposals in this chapter will stimulate further discussion regarding the development and implementation of a regional accreditation system.

11

Standards for Library Systems

INTRODUCTION

Librarians have recognised and supported, long before the dawn of computers, the need for standards to aid in collection management, share resources with other libraries, and improve access for library patrons.

The widespread use of *Integrated Library Systems* (ILS), global communications via the Internet, and growing numbers of digital library initiatives have made the need for compliance with standards more critical than ever.

Implementing information products and systems that support standards can ensure that libraries will be able to:

- Integrate electronic content products from multiple vendors;
- Resource share on a wider geographic scale, even globally;
- Participate in more cooperative programmes with other organisations, including ones outside the library community;
- Speed up the 'time to market' of library materials, *i.e.*, the time to acquire, catalogue, process, and circulate an item;
- Provide remote access to library services;
- Reduce the need for user training;
- Operate successfully with their parent organisation's computing infrastructure;

- Migrate cost effectively to newer systems; and
- More easily adopt new technologies.

But which standards are important when considering a library system? And how can one determine if a vendor's product really complies with a standard? The RFP Writer's Guide to Standards for Library Systems was created to answer these questions. It is intended for those who are writing Request for Proposals (RFPs) for library systems or evaluating RFP responses and software products.

Standards compliance needs to be considered from the very start of planning for an information system—during the needs assessment. This guide identifies the current U.S.,. national and international standards that are most important for all types of libraries.

Once the standards have been identified, conformance requirements specific to the library system need to be clearly stated in the RFP that is sent to potential vendors. The guide assists in this effort by providing sample language for inclusion in the RFP. When evaluating systems, it is not enough to accept a general statement from the vendor that the product 'complies' with a particular standard.

In many cases, there are different approaches that can be taken in implementing a standard or the product may support some parts of a standard and not others. This guide will discuss known issues regarding compliance with a standard as it applies to library systems and suggest questions to be asked or tests to be performed to validate a product's conformance.

BIBLIOGRAPHIC FORMATS

MARC 21 FORMATS

The Machine Readable Cataloguing format (MARC) was originally developed by the Library of Congress to automate the production of catalogue cards.

Over time, MARC has become widely used internationally and expanded to support advances in technology and library practices. The USMARC formats have evolved into the MARC

21 specifications, becoming the defacto standard for bibliographic formats in library computer applications.

The MARC 21 formats specify three content designators:

- *Tags*: A 3 digit number that uniquely identifies all the possible 'fields' of the cataloging record, such as title, author, series, etc.
- *Subfield codes:* A lower case letter or digit, preceded by a delimiter, used to further differentiate the data within a field.
- *Indicators*: Two one-character positions for single digit numbers whose use or meaning varies depending on which field tag the indicator follows.

The specifications address the format encoding necessary for representation and exchange of bibliographic data between systems. Display formats and database storage technologies are not included in the specification and are determined by the design of the particular information system product.

There are five MARC 21 format or content specifications, each addressing a specific type of data:

- The MARC 21 Format for Bibliographic Data.
- The MARC 21 Format for Holdings Data.
- The MARC 21 Format for Authority Data.
- The MARC 21 Format for Classification Data.
- The MARC 21 Format for Community Information.

At this time the only system using MARC 21 classification data is the centralised database of Library of Congress Classification records maintained at the Library of Congress. Other libraries would not reference the classification data standard in their RFPs. The Library of Congress is the official Maintenance Agency for the MARC 21 specification.

MARC 21 FORMAT FOR BIBLIOGRAPHIC DATA

Bibliographic data is the core component of an automated library system. It forms the basis of all online catalogues and shared cataloguing processes.

All the functional modules of an integrated library system utilise or interact with the bibliographic data in some way. In earlier versions of MARC, each type of material had a separate format defined. In the 1990s, however, the concept of 'format integration' was implemented—now all material types are addressed with one format and all MARC 21 fields may be used with any material type.

Sample RFP Language

The following are examples of language that could be included in an RFP to address MARC 21 bibliographic format compliance:

- The system must encode all bibliographic records in MARC 21 Format for Bibliographic Data without limitation on record length. Describe how the system supports this format. Discuss any limitations on the use of 9XX or X9X locally defined tags and fields.
- The system must be capable of importing and exporting bibliographic records in MARC 21 Format for Bibliographic Data without vendor intervention and with full preservation of all content designators. Discuss how import and export is handled. Address whether 9XX locally defined fields are included in import and export.
- The system must provide for display of all MARC content designators on the cataloging workstation and suppress display of codes on all patron access workstations. Describe how record display is handled for each of the following clients: librarian/cataloger workstation, OPAC, Z39.50 client, and Web browser.

Assessing Compliance

A library will want a system that supports the full MARC 21 bibliographic format, allowing use of the complete spectrum of content designators, even when it is not intended to use all of them. It is desirable that the system has some validation mechanisms for content designators and selected controlled values.

Additionally, the system should accurately import and export records with all content designator tags intact. The system should preserve the order of MARC fields as created or imported, so as not to lose context of related data. The many data elements contained in MARC can result in a powerful search system; the evaluation team should assess how effectively the system uses the wealth of data in the record. The system should support all functionality expressed through indicator values. For example, if an indicator is defined as meaning a display constant should be supplied or a certain number of characters are non-filing, then the system should provide that functionality.

Format changes to MARC 21 are issued annually and the vendor should discuss how the system is kept current with these changes. If the system uses a vendor-supplied tag table, ask about the update frequency of these tables by the vendor and the lag time from when tag changes are issued by the Library of Congress and incorporated into the vendor's tables. Since, record display is not specified in MARC 21, demonstrations of display on different types of workstations for different types of users—cataloguing workstations, OPAC terminals, Z39.50 clients, and Web browsers—should be performed to determine how each display might differ

MARC 21 FORMAT FOR AUTHORITY DATA

Authority data acts like an online thesaurus, allowing for control of authorised names and subjects used in designated fields of bibliographic records.

These records may also generate cross references from unused to preferred terms and interrelationships between authority entries. The MARC 21 Format for Authority Data identifies seven kinds of authority records—established heading, reference, subdivision, established heading and subdivision, reference and subdivision, node label—and defines how each type is to be encoded.

Sample RFP Language

The following are examples of language that could be included in an RFP to address MARC 21 authority data format compliance:

- The system must support MARC 21 Format for

Authority Data and allow all relevant bibliographic fields to be authority controlled. Describe how the system implements this format and identify which fields can be authority controlled. Describe the default authority control policies and the ability to customise these policies.

- The system must generate SEE and SEE ALSO references from authority records and display them in the OPAC. Discuss how the system creates, manages, and displays cross-references.
- The system must be capable of importing and exporting authority records in MARC 21 Format for Authority Data without vendor intervention.
- The system must be capable of editing authority records individually and globally and allow easy access to authority records editing from within the bibliographic module.

Assessing Compliance

The system should be evaluated for the ability of authority records to interact with bibliographic records in generating references and validating entries. Compliance issues generally relate to the implementation of cross references—specifically how and when the system displays simple and complex cross references from the tracings information.

Additionally, authority records have import and export requirements that differ from those of bibliographic records and thus should be tested separately. Libraries that import authority control lists from more than one source should determine if and how these lists are merged and how overwriting is prevented.

MARC 21 FORMAT FOR COMMUNITY INFORMATION

Many libraries, especially public ones, identified a need for storing and making accessible to patrons local information about their organisation and community that cannot be described by the traditional bibliographic record.

The MARC 21 Format for Community Information was the answer to that need. It identifies five types of community information records—individual, organisation, programme or service, event, and other—and defines how each type is to be encoded.

Sample RFP Language

The following are examples of language that could be included in an RFP to address MARC 21 community information format compliance:

- The system must support MARC 21 Format for Community Information. Describe how the system implements this format.
- The system must be capable of importing and exporting Community Information in MARC 21 format without vendor intervention.
- The system must be able to limit searches to the community file only. Describe how this is accomplished.
- It is desirable for the system to provide linkages to an authority file. Describe how authority records for Community Information are handled.

Assessing Compliance

There are minimal requirements for community information format compared to the other formats. Support for all the identified data elements, import and export capability, and the validation routines should be verified. If authority control is desired for community information, determine if a separate authority file is available.

MARC 21 FORMAT FOR HOLDINGS DATA

The holdings data describes the particular items and copies in the library's collection that are associated with a bibliographic record. Proper holdings format and coding is critical to the operation of circulation related functions, serials check-in, and integrated acquisitions.

The MARC 21 Format for Holdings Data specifies data fields and tags for three types of holdings—single-part items, multi-part items, and serial items—as well as rules for embedding holdings in or linking holdings to the bibliographic record. The current version of the standard has incorporated the required holdings elements specified in ANSI/NISO Z39.71 and includes a chart mapping MARC data elements to those in Z39.71. An encoding level tag has been added to identify the specificity of the holdings statement at 5 defined levels.

Sample RFP Language

The following are examples of language that could be included in an RFP to address MARC 21 holdings format compliance:

- The system must support MARC 21 Format for Holdings Data at both summary and detailed levels, and as either embedded or linked records. Describe how the system supports this format. Discuss the ability of the system to automatically generate summary holdings. Discuss how the system is kept current with modifications to the holdings format.
- The system must be capable of importing and exporting holding records in MARC 21 Format for Holdings Data without vendor intervention and with full preservation of all tags.
- The system must provide for display of all MARC 21 holdings tags on the librarian workstation and suppress display of codes on all patron access workstations. Describe how record display is handled for each of the following clients: librarian/cataloguer workstation, OPAC, Z39.50 client, and Web browser.
- The system's serials check-in system should automatically update the MARC 21 holdings record including all content related to the 85X/86X paired fields. Describe how the system serials check-in module integrates with the MARC holdings records.

Assessing Compliance

Full compliance to the MARC 21 Format for Holdings Data is not as widespread in current library systems as is compliance with the bibliographic format. Libraries frequently differ in their interpretation of what constitutes a 'copy'; the evaluation team should determine whether the system will support their local definitions and handling. Identify any limitations on the number of holdings records that can be linked to a bibliographic record. Serials holdings can be especially complex due to the 'pattern' variety of issues, irregular issues, and special extra issues.

The integration between the serials check-in functions and the holding records should be discussed. Ideally, the pattern information in the 853 field should match the pattern used for serials check-in and the 863 field should update automatically as an issue is checked in. Import capability is important when migrating from one system to another.

Export capability in either detailed or summary format should be reviewed if there is any expectation of contributing to a union catalogue or listing. Tests of holdings data should include embedded and linked holdings records, summary and detail holdings, and how the different types of holdings are displayed. Import and export of a sample of the libraries holding data should be tested to ensure that field codes are intact.

HOLDINGS STATEMENTS FOR BIBLIOGRAPHIC ITEMS

Z39.71, supporting the concept of format integration, supersedes and merges two holdings standards, Z39.44 for serials and Z39.57 for non-serials.

The NISO standard was based on the international standard, ISO 10324 Information and documentation–Holdings statements—Summary level, but goes further in defining holdings at a detail level. Use of the specified display formats provides consistency in the communication and exchange of holdings information among libraries and between disparate information systems.

Z39.71 works in conjunction with the MARC 21 Format for Holdings Data; MARC defines the structure and encoding for implementing holdings data while Z39.71 addresses the content and display of those holdings.

The standard defines four levels of specificity of holdings, mandatory and optional data elements for each level, punctuation / format to be used for the data content, and display options.

Sample RFP language

The following are examples of language that could be included in an RFP to address Z39.71 holdings statement compliance:

- The system must support holdings statements of both serial and non-serial multi-part items as defined in ANSI/NISO Z39.71 Holdings Statements for Bibliographic Items, including summary and detailed holdings, mixed level holdings, itemised and compressed formats, and enumeration and chronology displays. Describe the system's support for all mandatory data elements at all four levels and discuss how optional elements can be utilised.
- The system must support holdings display as defined in ANSI/NISO Z39.71 Holdings Statements for Bibliographic Items, with respect to formats, punctuation, and order of data. Describe how holdings statement display is handled for each of the following clients: librarian/cataloguer workstation, OPAC, Z39.50 client, and Web browser.
- The system must support export of holdings data, with full retention of content formats as defined in ANSI/NISO Z39.71 Holdings Statements for Bibliographic Items, to allow participation in union lists or library data exchanges.
- Describe how the system links holdings data and bibliographic data.

Assessing Compliance

Full support of holdings data at any of the four levels defined in the standard is the main compliance issue. The system should accept the newly defined option of having an open-ended holding in an OPAC display.

Available display options should be verified and tested on all types of clients that the library intends to use. Linkages between holdings data and bibliographic data should use an item identifier. While not specified in the standard, limitations, if any, on number of holdings linked to a given bibliographic item or holdings record length should be determined. Z39.71 accommodates the use of holdings data created under the earlier standards. Libraries that plan to migrate data using older formats and use the new standard requirements for future holdings should understand how the system will handle and display both the old and the new formats.

RECORD STRUCTURE, CHARACTER SETS AND EXCHANGE MEDIA

In addition to the MARC 21 format specifications, there are also specifications that relate to the more technical structure, coding, and labeling of data that is needed for the exchange of information between computer systems. The MARC 21 Specifications for Record Structure, Character Sets, and Exchange Media define the standards for ensuring that all the bibliographic formatted information is retained, understood, and translated correctly.

MARC 21—RECORD STRUCTURE

The record structure is the key for the computer's understanding all of the MARC bibliographic formatted data and is an integral reference in all the format specifications. The MARC 21 record structure specification is an implementation of ANSI/NISO Z39.2, Information Interchange Format, and ISO 2709, Format for Information Exchange.

It defines how bibliographic and related records should be structured so that any compliant computer software can translate the codes and data into understandable, editable, and searchable information.

The specification details three parts of the record:

- The leader tells the computer how to process the subsequent record by defining the length and type of the record and kinds of coding being used.

- The directory provides an index to the record by identifying the field tags that are used in the record and their length and start position.
- Variable fields are all the control and data fields that make up the actual record.

Sample RFP Language

The following are examples of language that could be included in an RFP to address MARC 21 record structure compliance:

- The system must comply with the record structure specified in MARC 21 Specifications for Record Structure, Character Sets, and Exchange Media. Discuss how the system has been tested to validate this compliance and provide copies of relevant test documentation.
- The system must be capable of importing and exporting all types of MARC 21 formatted records without vendor intervention and with full preservation of all tags. The system must be able to import and export individual records as well as the entire database in MARC 21 format.
- Describe the system's capability of importing and exporting bibliographic utilities' versions of MARC records, *e.g.*, OCLC-MARC and RLIN-MARC.

Assessing Compliance

The system should accurately import and export records of all MARC 21 format types with all structure and content designator tags intact. The system should provide all the tools and utilities needed to do imports and exports without additional programming or services from the vendor.

Some bibliographic utilities, such as OCLC and RLIN, have subtle differences in their implementation of the Z39.2 standard, usually in the leader format and how records are blocked on tape.

The library evaluation team should determine if import and export of MARC records from the bibliographic utility they use has been implemented and tested. Since, record indexing and storage are not specified in MARC 21and could vary greatly from one system to another, the evaluation team should ask for a full explanation of the underlying database structure and indexing routines.

MARC 21—CHARACTER SETS

All computerised characters have to be encoded at the binary level. While early automation systems used the EBCDIC character set, since, the 1970's ASCII has been the most commonly used code across all types of computer applications. But ASCII, which has only 256 possible combinations, falls short when a single application, such as the typical library catalogue, utilises multiple languages, translitreations, and diacritics.

The MARC 21 specification defines two character set formats:

- MARC-8, an 8-bit coding system which utilises the ASCIJ set from ANSI X3.4 and its international counterpart ISO/IEC 646, the ANSEL extended Latin character set, the East Asian Character Code, as well as a number of other sets specific to particular languages and symbols.
- UCS/Unicode UTF-8, a variable 8/16-bit coding system based on the Unicode and UCS standards. Unicode defines a single character set that encompasses most written languages. The MARC standard does not currently define the full Unicode character set. The supported MARC-8 character codes have been mapped to Unicode with the intent of enabling transition from 8 bit to 16 bit systems and round trip movement of data without loss of information.

The character sets supported in an automated library system will determine how bibliographic text is input, stored, and displayed. To accurately import records in electronic format, the library system must either natively support the records' character set or have a reliable conversion programme. While all types of libraries may encounter character set issues, libraries with diverse multilingual collections will need to be most concerned with how a potential system implements character sets.

Sample RFP Language

The following are examples of language that could be included in an RFP to address MARC 21 character set standards compliance:

- The system must support the importing, inputting, editing, displaying, printing, storing, and exporting of all characters defined in the character sets of MARC 21 Specifications for Record Structure, Character Sets, and Exchange Media. Identify any character sets specified in MARC 21 that are not fully supported by the system for importing, inputting, editing, displaying, printing, storing, and exporting. Explicitly describe the areas of non-support.
- The system must support the MARC 21 character sets utilising standard hardware peripherals for input, display, and printing. Describe any specific requirements for peripheral hardware to ensure this support.
- Describe how non-Roman alphabets, Latin script characters, and specialised symbols are handled with a standard Web browser client.

Assessing Compliance

Each character set that the library plans to use should be tested separately in the proposed system. After testing input on a cataloging workstation, the display and printing of the characters should be tested on the different types of peripherals the library expects to use. Display should also be checked using a Web browser.

Sample records utilising the different character sets should be imported and checked for editing, display, and printing. Record exporting options should also be tested and round trip export/imports should be tried.

MARC 21—EXCHANGE MEDIA

The MARC 21 Exchange Media specifies media format and labeling for mechanisms that may be utilised to exchange MARC 21 encoded records between computer systems.

The requirements for labeling, volume, organisation, and sequence of data are defined for three types of exchanges: electronic file transfer, microcomputer diskettes, and magnetic tape. Magnetic tape interchanges are based on three related ANSI standards: ANSI X3.27, ANSI X3.39, and ANSI X3.54.

Sample RFP Language

The following are examples of language that could be included in an RFP to address MARC 21 exchange media compliance:

- The system must support the MARC 21 Specifications for Exchange Media with the capability to import and export, without vendor intervention, by FTP electronic transfer, disk, and tape.
- Describe all tools and utilities that come with the system, or are available as separate modules, which are utilised to import or export MARC formatted records.
- Describe all tools and utilities that come with the system, or are available as separate modules, which are utilised to import MARC records from bibliographic utilities.

Assessing Compliance

Adherence to media format and labeling specifications is essential for successful exchange of MARC 21 records. Vendors should be asked for documented test results or demonstrations for the type of transfers the library requires.

Electronic file transfers utilising Internet File Transfer Protocol (FTP) can be easily tested using the library's own data or sample data files. Magnetic tape transfer specifications were changed in 1977 to support record spanning across media. Libraries should verify that the vendor supports the new tape specifications.

SERIALS

SERIAL ITEM AND CONTRIBUTION IDENTIFIER (SICI)

The SICI standard defines a coding structure to assign unique identifiers to serials. The code builds on the International Standard Serial Number (ISSN) for the serial item portion of the identifier.

The SICI code is derived algorithmically from bibliographic information about the serial and/or article and may be generated by the creator/publisher of the items and contributions, by a third party vendor such as a document delivery supplier or abstracting and indexing service, or by the library which acquires and holds the materials.

Use of the SICI code in a computer system allows the items and contributions to be uniquely identified in many library automated transactions including ordering, claiming, bibliographic database linking, ILL and document delivery, check-in, reserve room, and rights management and royalty collection.

The code was designed to be compact enough to be easily converted to a barcode. SICI has also been assigned a use value in the Z39.50 bib-1 attribute set. This assignment allows the SICI to be used as a qualifier in a Z39.50 information retrieval search. SICI also could be used as the identifier in conjunction with an ILL Protocol request, EDI order, or a GEDI electronic document transmission.

Sample RFP Language

The following are examples of language that could be included in an RFP to address SICI compliance:

- The system must support the use of the Serial Item and Contribution Identifier as specified in ANSI/NISO Z39.56. Describe how your system implements SICI for both serials and contributions. Discuss how the SICI is stored, indexed, and searchable.
- Discuss how your system does SICI code matching and validation.

Assessing Compliance

It is more likely, currently, to find support of SICI at the Serials Item level than the Contribution level in a library system. However, the use of the Contribution Identifier through the entire ILL or document delivery cycle is becoming more crucial.

Even libraries that do no currently identify items at the contribution level should look for a system that allows the code's use. Since, the standard allows that some data elements can be omitted when creating a SICI, the algorithms a system uses to match or validate SICI codes can be complex. Demonstrations and tests of this functionality should be requested from the vendor.

The 1996 version of the standard changed the rules for Title Code, clarified the distinction between serial items and contribution identifiers, added a method for indicating the medium of the material, and better delineated the segments of the identifier. Libraries should confirm that the system supports the changes in this version.

DATA ELEMENTS FOR BINDING LIBRARY MATERIALS

Z39.76 identifies and defines common data elements used to process and track library materials for binding when information about the material is exchanged between a library management software system and a binding preparation software system.

Use of the specified data elements in an automated library system can reduce duplicate data entry when preparing binding orders, improve accuracy and consistency of binding labels, and allow for more automation of binding processes. The standard incorporates other identifying codes and standard numbering systems such as ISBN, ISSN, and SICI. Holdings information fields are based on the MARC 21 Format for Holdings Data. The standard does not define any of the communications protocols required for the information exchange, but the expectation is that EDI is utilised for the transfer of data.

Sample RFP Language

The following are examples of language that could be included in an RFP to address Z39.76 binding data elements compliance:

- The system must support ANSI/NISO Z39.76 Data Elements for Binding Library Materials. Define which binding element fields are included by default in the system and discuss how optional elements are handled.
- Describe how binding element information is input and how it is linked to the bibliographic and holdings record information to ensure consistency.
- Describe the process for generating binding information from the system to send electronically to a vendor. Describe the methods and formats for exporting binding information to a file.
- Identify which communications protocols can be used to transmit binding information.

Assessing Compliance

A small subset of the data elements defined in the standard is considered mandatory; these elements should be supported in the selected system. Many of the optional fields are defined as such only because they would not be utilised with every binding order thus it is likely that many of the optional fields would be desirable to have.

Additionally, some libraries may be using a binding preparation software package that might require some of the standard's optional data fields. The evaluation team should review all the optional elements and identify the additional fields that would be 'mandatory' to their library's binding process. Determine how the desired optional data elements are supported and how easily additional data elements can be added at a later time.

Ask if there are any limitations on the number of binding related fields which the system can support. Determine that the system supports both serial and non-serial materials in the binding processes and that the binding module can access needed data from the serials and acquisition modules. Have the vendor create a test file of binding data from the system as it would look when transmitted and verify that the information is compiled and reported correctly.

If the library's binding vendor accepts electronic transmissions, a test transmission to that vendor and the vendor's verification of how the data was received would be useful. Clarify with the vendor which communication protocols are supported for binding information. If the system supports EDI transmission for acquisition and claiming activities, can it also be used for the binding transmission? If the binding data is exported to a file, determine what file formats are available and if these are compatible with what the library and the binding vendor use.

CIRCULATION

NISO CIRCULATION INTERCHANGE PROTOCOL (NCIP)

The NISO Circulation Interchange Protocol (NCIP) defines and specifies the objects, services, messages, and data elements needed to facilitate interoperability between dissimilar circulation systems.

Three applications are addressed: direct consortial borrowing, circulation/interlibrary loan interaction, and self-service circulation. Functions that permit a circulation system to manage controlled access to electronic materials, such as e-books and music files, are also included in the protocol. Currently, many libraries have to record an interlibrary loan in both their circulation system—to track the patron's check-out or the item's non-availability status—and in the shared ILL system—to track the loan or outstanding loan request.

Use of the NCIP will allow disparate circulation systems and ILL systems to communicate, exchange information about users and items, and update status automatically—eliminating duplicate data entry, lessening manual interventions, and ensuring consistency in loan information and updates. Library consortiums where individual libraries are using different library systems can utilise NCIP to turn consortial loans into circulation transactions. Self-service circulation transactions can be improved and expanded beyond the patron's home library.

The NCIP standard separates the specification of services and data objects from implementation details to allow the protocol to be deployed using different encoding and transport methods, as well as permit the use of future technologies without rewriting the entire standard.

Implementation specifics are handled through Implementation Profiles, which specify methods for message exchange using particular technologies, and Application Profiles, which describe the particular service requirements needed to support typical circulation applications. Templates and rules for developing these profiles are provided in the standard.

A basic Implementation Profile, utilising current Web and XML technology, is included as part 2 of the standard. Eight Application Profiles associated with Implementation Profile 1 have been defined and are available on the NISO NCIP web site along with the schemas referenced in the Implementation Profile.

Sample RFP Language

The following are examples of language that could be included in an RFP to address NCIP compliance:

- The system must support the NISO Circulation Interchange Protocol, ANSI/NISO Z39.83. Describe any successful demonstrations of NCIP implementation between:
  - The system's circulation module and other ILL systems, and
  - The system's ILL module and other circulation systems.
- The system must support NCIP Implementation Profile 1, ANSI/NISO Z39.83, Pt. 2. Describe how the system implements this profile.
- Identify the specific NCIP Application Profiles which the system supports.

Assessing Compliance

NCIP Implementation Profiles and Application Profiles include conformance requirements, specifically, which of the services, messages, and data structures are required as well as the rules defining behaviour for conformance. Implementation Profile 1, provided with the standard, defines two levels of conformance: strictly conformant and conformant, each of which is further explained in the profile.

This particular Implementation Profile requires the use of XML for message encoding, DTD to encapsulate the structure, Unicode UTF-8 for character encoding, and one of three transport protocols—HTTP, HTTPS, or TCP/IP. Current implementations of NCIP should demonstrate compliance with these protocols and schemas. Libraries should determine which of the eight application profiles are relevant to their environment.

The event tables in the application profile can be used as a kind of checklist to determine if the system being evaluated supports the services needed in the desired application environment. NCIP was approved in mid-2002 and a newly formed implementors group plans began meeting in October 2002. It is expected that this group will develop further guidelines on conformance interoperability.

BARCODES

A barcode is an optically readable array of black and white 'bars' of varying widths where a fixed pattern of bars and spaces represents a particular machine-readable character. An optical scanning device 'reads' the barcode and sends the information to a decoder which converts the scan to its correct machine-readable characters.

The ratio of the bar widths, the print density and quality of the label, the accuracy of the scanning device, and the capability of the decoder all play a part in whether the right information is ultimately fed into the computer system. Libraries typically use barcodes to uniquely identify a physical library collection item and link the physical item to a bibliographic and holding record.

Barcodes are also used on library patron identification and link to the patron's database record. During a circulation transaction, the barcodes of the library item and the patron are scanned resulting in a faster and more accurate circulation transaction.

An accurate and effective barcode scan is dependent on the interaction of the barcode label, the barcode reader, the decoder, and the library system software interface. Readers and especially the labels are often purchased from different vendors than the library system supplier, which makes standards conformance of all the vendors critical. There are over 200 barcode symbol 'languages' in existence worldwide. Each 'language' specifies rules for how data is encoded into the 'bars,' label printing requirements, decoding rules, and error checking. Only a fraction of the bar code specifications are in wide use. The two bar code standards most in use by libraries are Code 39 and Codabar.

CODE 39

Code 39 is a general barcode standard utilised in many industries. It is sometimes called the '3 of 9 code' as it uses 9 bars, 3 of which are wider than the others, to define a character. An alphanumeric system is used which can have up to 43 characters with 1 start/stop code pattern. Code 39 is considered one of the easiest codes to use because of its self-checking capability.

CODABAR

Table 11.1 Codabar is a Library Specific Barcode that Utilises a 14 Character-numeric Label Broken Down as Follows.

Digit Position	Description
1	Type of barcode. A '2' signifies a patron label. A '3' signifies a title label.
2 – 5	Four digit library identifier
6 – 13	Consecutive number
14	Check digit

Codabar is strictly numerical and is considered to have one of the highest resolutions of all bar codes.

Sample RFP Language

The following are examples of language that could be included in an RFP to address barcode compliance:

- The system must support the use of both Codabar and Code 39 barcodes for bibliographic items and patron IDs, with the ability to interpret a minimum of 14 digits.
- The system must accept input from third party suppliers' barcodes and readers, or another library system barcodes, that comply with Codabar or Code 39 standards. Describe any limitations on support of these standards or standard-compliant third party products.
- Barcode numbers on items or patron-IDs should be able to be scanned or manually entered into the system.
- The system must be able to create output that can be used by a vendor to create Code 39 or Codabar standard barcodes.
- Barcode numbers should be entered into MARC field 949 or an appropriate 8XX field of the record.

Assessing Compliance

Bar code technology and readers supporting both Code 39 and Codabar are fairly commonplace. Their commodity nature has caused libraries to shop around to find the best prices.

As a result, it is not unusual for different vendors to supply the barcodes, the readers, and the system software. Thus it is important that tests be performed using the proposed products from all vendors involved to ensure accurate interoperability. In particular, test check digit computation, readability, and reliability should be verified.

RESOURCE SHARING AND INTERLIBRARY LOAN

ILL PROTOCOL

- ISO 10160, Information and documentation—Open Systems Interconnection—Interlibrary Loan Application Service Definition
- ISO 10161-1, Information and documentation—Open SystemsInterconnectio—InterlibraryLoan Application Protocol Specification—Part 1: Protocol specification
- ISO 10161-2, Information and documentation—Open Systems Interconnection—Interlibrary Loan Application Protocol Specification—Part 2: Protocol implementation conformance statement proforma

The ISO ILL Protocol standardises the exchange of interlibrary loan information between computer systems. Currently, most automated ILL systems or consortia require the borrowing and loaning libraries to access a common database and system.

Loans are generally available only from those libraries participating in the common system. Loans outside of the common system usually have to fall back on paper ILL requests that are mailed or Faxed. The ISO ILL Protocol takes a distributed view to handling automated ILL transactions. Borrowing and lending libraries, whose systems are compliant with the standard, would enter information into their own systems which would then send messages in the standard protocol format directly to each other or through an intermediary.

In addition to allowing the library to use the ILL system of its choice or the ILL module in its own integrated library system, use of the ISO protocol approach widens the resource sharing base—potentially to anywhere in the world where the protocol is being used—an increasingly important capability in today's global society. The ILL Protocol breaks transactions down into separate activities or tasks, each of which is defined as a 'service.' These services have defined specific data elements and 'messages' that get transmitted during the ILL transaction in a specified sequence.

Three standards make up the full protocol:

- ISO 10160 defines the ILL roles, models the different role combination interactions, and defines the various ILL services, messages, status states, and sequencing rules.
- ISO 10161-1 is the 'meat' of the protocol, specifying the 'ILL Protocol Machine's' behaviour requirements and the procedural rules to support the services defined in ISO 10160.
- ISO 10161-2 details the requirements for completing a conformance statement.

Three roles—requester, responder, and intermediary—are defined along with their respective events, actions, and procedural rules. Services supported by the protocol include ILL requests, renewals, recalls, tracking, and overdue notification. Provision is made for the identification of the delivery mechanism and the item medium/format; however the standard does not prescribe the actual delivery mechanisms or telecommunication transport protocols. The National Library of Canada is the official Maintenance Agency for the ISO ILL Protocol standards.

Sample RFP Language

The following are examples of language that could be included in an RFP to address ISO ILL Protocol compliance:

- The system must support the ISO ILL Protocol standards, ISO 10160 and 10161-1. Describe how the system enables input and output of ISO ILL Protocol requests. Discuss any implementation decisions related to optional protocol requirements.
- The system must conform to the Interlibrary Loan Protocol Implementors Group (IPIG) Profile. Vendors should submit a copy of their completed IPIG Profile Conformance Statement Requirements List.
- Identify which communications protocols can be used by the system to transmit ISO 10160 and 10161-1 compliant ILL protocols.
- Describe how the system's ISO-compliant ILL

Protocol Machine application interacts with the other modules of the library system, particularly circulation and finance applications.

Assessing Compliance

A system can be compliant with the protocols for one or any combination of the three roles and only the simple transaction functions are mandatory.

In order to effectively evaluate a system's compliance, the library needs to be clear about which role(s) it intends to perform and which optional services and parameters are needed for its particular ILL operations. The Interlibrary Loan Protocol Implementors Group (IPIG) was established by the North American Interlibrary Loan and Document Delivery Project to facilitate implementation of the protocol. To address the complexity of understanding and implementing conformance with the protocol, IPIG created the ILL Protocol Implementors Group (IPIG) Profile for the ISO ILL Protocol reflecting a common set of decisions, options, and values for implementation.

The IPIG Profile imposes some additional constraints on implementation, beyond those specified in the base application standards. A claim of conformance to this IPIG Profile is a claim that all requirements in the relevant base standards are satisfied and that all the requirements of the Profile are satisfied. The library evaluation team should go through The library's requirements can then be compared to the completed forms submitted by the vendors. For those features which are designated as having conditional support, the evaluation team should determine whether the identified conditions would be relevant in their implementation.

A separate publication, IPIG Guidelines for ILL Application Developers, provides advice for understanding and achieving conformance with the ILL standard and IPIG profile. Although created for developers of ILL computer systems, the guidelines can also be useful to the library evaluation team in understanding the standard, developing their own requirements, and interpreting the vendor's conformance statement and implementation approach.

The ILL Protocol Maintenance Agency web site includes resources on how to conduct system tests including a list of participating testbed sites. The ILL Protocol Implementor Group web site includes updated information on the status of system testing by IPIG members.

GENERIC ELECTRONIC DOCUMENT INTERCHANGE (GEDI)

- ISO 17933, Generic Electronic Document Interchange (GEDI)

The Generic Electronic Document Interchange (GEDI) standard defines the formats and protocols for exchanging electronic documents. It was created to avoid the development of disparate non-standard automated systems as electronic document delivery continues to grow in availability. A standard set of formats and transport mechanisms will encourage the use of electronic document delivery, allow the use of automated systems to increase speed and lower delivery costs, and utilise the same networking technology for ordering and delivering documents. The GEDI format consists of two parts: the header or cover information and the electronic document itself.

To facilitate use of GEDI with the ISO ILL Protocol, the header tags have been mapped to equivalent data elements defined in ISO 10161-1, Interlibrary Loan Application Protocol Specification. Document formats currently supported are TIFF, PDF, and JPEG, however the standard is designed to accommodate registration of additional formats as they become widely accepted. While the standard is designed to allow utilisation of any transfer protocol agreed upon by the involved parties, it defines profiles for FTP and MIME e-mail transmission. Three roles of participating organisations are defined—Supplier, Consumer, and Relay—the latter being an intermediary store-and-forward facility.

Sample RFP Language

The following are examples of language that could be included in an RFP to address GEDI compliance:

- The system must support the transfer of electronic documents in compliance with ISO 17933, Generic Electronic Document Interchange (GEDI). Describe how the system provides these capabilities. Identify which document formats and transfer protocols are supported.
- Describe how the system integrates ISO ILL Protocol (ISO 10160 and 10161) functionality with GEDI functionality.

Assessing Compliance

The GEDI standard specifies the conformance requirements based on the role being performed—Supplier, Customer, or Relay. An information system at the highest level of compliance would have to both send and receive in all the listed formats and transfer protocols, receive and interpret all header data elements, and even accept and ignore non-standard header elements.

Libraries should identify which role(s) they intend to perform and identify which formats and transfer protocols are needed to perform those roles in their environment. Except for mapping of the header data elements, the standard does not specify the integration functionality with the ISO ILL Protocol or a library system's ILL transaction module. Discussions with the vendor will be necessary to determine if this integration exists and how it was implemented.

ELECTRONIC DATA INTERCHANGE (EDI)

- ANSI X12, Electronic Data Interchange (series of standards)
- ISO 9735, Electronic data interchange for administration, commerce and transport (EDIFACT)—Application level syntax rules

EDI, the electronic exchange of information to conduct business transactions is commonplace today in many industries, especially for purchasing and invoicing. Both the customer and supplier can benefit by the use of EDI through reduced data entry time, improved accuracy of data (no rekeying errors), and faster speed of response and transaction fulfillment. Many publishers and book/serial agents are set up to utilise EDI with libraries for orders, invoices, claims, claim responses, and shipping notices.

EDI implementation requires the use of a highly structured format. Two major standards: ANSI X12 and EDIFACT are the specifications utilised most widely, X12 in the U.S.,. and EDIFACT internationally, especially in Europe. Each standard defines the EDI messaging structure, syntax, codes, transaction sets, directory of elements, and rules of behaviour. Both of these standards are quite complex; in fact, each is actually a series of standards. Additionally, neither X12 nor EDIFACT are static standards; new versions and interim releases are scheduled periodically to address technology and industry changes. Different releases are not always fully compatible with one another. To ensure interoperability, the two communicating systems must be supporting the same version and release level for transaction sets, segments, and data elements. Like many standards, there are numerous elements designated as optional, further complicating implementation.

To address the complexity and options of the standard, many industry groups have developed guidelines 'translating' the standards to specific recommendations for their industry's applications and specifying particular transaction sets or subsets.

Several organisations in the publishing and library community have created such guidelines. BASIC, a standards group formed through the merger of BISAC and SISAC has developed formats for EDI for the publishing community based on ANSI X12. ICEDIS has published formats for subscription orders based on X12.

Basically, the BASIC and ICEDIS guidelines identify selected X12 transaction sets and map them to book and serial related activities.

The X12 transaction sets that are typically used in library applications include:

- 810 Invoice
- 850 Order
- 855 Order acknowledgement
- 997 Functional acknowledgement

- 869 Order status enquiry/ Claim
- 870 Order status response / Claim response

Both BASIC and ICEDIS are migrating their guidelines to EANCOM, a widely used subset of EDIFACT developed by EAN International. EDItEUR has already taken the X12 guidelines for serials developed by SISAC and created EDIFACT versions.

Sample RFP Language

The following are examples of language that could be included in an RFP to address EDI compliance:

- The system must support *Electronic Data Interchange* (EDI), in conformance with ANSI X12 standards, for ordering, claiming, canceling, invoicing, and reporting for both monographic and serial materials. Describe how the system implements EDI. Discuss how the system verifies EDI data elements and provides error alerts.
- Describe your plans and timeframe for EDIFACT support for EDI transactions.
- The system must support all of the X12 transaction sets as specified in the BASIC (BISAC/SISAC) Guidelines. Describe any deviations from the guidelines.
- Describe how data sent and received in EDI transactions is integrated with the different modules of the library system, particularly bibliographic, serials, acquisitions, and finance.
- Describe to what extent and how EDI related transactions can be completely automated, *e.g.,* claims sent without operator initiation.
- Identify which telecommunications protocols can be used for EDI transmission.

Assessing Compliance

The critical compliance issues for EDI relate to both the handling of the needed transaction sets and the methods in which the library system creates and receives this transaction information. Many systems have a software module that 'translates' the relevant information in the library system to and from an EDI formatted message.

The library evaluation team will want to understand which data fields are extracted for sending transmissions and in which fields received data is loaded. In particular, support of the subscription renewal invoice from a serials agent can be more problematic than dealing with individual book orders or new subscriptions.

The timing of the EDI transmission data extracts/loads and the amount of operator intervention needed can also be issues. There are both pros and cons to real-time vs. batch functioning as well as totally automated vs. operator-initiated actions. The library team needs to consider how these choices fit in with their processes and which options are available within the system. Earlier implementations of EDI transmission generally required the use of a *Value-added Network* (VAN) communications supplier, which can add to the costs of using EDI. Some implementations now support transmission over the Internet. The various transmission options should be discussed along with their costs and available security controls. Most library system vendors and major book/serial agents have experience in EDI interchanges between their respective systems.

The library evaluation team should discuss with the library system vendor which book/serial agents they have worked with directly and ask for documented tests of interoperability. Likewise, the current book and serial agent used by the library should be consulted for input on their experiences with different library systems and any issues the library will need to address with a particular system, if chosen.

INFORMATION RETRIEVAL

Z39.50

Z39.50 defines a standard protocol for two computer systems to communicate for the purpose of information retrieval. Based on client/server architecture, the protocol standardises the messages that clients and servers use, regardless of the underlying software, systems, or platforms. A client system that implements the Z39.50 protocol allows communication with diverse servers, and a server system that implements the protocol is searchable by clients developed by different vendors.

The protocol is independent of the underlying transport mechanism, however most current implementations are done using TCP/IP over the Internet. Originally Z39.50 was designed to help with searching library bibliographic catalogues utilising different library system software. Today Z39.50 is used to access a wide range of databases in many disciplines across a variety of organisation types. A library implementing Z-client technology can provide their users access to any Z-server compliant database without the user having to know that system's native search interface. A library implementing Z-server technology can open up their catalogue to other libraries' or organisations' users without individual customised set-ups. Z39.50 has a 'broadcast search' capability that allows a user to simultaneously search multiple databases from different providers.

Libraries can adopt a single standardised Z39.50 interface for their patrons to concurrently access the library's catalogue, purchased CD-ROMs, subscriptions to online databases, and Internet resources. And data from a variety of sources can be extracted, using the protocol, to a common format for offline use or import into a local database. The Z39.50 standard identifies a number of 'facilities,' *e.g.* Initialisation, Search, Retrieval, etc. Each facility contains one or more 'services' which are the specified protocols to perform a particular task within the facility, *e.g.* Sort.

Queries are qualified by various 'attributes' which are grouped into types. A 'Use' type of attribute indicates the query access points, such as title or author. A 'Relation' type of attribute qualifies the relationship of two query values to one another, *e.g.*, less than, greater than, or equal to. Other attributes that control queries include truncation or omitting of characters in search terms and the structure of the query itself.

Attribute types and values are clustered into related sets. An example of an 'attribute set' is 'bib-1', which specifies the attributes that could be used in a typical bibliographic query. The specification for 'extended services' in version 3 allows libraries to go beyond catalogue searching and utilise Z39.50 protocols for many other library processes such as finding and importing cataloguing records, creating 'virtual' union catalogues, making ILL requests, saving and running Selective Dissemination of Information (SDI) profiles, and updating databases. Additionally, the Z39.50 standard is becoming accepted as a solution to the challenge of retrieving multimedia information including text, images, and digitised documents. The Library of Congress is the designated Z39.50 Maintenance Agency. A voluntary group, the Z39.50 Implementors Group (ZIG), meets regularly to discuss implementation issues and recommend improvements to the protocol.

Sample RFP Language

The following are examples of language that could be included in an RFP to address Z39.50 compliance:

- The system must include a Z39.50 client and server that are compliant with ANSI/NISO Z39.50 version 3. Describe how the system has implemented Z-client and Z-server, and indicate how compliance has been tested and verified. Discuss how new Z-connections are set-up for both client and server, how customisable the set-up configuration is, and the skill set required to create and maintain set-ups.
- Identify and describe any Z39.50 optional facilities, services, or extended services that have been implemented.
- The system's Z-server must be accessible over a TCP/IP connection by at least two different remote Z-clients that are not the vendor's own products. Vendors will be required to demonstrate this capability or provide test documentation.
- The system must provide a Z39.50 version 3 client interface integrated with the system's patron Web

client or has the same 'look and feel.' Vendors must be able to demonstrate that searches via their Z39.50 client and the native search interface return the same records.

- The system must include bibliographic data, holdings, circulation status, and user-understandable diagnostic messages in Z39.50 result displays. Identify the holdings schema that is utilised.
- It is desirable that the system include a Z39.50 cataloging client which supports import/capture of MARC bibliographic and authority records from any Z39.50 compliant server. Describe the system's Z39.50 support of the MARC records structure and identify any other record syntaxes that are supported.
- The system must have the ability to enable broadcast searches of Z39.50 servers. Describe how multiple Z39.50 connections and simultaneous searches are handled and how retrieval sets are merged, sorted, and displayed.
- Describe how the system will support seamless Z39.50 search and display interface with non-MARC internal or external databases (CD-ROM or online) that support the Z39.50 protocol. Identify any particular systems or databases which have been pre-configured for Z39.50 access from the library system.

Assessing Compliance

Libraries should first determine if they need both the Z-client and Z-server functionality. If only database searching of other Z39.50-compliant systems is envisioned, then the Z-client functionality may be all that is required.

Z39.50 implementations can vary depending on which version of the standard is supported. Generally, libraries will want a system that complies with version 3, which adds more powerful Boolean and proximity searching; greater security, authentication, and resource controls; and a number of 'extended services' that provide mechanisms for Z39.50-enabling systems. Many of the added features in version 3, especially the extended services, are optional.

A system could be in conformance with version 3, but not provide many features that the library might want. It is important that the library evaluation team understands the various options in the standard and identifies those facilities and services which are needed or desirable for their application.

Examples of some enhanced version 3 features libraries might want are Scan, which allows index browsing; Explain, which allows users to obtain information about the target system; and Persistent Query and Periodic Query, which allow the saving and re-running of searches. When evaluating the system's Z39.50 broadcast search capability, the evaluation team should determine any limits (or ability to set them) on the number of targets or result set sizes, how result sets are sorted and merged, and if preliminary results from one target can be displayed while others are still being searched.

Even if a library implements version 3 compliant protocols, there may still be interoperability issues with other target systems that have implemented earlier versions or chosen different optional features. The University of North Texas is conducting a Z39.50 Interoperability Testbed Study whose goal is "to develop rigourous methodologies, test procedures, and measures to assess interoperability between systems using the Z39.50 standard protocol for information retrieval.'

The results of this project should help both libraries and vendors in understanding and improving interoperability. A Z39.50 Register of Implementors is available on the Maintenance Agency's web site. To further aid in both the selection of optional features and the interoperability issues, profiles have been developed that further define conformance requirements in specific application areas.

Z39.50 PROFILES

Ensuring that separate Z39.50 implementations interoperate can be challenging due to the different options that can be chosen. To address these challenges, many organisations and user groups have developed 'profiles' which detail a subset of Z39.50 features and functions that an implementation conforming to that particular profile will support.

When all the databases being searched support the same profile, search results should be more consistent and accurate. Some 25 profiles have been registered with the Z39.50 Maintenance Agency, crossing numerous organisation types, geographic areas, and subject disciplines, including geospatial data, museum information, and thesaurus navigation. There are three profiles of particular interest to most U.S.,. libraries: the Bath Profile, the U.S. National Profile, and the GILS Profile. Other library related profiles exist or are in development that may be of interest in other geographic regions or particular subject disciplines. Consult the Library of Congress Z39.50 Maintenance Agency site for a list of these profiles.

BATH PROFILE

The Bath Profile was developed to improve interoperability of Z39.50 accessible library catalogs. It was designed to be international in scope with the expectation that it would be incorporated into more detailed national, regional, or provincial profiles.

Release 1.1 of the Profile has been endorsed as an ISO Internationally Recognised Profile (IRP). Release 2 is expected to be issued in late 2002.

Three functional areas are addressed in the current release:

- Basic bibliographic search and retrieval with primary focus on library catalogs,
- Bibliographic holdings search and retrieval, and
- Cross-domain search and retrieval.

For each area, three levels of conformance are defined, with each higher level inheriting the requirements of the lower level(s). Conformance Level 0 has limited requirements as it was intended to encompass as many existing Z39.50 products as possible.

Conformance Level 1 adds requirements to improve searching and interoperability; libraries specifying new or enhanced Z39.50 systems should require adherence to at least this level. Conformance Level 2 defines a number of enhanced functions that may not yet be widely available in existing implementations.

Level 2 requirements are not detailed in the current release of the specification but are included in the forthcoming Release 2. The profile also defines a core set of typical library user searches and how to express those searches using Z39.50 "vocabulary." The National Library of Canada is the Maintenance Agency for the Bath Profile.

U.S. NATIONAL PROFILE

The soon-to-be issued U.S. National Z39.50 Profile for Library Applications is a compatible superset of the Bath Profile. It includes additional specifications and requirements than the Bath Profile to address national requirements for U.S.,. and Canadian libraries.

The first version of the U.S. National Profile focuses on two areas;

1. Bibliographic search and retrieval from library catalogues; and
2. Bibliographic holdings retrieval. It follows the same modular structure as the Bath Profile, using functional areas and conformance levels, but has some different requirements and criteria for each level.

The U.S. Profile also specifies exact Z39.50 attribute combinations for expressing a set of typical library catalogue searches. The Holdings functional area currently focuses on presenting holdings information related to bibliographic records retrieved from a search. Searching of holdings will be addressed in a later release of the profile.

GILS (GLOBAL INFORMATION LOCATOR SERVICE)

The Global Information Locator Service (GILS) is a Z39.50 profile developed to provide a uniform search and retrieval method for accessing U.S.,. federal government information. The U.S. Government's information runs the gamut of disciplines from the arts to sciences, social sciences, and legislative information; the complexity of both the government's information and its management bureaucracy makes it difficult to prescribe any standard formats for its vast array of resources.

GILS seeks instead to specify a common set of access points and a search and retrieval gateway to the information regardless of where it is located as long as the server is GILS-compliant.

The GILS Profile specifies a 'GILS Core' utilising Z39.50 requirements and, in addition, provides specifications relating to other aspects of GILS conformant servers that are outside the scope of Z39.50. Servers compliant with the ISO 23950 Geospatial Profile (GEO) or the Catalogue Interoperability Profile (CIP) are also compliant with the GILS standard. Although developed for federal information, GILS is widely used for state information and many state libraries have implemented GILS. Government libraries, libraries doing cooperative ventures with government agencies, or libraries in government contractor organisations will want to seriously consider including GILS conformance in their RFP specification. Any libraries that want to make government information more accessible to their patrons will want to have GILS interoperability at least at the Z-client level.

Sample RFP Language

The following are examples of language that could be included in an RFP to address Z39.50 profile compliance:

- The Z39.50 client and server functionality provided with the system must comply with Conformance Level 1 of the Bath Profile for all Functional Areas defined. Describe any deviations from this conformance and indicate how compliance has been tested and verified.
- The Z39.50 client and server functionality provided with the system must comply with Conformance Level 1 of the U.S. National Profile for all Functional Areas defined. Describe any deviations from this conformance and indicate how compliance has been tested and verified.

- Identify and describe any Z39.50 client or server functionality that conforms to Level 2 of the Bath or U.S. National Profiles. Where Level 2 functionality does not currently exist, describe any plans for adding this conformance.
- The Z39.50 client and server functionality provided with the system must support the GILS profile specification. Describe any deviations from this conformance and indicate how compliance has been tested and verified.

Assessing Compliance

Z39.50 profile-specific compliance issues relate to whether specific features from the standard have been implemented as specified in the profile. Ideally, the system will be pre-configured to support the desired profile, however, since, these profiles are relatively new and still evolving, their support may not be widely implemented yet.

The profiles will also have changing and/or added requirements as new releases are issued. Vendors should be asked which release they have implemented and if not the current one, what the timeframe is for supporting the latest release. If the profile is not supported 'out-of-the-box,' the library evaluation team will first need to determine if the profile can be supported at all.

If the native system, as well as the default Z39.50 implementation, doesn't include a service or facility that is identified in the desired profile, no amount of configuration will make the system profile-compliant. If the features are available, then the library will want to know if the vendor will do the configuration as part of the local installation (and at what cost) or if and how the library can do the configuration itself.

The configuration tools or process to match a desired profile should be fully understood, including the required skill set needed by someone doing such a configuration. Another issue to consider is that local database indexing choices can impact a library's ability to conform to any of the Z39.50 profiles regardless of the information system's conformance level. For example, a library may have chosen not to index a particular field that is identified in the profile, or may have indexed a field in a way that would not support features like truncation or proximity searching.

Full compliance with any of the Z39.50 profiles may require a library to change their indexing policy and reindex their database. Guidelines have been developed as part of the Z39.50 Interoperability Testbed Study to assist libraries in making indexing choices to best support Z39.50 profiles.

Command Searching

ISO 8777 names and defines 30 search and retrieve commands, eight symbols or punctuation used to qualify the commands, and the expected system response to each command. The goal is to provide a common language for conducting searches in a command mode. With the widespread use of browser-based graphical user interfaces, command searching is not utilised as much in library systems, particularly in the patron access modules. However, it may still be useful to have commands as an alternate search method for those who are familiar with and like Boolean searching.

Command searching can be very useful for library technical staff to find and retrieve records for administrative, maintenance, data clean-up, and reporting purposes. A number of Integrated Library Systems offer 'CCL' searches as an 'Expert Search' or 'Command Search' option because of the power of such a search and the speed of entering the search criteria.

Sample RFP Language

The following are examples of language that could be included in an RFP to address command searching compliance:

- The system must support command level searching utilising the standard commands as defined in ISO 8777, Commands for interactive text searching. Describe any deviations from this standard.
- Describe any additional search command functions or languages, different from those defined in ISO 8777, that are available with the system.

- Describe any database records and system functions or modules that cannot be accessed with a command level search.

Assessing Compliance

The standard defines an information retrieval system as being in conformance "when it recognises and responds to every command specified by this International Standard.' The commands and qualifiers listed in the standard are fairly basic, thus missing any of them would definitely limit the retrieval capabilities with a command method.

It is likely that a library would want more retrieval commands and functions than the standard defines. If that is the case, the RFP should state any additional requirements. A system may utilise a proprietary search language, however the vendor should be able to map the commands and functionality in their proprietary system to those in the standard. Where the commands perform the same function, it is desirable that the proprietary system would use the standard's command name.

METADATA

Metadata is typically defined as 'data about data.' Many libraries are looking to non-MARC/AACR2 schemes for cataloging certain types of materials, including but not limited to Web-accessible electronic resources and items in locally digitised collections.

Metadata schemas are rapidly being developed as a solution not only for libraries but also for many other organisations that collect or develop information resources and want to make them more accessible.

The use of metadata to 'catalog' information resources can:

- Improve accessibility and retrievability;
- Provide more effective relevance ranking of search results;
- Act as a surrogate for a resource such as a large file that could be time-consuming to download or view, raw data that requires an explanation to understand,

or even a resource not available in electronic form; and

- Aid in legal issues of intellectual property rights identification, tracking, and management.

The kinds of metadata associated with an information resource can address different aspects. Descriptive metadata identifies the resource and provides data about its content. Administrative metadata is used to help manage the resource; version numbering is an example. Technical metadata provides system related information about the resource such as the file type or format or resolution level of an image. Use metadata can keep track of usage and users.

Metadata may be added manually, created through the use of an automated process like an indexing algorithm, or computer generated 'on the fly'.Most Integrated Library Systems are still bibliographic/reference based—they were not designed for the storage and retrieval of full text and multimedia.

However, because of the increased demand for systems to support digital libraries, some ILS vendors have created add-on modules; others are providing integration 'hooks' for third party products or tools that can be used to add access to full text documents or images. These modules and tools increasingly include support for the creation, maintenance, search, and display of non-MARC metadata schemes. Numerous metadata standardisation projects exist.

Many are detailed schemas that build on a more general one; some are discipline or data type specific; most can be mapped to other metadata schemas to create interoperability. ISO, ANSI, and the World Wide Web Consortium (W3C) all have committees working on metadata-related standards and registries of metadata schemas.

Three metadata standards of particular interest to libraries are the Dublin Core, the VRA Core, and the Encoded Archival Description (EAD). Following discussion of these schemas, a protocol for harvesting metadata information that libraries should be aware of is described.

Metadata Schemas

Dublin Core

The Dublin Core Metadata Initiative began at a 1995 workshop (in Dublin, Ohio-thus the name) to improve discovery for networked information resources. Since, then, the Dublin Core has developed into an official ANSI/NISO standard and today is probably the most well-known and referenced metadata standard. Dublin Core's strength lies in its simplicity.

Fifteen elements are defined for describing any type of resource: Title, Creator, Subject, Description, Publisher, Contributor; Date, Type, Format, Identifier, Source, Language, Relation, Coverage, and Rights. Each element is optional and may be repeated as needed within the set. Most elements also have a limited set of recommended qualifiers which can be optionally utilised to further refine an element's content or to indicate the encoding scheme used in recording the element's value.

Information systems can conform to the standard without supporting qualifiers-such implementation of the standard is known as Dublin Core Simple. Dublin Core is ideally represented in XML (eXtensible Markup Language) syntax. However, Dublin Core Simple can also be represented in HTML (using 'DC' elements in the 'meta' tags) or even in a generic format (using Element="value").

Communities are encouraged to build on the Dublin Core to develop their own more specialised metadata element sets and many have done so. In theory, if a metadata scheme is based on the Dublin Core, cross-domain searches of the core descriptive information could be done more effectively while still providing specialised access points within a domain. Dublin Core has been given official standing with the World Wide Web Consortium (W3C) and Z39.50 standards initiatives. Dublin Core Simple is specified for the schema for the Z39.50 Bath Profile cross-domain searching conformance.

It has also been mapped to the MARC format to simplify development of automated methods for interchanging Dublin

Core and MARC data. The Dublin Core Metadata Initiative (DCMI) is the Maintenance Agency for the standard.

DCMI has several working groups including one for libraries which is developing a Library Application Profile to clarify the use of the Dublin Core Metadata Element Set in libraries and library-related applications.

VRA CORE

The Visual Resources Association (VRA) has developed a metadata set of 28 elements, called the VRA Core, designed to describe works of art, architecture, artifacts, and comparable cultural objects.

A visual resources collection frequently needs two or more records for a given item: one record to describe the physical object (the 'Work'), and one record to describe each surrogate of the object which is created for viewing on or offline (the 'Image'). The VRA Core includes a Record Type element used to clearly distinguish whether a record applies to a Work or an Image.

All category elements are optional and repeatable. The specification provides for the use of qualifiers to clarify a category's content and allows the addition of local use categories. Controlled vocabularies are recommended for many of the categories.

A guide to good practices for cataloging visual works using VRA Core is in development. It is assumed that most Work records will be linked to one or more related Image records but the specification does not define how record linking is to be done-that is left as a local database implementation decision. VRA categories have been mapped to Dublin Core and MARC format as well as to several other related visual art cataloguing schemas.

EAD (ENCODED ARCHIVAL DESCRIPTION)

The Encoded Archival Description is an encoding scheme for archival and manuscript collection finding aids, which provides access to other information by describing, often in detail, an archive's holdings.

The specification currently accommodates registers and inventories of any length. Currently, MARC records for archives are usually at more of a summary level than an individual finding aid. The EAD standard supports the interrelationship between the data content of catalogue records and finding aids by providing a MARC equivalency attribute, matching MARC field numbers, for related finding aid elements. The scheme can be represented as either an SGML (ISO 8879, Standard Generalised Markup Language) or an XML DTD (document type definition).

There are three parts to the specification: the SGML compliant DTD, a tag library with definitions of the standard elements and attributes, and an application guideline with extensive examples. The defined elements address both information about the finding aid itself and information about the archival materials covered by the finding aid. Attributes can be used to designate, for example, that a particular controlled vocabulary was used for a particular element's content. Use of controlled vocabularies or authority lists is not required. The Library of Congress, Network Development and MARC Standards Office is the Maintenance Agency for EAD, in partnership with the Society of American Archivists.

Sample RFP Language for Metadata Schemas

The following are examples of language that could be included in an RFP to address metadata schemas:

- The system must support the use of Dublin Core (ANSI/NISO Z39.85) metadata for digital information resources. Describe any built-in functionality or add-on modules that provide support of metadata for cataloging and/or search and retrieval including customisable templates for data entry and edit, user-readable display of metadata, and validation of data against authority lists.
- Identify any metadata schemas, other than Dublin Core that are supported and describe how they are implemented. Describe any conversion tools or

utilities that will translate from one metadata schema to another.

- Describe how search and retrieval of non-MARC metadata records and MARC bibliographic records are integrated.
- Discuss if the system's Z39.50 server allows both MARC data and non-MARC metadata to be searched. Describe if and how Z39.50 broadcast searches can be combined with metadata searches.
- Describe any tools within the system or available as separate modules that can be utilised to create, encode, and modify metadata records. Describe whether the metadata record can be embedded within the digital object, must be separate, or if either is supported. Describe to what level these tools can be customised. Define the skill sets that are needed to use these encoding tools.
- Describe how metadata records can be linked to one another within the information system's database. Identify whether one-to-one, one-to-many, or many-to-many linkages are available.
- Describe any data import/export functionality between MARC record cataloging and metadata encoding that would reduce duplicate cataloguing effort and ensure consistency.

Assessing Compliance

Currently, integration of library bibliographic systems and metadata encoding/searching is in the embryonic stage. Often, libraries use systems from multiple vendors to address both traditional and digital library system implementations.

This results in the traditional library catalogue and the digital library being totally separate with perhaps a low level of integration by providing a link within the MARC record that will take the user to the corresponding full-text or image. This situation is changing, but varies significantly from one system to another in what is supported, how it is implemented, and how transparently the two types of data are accessible.

Two main areas of concern in assessing metadata support are in the input/creation of metadata and in search and retrieval. On the input side, the library evaluation team will want to determine what kind of input tools are available to support metadata creation, which metadata schemas have built-in templates, and how user-friendly and customisable the tools and templates are. Ideally the metadata input templates should be similar in look and feel to the templates used for MARC record cataloguing. To reduce duplication of effort in cataloguing, the tools should allow data fields from a MARC record to be easily transported to a metadata record and vice versa.

Many of the metadata schemas have tools available to validate whether a particular record complies with the standard; these should be used to test sample metadata records created through the system's input tools and through any conversion tools from MARC to metadata or one metadata schema to another.

On the search and retrieval side, the system would ideally allow a single user interface to simultaneously search the library's MARC records and metadata records and present a single list to the user with associated records linked. A Z39.50 broadcast search combined with a metadata search of collections and resources outside of the library would also be desirable. If third party tools for search and retrieval are being considered, then the configuration requirements of both the library system and the third party tool need to be carefully assessed to ensure interoperability.

PROTOCOL FOR METADATA HARVESTING

The Open Archives Initiative (OAI) Protocol for Metadata Harvesting (PMH) was initially developed to support federated searching of metadata for distributed electronic archives of scholarly papers. The concept was deemed to have wider applicability and has since, grown to encompass a standard harvesting protocol for multiple forms of metadata in any type of information repository.

PMH defines a mechanism for a designated 'data provider' to expose its metadata to one or more 'service providers.' Designated service providers could use the protocol to harvest metadata and to offer value-added services, such as a metadata search engine. This architecture differs markedly from the Z39.50 model of distributed search and retrieval. While lacking in some of the advanced functionality of Z39.50, PMH has a simpler implementation and shifts the operational responsibility and processing away from the data providers to the service provider. It is considered particularly useful for collections of locally digitised or born-digital materials, which can now be included in the databases of large search engines.

Currently, the protocol requires all data repositories to be able to export their metadata for harvesting in an XML schema. All repositories must also support export in the Dublin Core Simple metadata set to ensure a common baseline. However, the protocol does support the concept of multiple types of metadata sets and data providers may offer their metadata in additional schemas as well.

The protocol also requires repositories to datestamp all records at time of creation or modification to allow service providers to do selected harvesting within a specified date range. OAI maintains a registry of PMH compliant data providers, but registration is optional so it is expected that more providers are using the protocol than have registered. The protocol and its related documentation do not currently provide guidelines related to issues of intellectual property protection and acceptable use of exposed metadata.

Libraries that become PMH data providers need to consider what their policies for these issues will be and how they will address enforcement of those policies by service providers who harvest their data.

Sample RFP Language

The following are examples of language that could be included in an RFP to address OAI Metadata Harvesting compliance:

- Describe how the system supports the OAI Protocol for Metadata Harvesting (PMH) for a data provider.

including any optional features that have been implemented. Discuss in particular how selected metadata records can be restricted from harvesting and how datestamping is handled.

- Identify any metadata schemas other than Dublin Core which are supported for exposure to the OAI Protocol for Metadata Harvesting (PMH).

Assessing Compliance

Many of the data providers' compliance issues for the OAI PMH specification relate to how the metadata gets created and encoded. Some additional questions which the library evaluation team will want to explore include how the metadata gets XML-encoded (if not natively in that format), how the system assigns the required unique identifiers, how datestamping is done to allow for accurate incremental harvesting, and how access controls are applied to restrict selected metadata records from being harvested.

Metadata and protocol harvesting support may not be provided as an out-of-the-box implementation, but instead be supported through the availability of toolkits. In such cases, the flexibility, ease of use, and learning curve for the toolkit will be a key factor.

WEB ACCESS

WEB ACCESSIBILITY INITIATIVE

The Web Accessibility Initiative (WAI) is an activity of the World Wide Web Consortium (W_3C) to make Web content accessible to people with disabilities. The guidelines do not discourage the use of multimedia in Web content, but rather they explain how to make such content more widely accessible. Many libraries have an interest in making their information more accessible to disabled people and some have already incorporated the accessibility guidelines into the inhouse development of their Web pages.

This same accessibility should be required of the Web interface to the library system. There are three different guidelines, each directed to a different participant in the provision of Web content.

Each specification details the guidelines, associated checkpoints, priority, (*i.e.*, criticality) levels for each checkpoint, and conformance level requirements. The Web Content Accessibility Guidelines are directed to Web content developers.

The Authoring Tool Accessibility Guidelines are directed to developers of Web page creation and editing tools or Web site management tools. The User Agent Accessibility Guidelines are directed to developers of Web browsers or other user interfaces to Web content. Separate supporting documents for each guideline provide information on implementing the checkpoints and testing and validation of the content or Web software products.

Sample RFP Language

The following are examples of language that could be included in an RFP to address Web accessibility compliance:

- All Web-based interfaces in the system must comply with the Web Accessibility Initiative Web Accessibility Guidelines (WAG) or supply alternative versions of Web pages that comply with the guidelines. Describe how your system addresses Web accessibility support and identify the level of conformance with each of the WAG guidelines. Indicate how compliance has been tested and verified.
- Describe any Web page development and editing tools, available with the system or as add-ons, and discuss how the tools support creation of Web pages that comply with Web Accessibility Initiative Web Accessibility Guidelines (WAG).

Assessing Compliance

There are a number of tools available to verify that a Web page meets WAI guidelines; these are listed on WAI's web site. Even if the system's default Web pages have been tested by the vendor using one of these tools, there is usually some level of customisation to the Web pages and interfaces during implementation.

Therefore, the library evaluation team will need to retest the final design of their Web pages. Since, Web page interfaces used with the library system will typically be modified and customised inhouse on some periodic (possibly even frequent) basis, the library should include a requirement of running a WAI compliance test as part of their ongoing Web page development and modification process.

OPEN URL

The OpenURL standard was designed to allow a library user who has retrieved an information resource citation to obtain access to the most 'appropriate' copy of the full resource. The standard defines a mechanism for attaching an OpenURL link to a reference, usually a bibliographic citation. When the OpenURL is clicked, the user is presented with an option to request the full-text. When the user selects the option, it is fulfilled with the given the user's and organisation's preferences related to cost, contractual and license agreements in place with suppliers, access rights, etc.

Consider the scenario of three users in three different libraries accessing the same vendor's database product and wanting to retrieve the full-text of a particular article found in a search. If the database product were OpenURL encoded and the three libraries had implemented OpenURL services, then UserA could have the article retrieved from an inhouse collection of electronic journals, UserB could have the article retrieved from a publisher's Web-based journal database which the library had licensed, and UserC could have the article automatically requested from a document delivery supplier under the library's volume purchase agreement.

All of the decisions, routing, and licensing necessary to make this happen would be transparent to the users.

An OpenURL differs from a standard Web URL (Uniform Resource Locator) in two ways:

- It delivers metadata as well as identifiers that can be used to initiate action requests beyond linking to a referred site.
- It is context sensitive, in that the request is processed

differently based on the context of the user initiating the request.

When the OpenURL is clicked, the associated metadata stored with the URL is sent to an OpenURL-compliant link server where the 'rules' about target link preferences for the particular user base are stored. The link server presents the user with the available extended services for that user, such as electronic full-text, and fulfills the requested service on demand using the method determined by the stored rules.

While electronic delivery of full-text articles was the initial impetus of OpenURL, the standard can be applied to the provision of other services such as ordering of full-text from document delivery suppliers, searches of selected library's holdings for ownership of a referenced title, citation searches of a referenced article, links to book reviews, author searches for additional works, links to author biographies and personal web sites, Web searches for related information on the same topic, etc.

A NISO version of OpenURL is currently in draft and expected to be issued for trial use in early 2003. However, the first version of the specification has existed for several years and has been implemented by a number of library and information suppliers. The forthcoming NISO version is expected to generalise and add to the defined syntax to better address extended services beyond scholarly journal articles.

Sample RFP Language

The following are examples of language that could be included in an RFP to address Open URL standards compliance:

- Describe any built-in or add-on capability to support a locally managed OpenURL-compliant link server. Discuss how this server interoperates with the various library system modules.
- Describe any capabilities of the system to integrate with a third party supplier of an OpenURL-compliant link server system or service. Discuss how this third party system would interoperate with the various library system modules.

- The system must support input and editing of OpenURL links as part of its cataloging/editing modules for both bibliographic MARC records and metadata records. Describe how the system supports OpenURL link input and discuss options for handling OpenURL identifiers.

Assessing Compliance

The standard focuses on the syntax for the OpenURL but does not address or specify software design for link server management or technologies to manage the user identification, which is where many of the difficult implementation issues reside. These technologies would generally be supplied through some type of add-on modules or through a third party product or service. Thorough testing of all the technologies and interfaces with the library system will be needed, as this is not currently a plug-and-play type of implementation. Similar to the situation with many library's digital resource collection, current implementations of the OpenURL and link server technology are often separate from the integrated library system.

If the OpenURL related functionality is integrated with the library system, the main compliance issues will be with the creation and management of OpenURL links, how the system handles the links in their Web interface, and how the system and its Web interface would interoperate with a link server. Many library systems allow the storing of a URL in a MARC 856 field and present it as a live hyperlink in the Web interface. This type of implementation should be tested to ensure that it can support the input and storage of an OpenURL (which is both longer and more complex than a standard URL) and pass the entire OpenURL intact to the Web interface.

Other questions for the evaluation team to ask the library system vendor are: How does the library system recognise an OpenURL vs. a standard URL and how are they handled and displayed differently? When an OpenURL link is clicked in the library system's Web interface, does the system recognise it as an OpenURL and pass it correctly to the designated link server? How is the user's identity and preferences handled so that they are included or referenced correctly when the OpenURL is sent to the link server? If the library system is using a common Z39.50 interface to access additional resources beyond the library's catalogue, such as an abstracting and indexing service database, how are OpenURL links embedded in those resources handled? Can the common search interface correctly display and act on an OpenURL link of a retrieved citation from another Z39.50 compliant product?

XML

The eXtensible Markup Language (XML), one of the latest incarnations of 'markup' languages, is quickly becoming the universal format for structured documents and data on the Web. While HTML, also a markup language, addresses the presentation and look of information, XML defines the structure of the information and describes the role of its structured components.

XML is a subset of SGML, the international Standard Generalised Markup Language defined in ISO 8879, which was developed for technical documentation before the Web existed. XML kept the best, most functional features of SGML and dropped many of the optional, complex aspects to make a markup language suitable for the Web environment.

Some key components of XML that make it such a powerful tool are:

- *Open system approach:* XML is non-proprietary and utilises ASCII, making XML data machine-independent and accessible across computing platforms.
- *Separation of Content and Display*: XML coding focuses on the structure of the document with the intent that it can then be re-used and customised for different purposes. Separate stylesheets can be created using eXtensible Style Language (XSL) (or other tools) to define particular display or print formats. This separation grows in importance with the widespread use of different sizes and types devices to read Web content, from PCs to PDAs to cell phones and whatever new device gets invented tomorrow.

- *Extensibility*: XML is called extensible because it allows the creation of customised markup tags and applications. The customised tags and rules to be used are defined in a Document Type Definition (DTD)—a name inherited from SGML—which is the collection of tags defined for a particular application. This allows groups of people or organisations to create their own customised XML applications for exchanging information in their domain, however they choose to define that domain.
- *Internationalisation*: XML utilises Unicode, a single comprehensive character set that encompasses virtually all of the world's written languages.
- *Database interoperability*: XML uses the concept of a document composed of a series of entities, which can contain one or more elements. This component nature of XML accommodates interfacing with a database, since, XML tags can be mapped to database fields, and makes it very suitable for storing the XML in a database, as whole documents or in components for greater repurposing capability.
- *Extended linking*: XML's linking capabilities go beyond the simple HTML one-way hyperlinking from point A to point B. X-links can be to multiple targets, activate automatically, embed or replace information, or be defined 'out of line' in a separate document. Not many tools have implemented extended linking features yet, but the possibilities are there.
- *Metadata support*: The metadata describing a document can be explicitly tagged with XML, making the data much more useable and searchable than HTML's meta-tags allow.

XML offers many opportunities for library applications:

- *MARC:* The Library of Congress Network Development and MARC Standards Office is developing a framework for working with MARC data in an XML environment, including DTD schemas, stylesheets, and software tools. This would allow MARC data to be fully converted to XML format or to be selectively output to XML for publication or use in another application or schema. There is even some controversial discussion about whether XML should completely replace MARC.

- *Integrated Library System Interfaces*: By using XML as the common input/output format, the traditional library system could be more easily integrated with Web technology and other proprietary systems. Newly developed tools or systems would not require separate special interfaces to be written. A totally XML-based integrated library system is likely in future years.
- *A&I Databases*: Output from abstracting and indexing databases could be offered in XML format which allows the record to be more easily re-used in applications such as interlibrary loan.
- *Domain Specific Metadata Searching*: Organisations with common interests can define an XML-compliant schema for 'cataloging' their data or tagging multimedia documents, then create virtual databases of the combined data or export the data for harvesting by a search engine.
- *Digital Publishing*: XML is tailor-made for digital publishing and can provide a common format for e-books and other electronic documents The Open eBook Forum has developed a standard for encoding e-books in XML that would allow them to be read in a variety of reading devices.

XML is in its early development phases and its use in library applications is just beginning. Supporting tools and new applications are rapidly growing and it is clear that XML will have a significant role in electronic information management and delivery. A number of the standards discussed in this guide are already being implemented using XML and more XML implementation approaches are planned or expected in the future. RFP language is not included here as the RFP requirements need to be specific to the particular application which is using XML, e.g. EAD, or Dublin Core, or MARC-XML.

Bibliography

Ahmad, E.: *Standards for Accreditation of Master's Programmes in Library and Information Studies*, Cambridge: South End Press, 2002.

Ali, T.: *Accreditation Process, Policies and Procedures*, London: Picador, 1999.

Ansari, I.: *Procedures and Guidelines for the Recognition of First Award Professional Courses in Library and Information Studies*, New Delhi: Institute of Objective Studies, 2002.

Balagopal, K.: *The Library and Information Sector*, Hyderabad: Perspectives Publishers, 1998.

Banerjea, D.: *Library Organizations*, Kolkata: Allied Publishers, 2003.

Baruah, S.: *The Library and Information Sector: Core Knowledge, Skills and Attributes*, New Delhi: Oxford University Press, 2003.

Chattopadhyay, K.: *Accreditation Instrument*, Kolkata: ICSP Publication, 2006.

Cohen, S.: *Guidelines for Professional Library/Information Educational Programmes*, New Delhi: Oxford University Press, 2007.

Das, Dilip K.: *Academic Accreditation in Libraries: Challenges and Responses*, London: Scarecrow Press, 2007.

Raghavendra K.: *Library and Information Science Education in Asia,* New Delhi: Indian Institute of Public, 2005.

Roy, A.: *Library Organizations and Environments,* New Delhi: Oxford University Press, 2006.

Srinivasavaradan, T.C.A.: *Perceived Uncertainty and Environmental Scanning*, New Delhi: Allied Publishers, 2000.

Thomas, B.: *Concepts and Issues in Administrative Behaviour*, Delhi: Permanent Black, 2007.

Tilly, C.: *Effective Library and Information Centre Management*, Cambridge: Cambridge University Press, 2004.

Verma, J.S.: *Introduction to Library Science*, New Delhi: Universal Publishing, 1997.

Viswanathan, S.: *Modern Library System*, Chennai: Narayana Publishing, 2002.

Wilkinson, I.: *Encyclopaedia of Library and Information Science*, New Delhi: Oxford University Press, 2003.

Zareer, M.: *Academic Accreditation in UK Libraries*, London: BBC Books, 2006.

Index

L

M

N

P

Q

R

S

U

W